— Beatrice

Thank you for
the support. Spread
the truth !!

Justin Helou

THE STEPFORD EMPLOYEE FALLACY

THE **TRUTH** ABOUT EMPLOYEE ENGAGEMENT IN THE MODERN WORKPLACE

JONATHAN D. VILLAIRE

CONTENTS

Dedication

For every employee who has ever felt that he or she had no voice. This is the truth your leaders sorely need to hear. This is the truth about employee engagement in the modern workplace.

Acknowledgements

I would like to thank my family and friends for their love and unending support. I would also like to thank those who contributed their stories to this book and entrusted me with their truth. Finally, thank you to the leaders out there who believe in my message and who live it every day; we need you to keep up the good work now more than ever.

Author's Note

The modern workplace is not one where employees can safely tell the truth for reasons you will see in the coming pages. Names and certain details mentioned herein have been changed to protect the innocent. I have tried to recreate personal stories, including relevant events, locations, and conversations, based on my own recollection. Claims about the (mis)conduct of any organizations, business entities, and involved parties were obtained through the public domain via news reports, court filings, and other credible publications and sources. References to any copyrighted works have been made for the purpose of commentary and to support the themes and concepts discussed throughout this book.

INTRODUCTION

Leaders, how many of you out there have sat wringing your hands in frustration over less-than-stellar performance due to the poor state of engagement within your organizations? Wouldn't it be grand if your employees would just give 110 percent every day, their priorities aligned with yours at all times? Oh, how the shareholders would delight if only your employees would go above and beyond all day every day! The sales! The profits! The cost savings! And just imagine how much free time you would have if you didn't even have to lift a finger. The employees would just be constantly engaged because that's their job. That's how employee engagement works, right?

Let me ask you something: are you familiar with the term "Stepford wife"? It's a pop-culture reference used to describe a married woman who appears docile and eager to please. A Stepford wife is seemingly perfect in every way and gladly submits to her husband's will. The reason she is so content to do his bidding is because she is literally a robot. She is programmed to think, act, and speak in a way that pleases her husband without any pesky needs, opinions, wants, or rights to make things difficult.

Many leaders today believe their employees are nothing more than a means to achieve company goals. *Human capital* is expected to be fully engaged and invested in executing organizational priorities because they are paid to do so. But the thing is, employees are people. They aren't robots and they aren't going to be engaged because you expect them to be. They won't be committed to going above and beyond for the company cause if the employee experience at their organization isn't a positive one—a fact cast in stark relief by data showing that less than one-quarter of employees around the world are fully engaged in their jobs. Yet, the decision makers continue to labor under the delusion that their talent will exert discretionary effort while maintaining a positive attitude at all times regardless of what it's like to work for them. This is a dangerous fallacy that needs to be exposed for what it is: pure fiction.

I wrote this book with the intention of expelling the commonly held beliefs about employee engagement that are costing companies billions of dollars each year in turnover, absenteeism, low productivity, reputational damage, higher taxes to cover unemployment, and other factors that eat away at the bottom line. For a decade, I worked as a front-line employee within large organizations that purported to place a high priority on employee engagement. However, there was a critical disconnect between what these companies expected from their employees in terms of engagement and what their leaders were doing to engage them. I saw employees being scapegoated, ignored, manipulated, and treated unfairly while senior management reminded them that they should be fully engaged and contributing to the company's success. Anyone who raised a concern or voiced dissatisfaction with the quality of their employee experience was labeled a complainer who had an attitude problem, a malfunctioning piece of equipment that needed to be replaced. After witnessing so much toxicity in the modern workplace, I spent years studying employee engagement and the myriad ways organizations are getting it wrong. Now I make a living sharing my passion for doing engagement the right way. I even published a book about it, to boot.

In the following pages, I will be dismantling the contemporary understanding of employee engagement and debunking the beliefs of business leaders who have unrealistic expectations for their workforce. Using anecdotes from my consulting practice, third-party research, brain science, current events, and my own personal observations from the front lines, I am going to explain why so many organizations are failing to engage their employees and what their leaders can do to correct it. It is my assertion that, absent the factors necessary to create a compelling employee experience and value proposition, employees do not engage themselves. *Leaders* engage employees. They can also disengage employees. The problem is that these same leaders refuse to acknowledge the influential role they play in this dynamic. They are too far-removed from the experience of being an employee to truly appreciate the impact that their decisions, behaviors, and interactions have on talent and on the state of engagement. My aim with this book is to tell leaders what they probably already know, deep down, and what their employees are too afraid to say. Employee engagement is often referred to as a win-win situation for workers and their employers. It is, but only if employers let go of the falsehood that has become an unspoken managerial tenet of the modern workplace: The Stepford Employee Fallacy.

PART I

WHY AREN'T EMPLOYEES MORE ENGAGED?

Employee engagement has become *the* hot topic in business circles over the past several years. Countless experts have published statistics and factoids about the impact that employee engagement has on an organization's bottom line. Leaders are slowly coming to realize the importance of having an engaged workforce, and they have begun treating engagement as a measurable business outcome. With such a laser focus on employee engagement, it seems surprising that less than 25 percent of employees worldwide are engaged in their jobs. What gives? Shouldn't employees be more committed and going above and beyond, instead of just going through the motions? It's a mystery that continues to confound and frustrate business leaders and their HR departments. They hire consultants who help them concoct the newest, sexiest benefits and perks so they can be hip like Facebook and Google. They send out anonymous surveys and badger employees into submitting their responses. They form committees and councils to plan company picnics and softball games and pot lucks.

So much effort is spent that leaders must feel as though they are merely spinning their wheels, gaining no traction whatsoever. They start trying to forcibly mold their organizations' cultures into the ideal of what engagement is supposed to look like by punishing employees who share critical feedback on what isn't working. It becomes a vicious cycle. Leaders try ineffective and superficial engagement strategies and then can't understand why employees don't put in more effort. So they blame employees for not doing a better job of engaging themselves in spite of the elements that are causing *dis*engagement. Instead of looking in the mirror or actually listening to employees' concerns, managers and executives double down on their efforts to force engagement, creating a workforce marked by fear and apathy.

Part I addresses the *why* that so many leaders struggle to understand when assessing the poor state of engagement in their organizations. In their minds, they are doing all the right things. But, in reality, it is they who are to blame for the very disengagement that they fail to resolve. We'll begin by taking stock of how bad things really are. There are stories behind the numbers and they will serve to better illustrate why leaders are so clueless when it comes to the role they play in creating a work experience that disengages their employees. Leaders with disengaged employees suffer from delusions of infallibility and grandeur, seeing themselves as disciplined, brilliant captains of industry. In Chapter 3, we will see how their greed, hubris, and detachment from the employee experience have blinded them to the damage caused by their action or *in*action. Budget cuts, unrealistic goals, insufficient resources, and demands for more and better results all contribute to the current state of engagement. Or, should I say, disengagement.

It's hard for leaders to even consider the fact that they bear responsibility for the level of engagement within their organizations. I've had conversations with many management professionals in which I laid out my diagnosis for the disengagement epidemic. Their reactions were nearly all the same: defensiveness mixed with a bit of amusement. "So you think leaders are fully to blame?" Trying to be polite, I'd respond, "I think leaders and their employees co-create an employee experience that fosters engagement, but it begins and ends with great leadership." In other words, yes, it still boils down to leadership.

The problem, as I've mentioned above, lies specifically in the nature of leadership positions. They enjoy the luxury of being far-removed from the day-to-day operations under their purview, yet they dictate the strategy, budget, and expectations with which employees must work. As we will see in the coming chapters, that is a recipe for disengagement and can even lead to desperate or unethical behavior within an organization's ranks.

A well-known vehicle for demonstrating how the vast chasm between leaders and their employees causes disengagement is the television program *Undercover Boss*. The premise of this show involves bridging the aforementioned gap by having a senior executive dress in disguise and work among the rank and file for a few days. After witnessing firsthand what it's like to do their employees' jobs, nearly every boss has the same epiphany: "Wow, my employees have it pretty hard here." For whatever reason—inefficient tools, lack of support, poor training, or a toxic culture—the employee experience at these companies forces the undercover bosses to rethink the way they lead and the decisions they make. They have forgotten (or never knew) what it's like to be the low man on the totem pole when the you-know-what rolls all the way downhill, smacks you in the face, and there's nothing you can do about it.

What I try to make clear in the first chapters of this book are the reasons for disengagement throughout the business world. The truth about what causes disengagement might be difficult for leaders to grasp, but they need to open themselves up to taking ownership for rectifying the situation—because it won't get any better until they do.

CHAPTER 1

THE SAD STATE OF EMPLOYEE ENGAGEMENT IN TODAY'S WORKPLACE

What comes to mind when you think of work? What images or emotions does it conjure? For a majority of employees, going to work elicits feelings of despair, frustration, anxiety, boredom, or just plain indifference. They either lack the inspiration to care about their work or are too busy dealing with all of the nonsense present in today's workplace that makes caring almost impossible. Considering that we spend the majority of our waking hours during the week at work, it's pretty depressing to know that most employees are so dejected or at least not engaged in their jobs. Many associate work with servitude or drudgery and too many think that's just fine. They think work isn't *supposed* to be fun or enjoyable or inspirational, that employees get a paycheck and do their jobs and that's all there is to it. These are the same people in management positions who bleat and fume about poor business outcomes like customer dissatisfaction without realizing they are the toxic by-products of low engagement.

THE NUMBERS SPEAK FOR THEMSELVES

Gallup, the global leader in measuring employee engagement, regularly publishes its findings on the current state of engagement in the United States and worldwide. And the results paint a pretty bleak picture of how employees feel about work. In 2017, approximately 60 percent of U.S. workers were classified as feeling disengaged based on Gallup's survey and analytics.[1] To put that into context, the Bureau of Labor Statistics reports that there are approximately 123 million full time employees in the United States.[2] Out of those 123 million, almost 78 million employees are disengaged. That's more than the combined populations of California, Texas, and Michigan. That's a lot of unhappy workers.

Gallup estimates the cost of disengagement for U.S. employers to be between $450 and $550 billion per year.[1] Here's a little perspective: In 2017, the U.S. GDP was about $18 trillion.[3] Employee disengagement costs businesses the equivalent of nearly 3 percent of America's GDP. Clearly, the problem has a severe financial impact for organizations, and an argument could be made that it also affects the economy on a macro level. After all, goods and services aren't just selling themselves. People make companies successful and are responsible for their performance on a highly competitive economic playing field. It just makes good business sense to have employees on board and committed to helping their organizations achieve success instead of just barely giving enough effort to get by. Unfortunately, the facts and research show that less than one-quarter of employees worldwide actually fit the engagement bill.

What makes these statistics even more disturbing is the fact that employee engagement levels have remained mostly stagnant despite increased awareness among managers and executives. By now, most business leaders are at least generally aware of the employee engagement concept and understand that it connects to organizational outcomes. There are, of course, those for whom employee engagement is an unfamiliar notion, and they certainly can be blamed for some disengagement in the workforce. They simply don't know any better than to do business the way it's been done since the days of the Industrial Revolution. Employees today, like their factory worker forebears, are merely a means to an end. However, there is another group of leaders that combines this factory-era management mindset with a gross misunderstanding of how employee engagement actually works. The result is a bizarre work culture in which employees are still treated like pieces of machinery, but they get an ice cream social and company picnic in the summer and free yoga classes and ugly sweater contests in the winter.

I have a name for this perversion of the employee engagement concept. I call it the Stepford Employee Fallacy. Essentially, *engaged* employees are expected to come tap dancing into the office every morning wearing smiles so big that their facial muscles cramp up and cheerily exclaim, "Hi! How are you? Are you engaged? I sure am engaged! Oh boy! Oh gosh gee golly willikers! I love this company! I love my job! I'm going to give 110 percent every day just because I'm getting a paycheck!" They should act like high-performing robots with attitudes so positive that they leave rainbows in their wakes as they skip out of the office at 8:00 p.m. every night. It's easier for leaders to believe and reinforce this fallacy than it is to face the verity of how employee engagement really works and make substantive changes to their organizations' employee experience.

It is my observation that the leaders who perpetuate this dysfunctional model are more culpable than their oblivious counterparts for the mass levels of employee disengagement because they subscribe to the Stepford Employee Fallacy. They use the actual business benefits of employee engagement to justify their approach, telling employees, "We need and expect you to be fully engaged so we can beat our competitors/dazzle our customers/please our shareholders." They see business results as the ends and employee engagement as the means, but put forth superficial and perfunctory efforts toward the latter. Scratch the surface of many companies with a Stepford Employee mindset and beneath the facade of smiley employees working hard or having fun in the office egg-tossing contest, you'll see human beings putting on a performance just to make it through the workday. The same disengaging leadership behaviors, decisions, and interactions are present. There's just some extra-sugary coating to hide the bitter taste.

My first full-time job out of college was working for a company with this kind of culture. Employees were treated like toddlers instead of business partners. Managers reprimanded you if they felt you were misbehaving (i.e. raising valid concerns) and simultaneously insulted you with patronizing gestures that would have been more appropriate for preschoolers. One day,

I arrived at the office to find that one of the supervisors had left little stickers and cutesy knickknacks on everyone's desk for Employee Appreciation Day. This came from a management team who, around the same time, fired a single mother for taking too many absences to care for her sick child. Did the tchotchkes have any effect on our engagement? Nope. We threw them in the trash.

For years, I used to take the train every day to Boston where I worked at a job that, for several reasons, just wasn't making me feel happy or engaged. At the end of the workday, I and hundreds of other commuters would pile back on to the train, jockey for a seat—or at least a place to stand—and ride back home for just a few hours of rest before doing it all over again the following day. I can still remember the sight of crowds of workers shuffling along the train platform each morning, marching grimly toward jobs they probably hated. The image of employees slowly and miserably ambling into the office as if they were cattle headed for slaughter certainly reflects the sorry state of affairs for employee engagement in the modern workplace. There are more people disengaged in their jobs than there are those who feel engaged. And that trend doesn't seem to be getting much better anytime soon, unless the future promises some key changes to the way organizations treat their talent.

SOCIO-POLITICAL, TECHNOLOGICAL, AND ECONOMIC FACTORS AT PLAY

Over the past decade, there has been a fundamental shift in the way employees view and relate to their work. A powerful blend of socio-political, technological, and economic factors such as The Great Recession of 2008, the proliferation of social media, and the influx of millennial workers has influenced employee engagement in profound ways. Work is no longer synonymous with the dull, repetitive labor and strictly autocratic management model of the Industrial Revolution, though some organizations and their leaders still haven't come to terms with that reality. It also has lost the confidence granted by near-guaranteed stable employment, a clear career ladder, and shared prosperity typical of organizations in the late twentieth century. Now, constant uncertainty, downsizing, and slowed wage growth are the new normal in today's knowledge economy. Market volatility and disruption keep businesses in a constant state of flux while their employees work in fear and frustration, clinging to whatever livelihood pays the bills and puts food on the table. There's little reason for employees to feel engaged, and their leaders aren't helping the situation by creating an unattractive work experience that only makes things worse.

After a calamitous economic downturn in the late 2000s, millions of Americans were left unemployed, under-employed, and disenfranchised. U.S. corporations outsourced talent, froze salaries, cut benefits and pensions, and moved operations to cheaper locales, leaving the working class feeling powerless without much to be engaged about—until a wealthy non-politician stepped forward pledging to upset the establishment and return power to the people. The working masses have always been a prime audience for politicians eager to score votes with promises of improving their work lives, and the man who would become forty-fifth president of the United States sure gave them quite a show.

The 2016 presidential election resulted in one of the most shocking political upsets in U.S. history, and with it came much controversy and discourse over corporatism. Republican candidate Donald Trump ran his campaign on a platform of making America "great again" by returning jobs to those hit hardest by the recession while repealing job-killing regulations to usher in a new era of business growth that would benefit working families. After his narrow victory, the newly elected president began the process of staffing his cabinet with Wall Street insiders and corporate moguls whose agendas leaned toward removing "burdensome" worker protections and granting tax breaks to the wealthy. Whether trickle-down economics actually benefits average workers is and has been a subject of heated debate, and is beyond the scope of this book. However, the new administration's legislative goals certainly stirred vocal commentary and notable activism from the political left and right. With companies free to operate in a more *laissez faire* capacity, many Democrats and Independents feared Trump and his staff would turn back the clock on workers' rights, an action that would surely have an eventual effect on employee experience and hurt engagement. Regardless of voters' political leanings, the election made it clear that U.S. employees are not happy with the way work is currently *not* working in their favor. It's an indication of the underlying anger and disengagement people feel; a warning sign to organizations that whatever they are doing (or not doing) to address employee engagement isn't helping.

Along with socio-political elements like globalization, outsourcing, and deregulation informing the current state of employee engagement, technology is playing a major role as well. The threat of job loss to artificial intelligence has not yet been realized to the extent that so many feared. However, technology and the Internet in particular have made employee engagement a lightning rod topic for both workers and their leaders.

Social media has enabled employees with unprecedented access to information about companies and voices to instantly share it. Before the Internet, employees had to rely on their own circle of connections to learn what it was really like to work for a certain organization. Companies enjoyed a high degree of control over their reputations and could easily get away with mistreating workers or maintaining toxic work cultures. They also controlled pay data and held all negotiating power in the hiring process. With the advent of LinkedIn, finding a contact who works at a company where you plan to apply for an open position takes only a minute. Now, one can learn all the dirt about a company before they apply, leveraging digital networks and anonymous forums to understand more about the working world than was possible even fifteen years ago. Websites like Payscale and Salary give employees insights into wage equity and arm them with information proving they are underpaid in their jobs. Glassdoor gives current and former employees of companies across the world the opportunity to share their experiences, providing transparency for job seekers and accountability for employers.

This new era of knowledge sharing has riled many employers now that the cat's out of the bag and their less-than-perfect work cultures are put on display for the whole world to judge. Disengaged employees now have the means to give honest feedback without fear of reprisal for being insubordinate or disparaging the company. They raise awareness of their leaders' damaging behaviors and poor decisions, upping the stakes for employers who otherwise resist accepting and implementing employee feedback. Whereas employers could comfortably go about doing business as they pleased before ubiquitous Internet scrutiny, nowadays they actually have to put an effort into creating an attractive employee value proposition (why someone would want to work for their company and not a competitor).

Sites like Glassdoor not only publicly post reviews of employers—the good, the bad, and the ugly—but they also aggregate and score companies on the basis of what reviewers have to say. High-value or high-potential job seekers can instantly screen out an ill-suited employer with just a cursory glance at its Glassdoor page. Current employees can determine whether the grass is greener and jump ship if a competing organization offers a better employee experience. Some employers have resorted to posting fake reviews on Glassdoor to artificially boost their overall scores, while others have tried strong-arming the site's administrators into handing over the identities of reviewers. Neither tactic is recommended or very useful. The responses of these employers are very telling of how they view and handle criticism from the people they should really be trying to keep happy and engaged: their employees. They also show how much this area of IT has affected engagement and how workers express the reasons for their disengagement.

Discussion of social media and the Internet would not be complete without mentioning the people who use this technology. And the people most associated with all things tech are millennials. Having been the first generation to grow up with computers and demonstrate proficiency in web surfing, these twenty-to-thirty-somethings let their tech-savvy nature color the way they go about life, including work. Millennials are called the Glassdoor Generation for a reason. Just as they are likely to go on Yelp to read reviews in search of the best local sushi joint, this cohort will refer to Glassdoor as a primary tool for deciding on a potential employer and have no qualms about sharing their thoughts on employment experiences via the Internet.

An employee at Yelp was fired in 2016 for sending the company's CEO a letter criticizing various aspects of its employee experience and then posting the missive online.[4] Her actions sparked admiration from some and scorn from many others. Detractors flung the usual stereotypes about millennials her way: spoiled, entitled, and lazy. The endless discourse on Generation Y in the workplace is evidence that this age group has taken the business world in a new direction, one where employers must adapt and respond to their expectations, or at least consider the benefits of doing so. But that's how employee engagement actually works. It's interesting, though not surprising, that it took the youngest segment of the workforce to shape the practice and understanding of employee engagement. Really, it's not just about what millennials want out of their work; it's what all employees want. Every age group certainly has its common qualities, but individual employees have their own engagement drivers that leaders should learn and leverage.

Millennials pose a quandary for business leaders who aren't quite sure how to attract and retain them without appearing to give in to their demands. On one hand, the idea of flexing to meet your subordinates' needs, especially those who are much younger, might make some managers' eyes twitch. On the other hand, employers will soon have no choice but to cater to millennials. They are already closing in on becoming the dominant age group in the workforce. By 2025, they will make up 75 percent of the talent pool.[5] So, even if you tire of having to give Matty Millennial constant positive feedback while telling him for the tenth time that you can't promote him after just a year, and you decide to fire him, you will probably be replacing him with Missy Millennial or Mikey Millennial.

Some organizations are trying to capitalize on millennial talent, but in all the wrong ways and for all the wrong reasons. They create an image of having a cool startup culture with beer on Fridays and a ping pong table in the break room, or they play up their corporate social responsibility efforts to seem like a company that cares. It's all fluff covering a dysfunctional culture that lacks any true engagement levers. Employers will advertise the fun perks and quirks, appealing to candidates from an emotional angle in the hopes of luring enthusiastic, energetic, young talent. Meanwhile, their older workers, who've been around the rodeo and can see through the organization's saccharine facade, are being targeted for replacement. I've seen this scheme in action. Although the seasoned employees represent a wealth of institutional knowledge, they are also considered expensive liabilities. Why keep cranky Bev at $65,000 a year when you can bring on eager-to-please Jenni and pay her $35,000 to do the same job? Does it matter *why* Bev says she's "had it with this place"? Nah, just get rid of her and hire some new blood by waving Whole Foods gift cards, free beer, and other shiny objects in front of their faces.

Millennials are catching on, though. They're becoming just as burnt out and disengaged as the generations before them. That's why engagement levels among the different age groups are all roughly the same (i.e. not good). Modern Survey, a talent analytics think tank, published a report in 2015 showing that, among the three main generations at work—millennials, Generation X, and baby boomers—only about 14 percent of each cohort reported being fully engaged in their jobs.[6] When it comes to engagement, leaders expect discretionary effort from these groups while continuing to ignore the real factors that inspire employees to go above and beyond.

GENDER DISPARITY AND THE DIVERSITY STRUGGLE

The concepts of diversity and inclusion are fairly nebulous for plenty of business leaders and difficult for them to grasp. They understand on a superficial level that having a diverse and inclusive organization creates an attractive employee value proposition by giving the appearance of being a welcoming, progressive organization. They might even have an appreciation for the fact that diversity, like employee engagement, has a measurable effect on the bottom line.

What leaders fail to realize, or even accept, is that having a population of diverse talent merely paints a colorful picture of their organizations. The story behind the painting is quite different, though. In other words, executives set hiring quotas for traditionally underrepresented groups but don't address the underlying reasons why those people aren't being hired, or, if they are, why they aren't sticking around. They think of diversity and inclusion as a numbers game: attract diverse talent through targeted recruiting and retain them by pushing a designated percentage of them through the advancement pipeline. If they can get more women (or any other marginalized demographic) into senior leadership positions by setting ambitious goals for female advancement, then they've ostensibly succeeded at cultivating diversity in their ranks. But it rarely works, at least not for very long. Why? Because there are cultural barriers preventing women and minorities from stepping outside the traditional white male business paradigm and acting as authentic, unique individuals at work.

Further, there are biases and ideals that undermine the very meaning of diversity and inclusion while purporting to maintain institutional integrity for the sake of doing business *the right way*. All this mindset accomplishes is it reinforces the status quo. Never mind that there is no single correct way to operate a complex organization, just as there are different approaches to doing a job. Silicon Valley is known as the cradle of innovation where the technological revolution continues to be fought. What we are seeing in recent years, however, is that women working in technology face unintentional and even blatant discrimination despite noble efforts from industry leaders pushing for equality. Gender disparity of course is not isolated to one industry. The World Economic Forum published a report in 2016 showing that Information and Communication Technology actually represents the third lowest population of female talent out of the nine industries and 371 companies surveyed.[7]

IT is of particular interest because women have, until recently, typically felt left out of STEM (science, technology, engineering, and math) disciplines. One of their male counterparts offered a controversial explanation as to why so few women land and keep coding jobs at Google. The Google staffer's manifesto on diversity within the tech giant went viral during the summer of 2017, and he took a good deal of heat and praise for what he wrote.[8] In his memo, the software engineer—a young, Caucasian male—laid out his argument that diversity for its own sake is not necessarily beneficial for businesses and that programs specifically aimed at developing minorities is discriminatory toward anyone who does not fit into one of those groups. He also made the unfortunate assertion that the gender pay gap is a myth in spite of countless studies across every economic sector demonstrating women are, indeed, paid less than men for the same work.

However, for all of the confusing and inaccurate observations in this open letter, its author actually made some valid points while recommending effective cultural changes to promote sustainable diversity. One of his central arguments is about biological differences between the genders being detrimental to women in the workplace, which is true. Rather than recommending that women should find less stressful jobs because they are, on average, more prone to anxiety, he advised a shift in Google's culture as well as a redesign of certain roles so they allow both sexes to thrive. That's a good thing! Google is viewed from the outside as one of the most progressive businesses in the world, yet its workforce is comprised of mostly white men. The company's self-reported statistics on diversity and inclusion show that women only make up 31 percent of its employee population.[9]

One of the leading experts on gender diversity in the workplace, Barbara Annis, published a book several years ago introducing the concept of Gender Intelligence, which is an informed appreciation of the innate differences between the sexes.[10] In the book, Annis exposes the critical blind spots and communication gaps between men and women in the workplace and explains why women are leaving their employers. The result of Gender Intelligence is equality in *value*, not just equality in representation, for both men and women at all levels of an organization. Since women do not feel valued, that they cannot be themselves inside a male-oriented business model, they are "voting with their feet," as Annis describes, and going to work for competitors or starting their own businesses. The diversity problem is cultural, and it requires a commitment to change that starts at the very top. Sadly, the rate of change is slow. Women are unlikely to reach parity with men in the business world anytime soon, which is a shame because, as we've seen, the costs of disengaging such a large segment of the workforce are simply too great to be ignored.

It is my belief that the problem of diversity in the modern workplace and, by extension, the dismal state of employee engagement are attributable to a lack of empathy. Another point the Google engineer raised in his memo was that the company places too much emphasis on empathy in making policy decisions and should instead be more rational. He went on to dismiss Google's focus on microaggressions because, in his opinion, it increases sensitivity and makes perpetrators afraid to speak their minds. The main flaw with this train of thought is that it essentially gives anyone license to say whatever they want to colleagues without taking responsibility for how it might affect them mentally or emotionally. As I say throughout this book, however, human beings are emotional creatures. To ignore that fact, especially in business, is terribly short-sighted.

Under the former Googler's premise, microaggressions are necessary in everyday discourse if an organization hopes to foster open and candid communication among employees. He implied that, because microaggressions are unintentional, they should not be given such attention when considering effective strategies for diversity and inclusion. Well, that's just flat out wrong. Microaggressions may be unintentional, but they can nevertheless be harmful to engagement and will subvert efforts to increase diversity.

For example, consider the comment, "I'm surprised you've done so well coding! Women don't seem well suited for highly technical roles." That's the kind of unintended slight that, while appearing innocent to the person saying it, is insulting and denigrating to the recipient.

Culturally aware, empathetic managers truly are better equipped to lead and engage diverse teams. They know which levers to pull and how their decisions, behaviors, and interactions can affect those they manage. It isn't coddling. It's having the knowledge of how to engage people and of how to not disengage them. Samuel Culbert, professor at UCLA's Anderson School of Management, talks about being an other-directed manager in his book *Good People, Bad Managers.*[11] This stems from the concept of being a servant leader, which old-school-management types consider absolutely blasphemous. They don't understand the correlation between treating their workers how they, the employees, would like to be treated and higher engagement. While it might seem backwards, adjusting and flexing to employees greatly improves engagement. Yet, so few leaders grasp and accept this methodology, thus accounting for the low engagement we see today.

I once attempted to counsel a manager on becoming more culturally aware in her interactions with members of the diverse work group she led. One team member—I'll call her Xi—was an immigrant from Taiwan. This manager relied mostly on sarcasm to inject humor into situations and discussions that would otherwise be boring or straightforward. It was a well-intended attempt at bringing levity to the team dynamic. Unbeknownst to the manager, her sarcastic comments were causing confusion and stress for Xi because this form of ironic communication was totally inappropriate in her country of origin. Asian culture tends toward saving face and eschewing any type of language that might humiliate or embarrass someone. When trying to praise Xi in front of her teammates, the manager would say things like, "Xi completed her walk through of the requirements with all stakeholders and it went awful, just awful."

I tried to explain to the manager that sarcasm doesn't have the same humorous effect on someone from an Asian country as it would a Westerner, but she brushed off my concerns. When Xi led her first training session for a group of customers, I was mortified to hear that the manager prepared the class by telling them, "This is Xi's first time training, so please be sure to boo her and tell her what a terrible job she is doing." Xi eventually grew accustomed to her manager's sarcastic humor, but not before months of discomfiture had passed. Imagine this lack of empathy on a much larger scale to understand the gravity of the diversity struggle that so many employers can't seem to address.

Who would want to work in an environment where managers and co-workers lack the requisite empathy, cultural awareness, and emotional intelligence necessary to foster positive relationships with people from diverse backgrounds? It simply isn't realistic in today's globally interconnected economy where diverse talent views employee experience as the new currency. Those employers who offer the best employee experience for all, not just for the majority, are the ones who will win the war for talent and dominate their respective markets. Empathy and cultural awareness do not create overly sensitive leaders who lose sight of business priorities in favor of political correctness. Being empathetic *is* a business priority. I would argue that it should be a top priority because, as I say, organizations employ and do business with human beings. It's impossible to remove the human aspect of running a business without engagement and, ultimately, bottom-line results suffering. That is pretty clearly evidenced by the troubling statistics cited throughout this chapter.

LOOKING AHEAD

The current state of employee engagement appears pretty bleak. We've seen how a large portion of the modern workforce is disengaged and costing businesses billions of dollars each year. Next, we will try to understand how this came to be. In Chapter 3, I will point to the very nature of corporations as the smoking gun responsible for employee engagement's critical condition. But first, we must look at the way leaders react to what they perceive to be the problem, specifically that employees aren't engaging themselves and instead choose to disengage or even actively disengage.

Chapter 2 visits the notions of disengagement and active disengagement from an angle that some leaders will find a bit hard to stomach, because they knowingly or subconsciously subscribe to the Stepford Employee Fallacy. They view disengaged employees as the root cause of their employee engagement troubles, and they believe that purging these naysayers and complainers will miraculously transform their organizations into ultra-productive bastions of business supremacy. What we will see in the coming pages, however, is that disengagement is merely a symptom of underlying cultural or organizational weaknesses. It is workers' natural response to a poor employee experience, meaning one or more aspects of working for their employer is a factor *causing* them to be disengaged. Until leaders come to understand that they are responsible for creating an employee experience that engages (or disengages) their talent, they will continue to perpetuate the cycle that has caused the sad state of employee engagement in today's workplace.

NOTES

1. Gallup. *State of the American Workplace Report.* 2017. http://news.gallup.com/file/reports/199961/SOAW%202017%20FINAL.pdf

2. Bureau of Labor Statistics. *Labor Force Statistics from the Current Population Survey.* 2016. https://www.bls.gov/cps/cpsaat08.htm

3. Knoema. *World GDP Ranking 2017.* 2017. https://knoema.com/nwnfkne/world-gdp-ranking-2017-gdp-by-country-data-and-charts

4. Chew, Jonathan. "Yelp Fired an Employee After She Wrote a Post About Her Lousy Pay." *Fortune.* February 22, 2016. http://fortune.com/2016/02/22/yelp-employee-ceo/

5. Hais, Michael and Winograd, Morley. "How Millennials Could Upend Wall Street and Corporate America." Brookings. May 2014. https://www.brookings.edu/wp-content/uploads/2016/06/Brookings_Winogradfinal.pdf

6. Modern Survey. *Employee Engagement and the Generations.* July 2015. http://www.modernsurvey.com/wp-content/uploads/2015/07/Employee-Engagement-and-the-Generations-Report-Summer-2015.pdf

7. World Economic Forum. *The Industry Gender Gap: Women and Work in the Fourth Industrial Revolution.* January 2016. http://www3.weforum.org/docs/WEF_FOJ_Executive_Summary_GenderGap.pdf

8. Emerson, Sarah, Koebler, Jason, and Matsakis, Louise. "Here Are the Citations for the Anti-Diversity Manifesto Circulating at Google." *Vice.* August 7, 2017. https://motherboard.vice.com/en_us/article/evzjww/here-are-the-citations-for-the-anti-diversity-manifesto-circulating-at-google

9. Naughton, Eileen. "Making Progress on Diversity and Inclusion." *Google* (blog). June 29, 2017. https://www.blog.google/topics/diversity/making-progress-diversity-and-inclusion/

10. Annis, Barbara and Merron, Keith. *Gender Intelligence: Breakthrough Strategies for Increasing Diversity and Improving Your Bottom Line.* New York: Harper Business, 2014.

11. Culbert, Samuel. *Good People, Bad Managers: How Work Culture Corrupts Good Intentions.* New York: Oxford University Press, 2017

CHAPTER 2

REDEFINING WHAT IT MEANS TO BE DISENGAGED

We need to have a talk about the "actively disengaged" employee label. You see, businesses love labels. They love to categorize, collate, and quantify everything, including their employees. The problem with labeling employees is that doing so dehumanizes them. It ignores all of the complexities behind their behavior or work performance, or even their level of engagement. In terms of employee engagement, workers have traditionally been given one of three labels depending on how engaged they are: engaged, disengaged, and actively disengaged.

Gallup defines an engaged employee as one who is committed to, involved in, and enthusiastic about his or her organization (Gallup's analytics put about 33 percent of U.S. employees in this category). Disengaged employees are essentially going through the motions during their workday and don't really go above and beyond (roughly 50 percent of employees are considered disengaged). And finally actively disengaged employees—those who exhibit behaviors or attitudes considered detrimental to the organization's success—make up a little less than 20 percent of Gallup's sample population.[1] I'd like to give some much-needed clarity on this final engagement label because it is very often misrepresented by the literature surrounding it and misunderstood by those who apply it.

Actively disengaged employees are usually described as organizational pariahs who should be given a swift boot out the door. I've also heard some organizational development folks call them "terrorists," which I think is a bit much. Aon Hewitt published a white paper calling them "workplace prisoners" who don't say positive things about their employer or strive to do any more than the bare minimum, yet they have no plans to leave.[2] And we've all probably heard the rowing team analogy that describes actively disengaged employees as trying to sink the boat, which, again, is sort of a mischaracterization. Here's the thing: unless you inadvertently hired a sociopath or a criminal, nobody is *actively* trying to destroy your company just for the fun of it. In my experience, I have worked with many employees who finally became so fed up with their boss or the company, itself that they threw up their hands and said, "You know what? Screw this place! I don't care anymore!" That doesn't make them bad people, or terrorists, or even bad employees; it simply makes them human beings reacting to a negative situation that, nine times out of ten, is outside of their control.

The flawed model of employee engagement that continues to be circulated today is that employees are responsible for their own engagement, or that it is a two-way street. In a perfect world, yes, that would make sense. Employees would be able to bring their whole selves to work and love every minute of it. If they have any ideas for improving their work lives, they would freely approach management with suggestions and those leaders would implement changes to better engage their workforce. Unfortunately, the business world does not currently work that way. Employees are reluctant to share what's bothering them because they know their concerns would fall on deaf ears, or worse, they would be labeled troublemakers or complainers. That's the real issue with calling employees actively disengaged. Managers have carte blanche to slap that label on employees they feel are rocking (or sinking) the boat because the contemporary employee engagement model reinforces the notion that these employees are somehow defective and that their leaders should accept no culpability.

Some organizations take an extreme approach to handling disengagement that is both ineffective and a little creepy. Buffer, a social media advertising service, has what it calls a "no complaining" culture in which any form of negative expression is frowned upon.[3] The problem with such a culture is it creates a slippery slope that allows managers to dismiss any employee concerns and punish those who speak out about their experience. The thing about complaining in a modern organizational setting is that it gives employees at least some sense of relief or catharsis to vent their frustrations when leaders won't address their needs or expectations. Even if it seems petty or passive aggressive, employees actually derive a psychological benefit from complaining, which we will discuss later in the chapter.

A culture of forced positivity is one of the primary tenets of the Stepford Employee Fallacy. Employees are expected to always be positive, happy, and smiling regardless of how they are treated. Trying to ignore or penalize negative feedback is, at best, a naive attempt to give the appearance of an engaged workforce. If employees aren't complaining (or can't complain), then you've solved your disengagement problem, correct? Not quite. Disengagement, in all its forms, is merely a symptom of an underlying condition that leaders need to remedy: a negative employee experience.

I have seen how the present approach to employee engagement works from both an employee's perspective and a manager's perspective. Years ago, I worked for a company that wanted to create a culture of engagement and employees were pressured into completing "anonymous" surveys to share their thoughts about working there. I asked a few of my colleagues whether they participated and they either said, "No", or "Yes, but I didn't give honest answers." I asked why, and the response was always the same: "Because they know who wrote which answers and they'll find a way to punish you for being negative." It was true. This particular company didn't foster a culture of engagement; they forced it. They beat employees over the head with it. So the employees who were unhappy or disengaged just kept their heads down and their mouths shut, because those who did speak up were eventually forced out.

As a manager at another company, I was having a conversation with one of our executives about recurring meetings we had with our staff to discuss any roadblocks they were experiencing or changes we could make to our department. She agreed that we should continue the meetings as long as they didn't "turn into a bitch-fest." And that kind of attitude is not uncommon among managers. They view any dissent or dissatisfaction as "bitching" and the offending employees get slapped with the actively disengaged moniker. Well-meaning experts say that employees need to be constructive in their feedback and offer solutions. That's fair, but even if employees know what the solution is, I have seen that, more often than not, change never comes. Or when change does come, it's too little too late, and the employees are so disenfranchised at that point that recapturing their engagement becomes nearly impossible. Look at the tools employees use in their jobs, as an example. Far too many technology projects result in systems that are barely usable, leaving employees frustrated and unsupported by managers who still expect them to be engaged and crank out quality work. I've seen employees break down in tears at their desks or had them confess to me they feared losing their jobs because a system so inhibited their productivity.

The point is, employees do not wake up one day and decide that they want to sabotage your company's success because it seemed like a great idea. There is a reason why they say negative things about the organization to their coworkers, friends, and family. There is a reason why they withdraw effort or are apathetic. There is a reason why they are actively disengaged. It's because they are human, and humans are complex, emotional creatures.

BEHAVIORS AND COGNITIVE BIASES

The following paragraphs will explore some of the human behaviors that are interpreted as active disengagement, shed light on what causes these behaviors, and provide guidance to leaders for being more empathetic and open-minded in addressing them.

Passive Aggression

When you think of passive aggressive behavior, what comes to mind? Eye-rolling? Silent treatment? In an organizational setting, passive aggressive behavior manifests among employees in these ways and more, including slowed productivity, taking long breaks, or ignoring managers. At face value, these are all certainly counterproductive and would fall under the actively disengaged label. But if we look at the *why* behind these behaviors, things become far less cut and dried.

In a 2015 paper they published for *Personnel Psychology*, researchers from several universities concluded that employees who experienced hostility in the form of verbal attacks or intimidation actually countered the stressful effects of this abuse by retaliating with passive aggression.[4] Research participants reported lower levels of psychological stress after they retaliated against a hostile boss by withholding effort, complaining, or otherwise being passive aggressive in carrying out their work. It's a way of restoring equilibrium in the power relationship between employers and employees. The findings from this research validate the work of Janet Yellen, former U.S. Federal Reserve Chair, and her husband who jointly wrote a paper in the 1990s called *The Fair Wage-Effort Hypothesis*.[5] They theorized that workers will exert or withdraw effort in proportion to how fairly they are paid. If they are paid below-average wages, they will only exert partial effort as a way to compensate for the real or perceived inequity. I would say this hypothesis has been proven by research and that it extends beyond wages to any other factor comprising an employee's experience of working at her organization. I call this principle The Experience-Effort Correlation.

Figure 2.1 illustrates how The Experience-Effort Correlation works. In essence, the better the experience leaders create for their employees, the greater the effort employees will exert. So, an employee who is being paid well below market average wages and is mistreated by his boss has a negative employee experience and will put forth a negative effort by engaging in passive aggressive behavior. The negative behavior is caused by the negative experience. Conversely, an engaging work experience prompts a high level of effort.

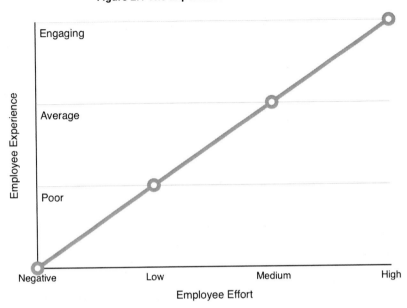

Figure 2.1 The Experience-Effort Correlation

Reactive Devaluation

Many managers have been trained to think that they shouldn't care whether or not their employees like them. They are encouraged to make unpopular decisions and ignore employee opinions. "I don't care if my employees hate me," they say. "I care about results!" But leaders, you should care if your employees hate you. In fact, you should be deeply troubled if your employees hate you. As humans, when we perceive another person as an enemy or antagonist, we are far less likely to buy into proposed change initiatives or engage as partners in action. This is due to a cognitive bias called reactive devaluation. It's why so many change efforts fail and why such a large population of the modern workforce is actively disengaged. The relationship between managers and employees accounts for the largest variance in engagement scores, according to Gallup.[1] Therefore, it is of the utmost importance for leaders to build open, trusting, and empathetic relationships with their employees. Otherwise the resistance from those who are disengaged and actively disengaged will have a dramatic effect on the organization's overall success. And leaders will only have themselves to blame. Except they seldom do.

What happens when managers refuse to accept accountability for creating and maintaining positive relationships with workers? They say these employees have an "attitude problem"; that they are actively disengaged and should therefore be transitioned out of the company as quickly as possible. The issue is never that the employee isn't being paid at least market average wages. No, the issue is that she is "entitled." The issue is never that the employee is forced to use tools and systems that are slow, unreliable, and counterintuitive. No, the issue is that he is "unproductive." The issue is never that the manager inflicts nonsensical and time-consuming processes on her employees. No, the issue is that an employee who raises concerns "isn't a team player." And then when these same managers need their employees to partner with them on change efforts or to buy into a new company initiative, they wonder why there is so much resistance. If your employees view you as their enemy, you must swallow your pride and take action to win back their trust.

Negativity Bias

Another cognitive bias that causes employees to be actively disengaged involves the powerful impact that negative experiences have on the human psyche. Negativity bias among disengaged and actively disengaged employees as a result of fear-based management practices, high levels of stress, or other unpleasant workplace experiences yields less innovation, less collaboration, and less trust. You've probably heard the oft-cited customer experience statistic which states that it takes twelve positive experiences to compensate for just one unresolved bad customer experience. In other words, if a customer has a bad experience with a particular brand, that company would need to offset the damage by creating at least a dozen positive experiences for that same customer in order to regain her trust and loyalty. That is an excellent illustration of how negativity bias works.

And this principle does not just apply to customer relationships. Employee relationships can be damaged just as easily (or even more so) by a negative work experience, thus requiring a strong effort from leaders to re-engage these individuals. Remember: Your employees are your first customers.

Sir Richard Branson said it perfectly when he described his philosophy on putting employees first [6]:

> If the person who's working for your company is not given the right tools, is not looked after, is not appreciated, they're not gonna do things with a smile and therefore the customer will be treated in a way where often they won't want to come back for more. So, my philosophy has always been, if you can put staff first, your customer second and shareholders third, effectively, in the end, the shareholders do well, the customers do better, and yourself are happy.

Negative work experiences can come in many forms, and what might seem totally inconsequential or even necessary to a manager could have a lasting impact on the employee experiencing them. A classic example would be the practice of micromanagement. Nobody likes to be micromanaged, especially grown adults, because it makes them feel incompetent or untrustworthy. A supervisor who micromanages might be an otherwise pleasant person, but the damage he is causing to his relationship with employees has a profound impact on engagement. The irony in these types of situations is, although the manager might intend to increase productivity or efficiency, the negative experiences he creates for his employees through harmful management practices have the exact opposite effect in the long term.

RE-ENGAGING EMPLOYEES

One of the fatal mistakes managers make in terms of handling employee grievances is taking the traditional "I'm the boss" approach that reinforces the unequal power dynamic between workers and their leaders.

For most adults, having a meeting with the boss to discuss workplace concerns usually leaves them feeling unheard and defeated. Picture Meryl Streep in *The Devil Wears Prada* glaring at you over the top of her glasses from behind her desk and then waving you away with a dismissive "That's all." This type of mindset stems from an outdated understanding of what leadership means. I've worked with plenty of managers who seem to have received the same combat training on how to do battle with their employees so that they always emerge victorious. They dig in their heels and refuse to concede when employees have raised a valid concern about something that is affecting their level of engagement. They pull the boss card and intimidate their employees into silence. What they don't realize—because they probably haven't been taught any different—is that this approach leads to a culture of begrudging compliance. And that's the best case scenario (read: disengagement). If left un-checked, the management behaviors, decisions, and interactions that trigger the previously discussed cognitive biases will cause active disengagement.

What, then, can leaders do to correct the situation? It's simple, really: listen and take action. The problem lies in the fact that neither of these is easy for most leaders to do because they are still stuck in the Dark Ages where a command-and-control management style reigned supreme. But this is a new era. A leadership style of empathy, humility, and curiosity is the only way to create an engaging work culture.

Listen

Listening with empathy, humility, and curiosity means taking off the boss goggles and setting your ego aside to have a human conversation with your disengaged employee. Far too many managers are so affronted that any of their employees would dare question them. I say this in the kindest way possible, but they really need to get over themselves. Scoot out from behind the desk, sit with your employee or take a walk, and just hear them out.

Here are a few dos and don'ts for listening with empathy, humility, and curiosity:

Do

- Do position yourself such that your employee doesn't feel inferior (facing a boss who is sitting behind her desk feels like going to the principal's office)
- Do set aside your own biases or preconceived notions
- Do encourage the employee to tell you why they feel a certain way
- Do reflect on a time you were in a similar situation and share it
- Do validate your employee's feelings by saying "I can see why you feel that way" or "If I were you, I would feel that way as well"
- Do thank your employee for being so candid, and assure them that you will do whatever you can to rectify the situation or ask if the two of you can brainstorm a solution together

Don't

- Don't interrupt
- Don't get defensive
- Don't be dismissive or insincere
- Don't threaten punishment or other consequences
- Don't ignore the employee's concerns and pivot to another topic
- Don't give a non-apology (i.e. "I'm sorry you feel that way.")
- Don't end the conversation on a sour note

Let's look at an example of how listening can turn a situation from one in which an employee could become actively disengaged to one in which the manager strengthens their relationship.

I once knew an employee who discovered that he and his colleagues were being paid less than the market average for their positions and, after discussing the situation, decided to raise the issue during his performance review. Upon telling his supervisor what he had learned, she said to him, "If you talk about your pay with another employee, you and I are going to have a problem." From that point forward, the issue never came up again, but the supervisor permanently damaged her relationship with the employee and poisoned his experience of working for that organization. Aside from the fact that what the supervisor did was illegal and actionable under the U.S. National Labor Relations Act of 1935, she also created a negative experience for her employee, one that sowed a bitter seed of disengagement.

Here's what a manager who was listening with empathy, humility, and curiosity would have said in this scenario:

> Look, you know I want us to be open and transparent with one another. I trust you and I want you to trust me. It's true that you're not getting paid what the market pays. We had to bring on more staff to meet customer needs, but couldn't pay market rates due to budgetary constraints. Right now, I don't believe we're in a position to raise everyone's base pay. But let's discuss other options, because I don't want you to feel like you're walking away with the short straw or that you're not being rewarded for your hard work. There are some professional development opportunities we could pursue for you; they would look great on your resume and get you exposed to other areas of the company. Also, in about a year you'd technically be eligible to get moved up to the next salary grade. But, based on your performance, maybe we can look into an early promotion. So tell me what you're thinking. I want to help you succeed.

Although paying employees below the market average is a disengagement factor in and of itself—remember the Fair Wage-Effort Hypothesis and the Experience-Effort Correlation—the supervisor's hypothetical response above at least showed that she wanted to make a genuine effort to re-engage her team member. That's the power of truly listening to employees.

Take Action

This one is a tough pill for many managers to swallow. They don't want to admit that they are wrong or appear as if they are making any concessions. Again, managers have been trained to adopt the mindset of "the boss is always right," and they have simply grown accustomed to leading that way. They tell employees that, if they do not like working for them, they should go ahead and find another job. That is the antithesis of a positive employee experience, and it breeds active disengagement within a workforce that could otherwise be executing organizational goals, if only they were inspired to do so.

Taking action requires a great deal of courage on a leader's part. It means validating workers' concerns and making a positive change to ensure a better employee experience, even if that takes standing up to executive leadership and challenging the status quo. Courageous leaders will graciously take their employees' feedback, even if it's negative, and use it to strengthen their organization's employee value proposition. Instead of telling employees to stop complaining and to just be grateful for their jobs, courageous leaders face their teams and say, "Thank you for telling me what isn't working. I want you to be proud of our company." This, of course, requires a culture of total openness and trust so employees feel comfortable sharing their feedback, a rarity in today's business environment. When leaders reprimand or threaten employees for expressing frustration over negative experiences, they are essentially inviting active disengagement into their organizations for reasons discussed throughout this chapter.

What does taking action look like? It looks like real, impactful change. It is cultural, procedural, organizational, and behavioral. It is not superficial or patronizing. Too many leaders look at employee engagement efforts as simple gestures to placate the masses without having to change the way they behave, be more realistic with their expectations, or dig into their pocketbooks. In their minds, giving employees silly tokens of appreciation and office pizza parties will somehow inspire them to be more engaged despite critical factors that are contributing to their *dis*engagement. This is one of the false beliefs comprising the Stepford Employee Fallacy which we will examine in Part II.

I'll use our earlier example of technology projects to illustrate why taking action requires great courage, but is absolutely necessary to prevent disengagement among employees. One of the first projects I worked on involved the upgrade of a legacy e-commerce system to a new web-enabled version. The system was developed over the course of two years and underwent significant testing. However, upon launch, it nearly crippled the department that would be leveraging it because usability was so poor. The interface was clunky and counterintuitive, and the processing time for even the simplest of transactions was so atrocious that it rendered employees incapable of meeting customer (or management) demands.

As is the common practice with many other large-scale technology implementations, the actual end users were not as involved in the development process as they should have been. The product itself had its own set of issues from the outset, but because senior leadership had already made the time and money commitment to upgrade, they saw no reason to reconsider their decision to proceed. This justification, known as the sunk-cost fallacy, is common among business leaders. Because they had already spent so many months and millions of dollars on their selected course of action, the project leaders and sponsor would not admit that they had bought an ineffective tool, even though it was harming the very people they expected to use it. Unfortunately, it was the employees who suffered most, and all their leadership did to support them was to document and suggest confusing workarounds that stifled productivity. The impact on engagement was palpable.

In this case, the leaders should have been courageous and taken action by reinstating the legacy system (which worked perfectly fine) and taken a step back to assess a better option. It would have been a pretty sizable financial blow to pull the plug and start over with more involvement and input from employees, but the investment would have paid dividends in terms of restored goodwill and engagement. Instead of forcing employees to use a system that didn't work and then labeling them as disengaged because they voiced their frustrations about it, the managers involved should have followed Sir Richard Branson's advice: put employees first! Leaders, I challenge you ask yourselves whether you are putting *your* employees first before you think about using that dreaded actively disengaged label.

LOOKING AHEAD

In this chapter, we took a critical look at the behavior that many leaders and Human Resources professionals classify as active disengagement. A number of practitioners recommend employers should simply remove or "transition out" disengaged employees, especially the actively disengaged ones. This is a dangerous and short-sighted approach to fostering an engaged workforce, because it doesn't bother to uncover what might have been causing disengagement to begin with. It is my assertion that leaders who endorse such a method of organizational development also subscribe to the set of misinformed beliefs comprising the Stepford Employee Fallacy. We will review and break down each of these components in Part II, starting with the belief that employees will engage themselves with nothing more than a paycheck as inspiration. But as far as disengagement goes, you really can't blame employees for their lack of commitment or for the current state of the modern workplace. In Chapter 3, we will see why the blame lies elsewhere and what exactly the true culprits have been doing to cause this problem.

NOTES

1. Gallup. *State of the American Workplace*. February 2017. http://www.gallup.com/reports/199961/state-american-workplace-report-2017.aspx

2. Aon Hewitt. *Actively Disengaged and Staying*. October 2016. http://www.modernsurvey.com/wp-content/uploads/2016/10/Actively-Disengaged-Staying.pdf

3. Widrich, Leo. "The 'No Complaining' Rule: What It Really Means to Create a Company Culture of Positivity". *Buffer*. July 20, 2015. https://open.buffer.com/no-complaining/

4. Tepper, B. J., Mitchell, M. S., Haggard, D. L., Kwan, H. K. and Park, H.-m. (2015), On the Exchange of Hostility with Supervisors: An Examination of Self-Enhancing and Self-Defeating Perspectives. Personnel Psychology, 68: 723–758. doi:10.1111/peps.12094 http://onlinelibrary.wiley.com/doi/10.1111/peps.12094/abstract

5. George A. Akerlof, Janet L. Yellen; The Fair Wage-Effort Hypothesis and Unemployment. *Q J Econ* 1990; 105 (2): 255-283. doi: 10.2307/2937787 https://academic.oup.com/qje/article-abstract/105/2/255/1864771/The-Fair-Wage-Effort-Hypothesis-and-Unemployment

6. Schurenberg, Eric. "Richard Branson: Why Customers Come Second at Virgin". *Inc.* https://www.inc.com/eric-schurenberg/sir-richard-branson-put-your-staff-first-customers-second-and-shareholders-third.html

CHAPTER 3

BLAME THE MBAS, BEAN COUNTERS, LAWYERS, AND BIGWIGS

Businesses have gotten a bad rap over the years, but hardly without merit. The tired caricature of a corporation as a soulless, well-oiled machine is so clichéd because we have become accustomed to working in and reading about organizations that treat employees as cogs in the greater business apparatus. There are rules, standards, and systems in place to ensure the business continues to run as its managers see fit, pursuing higher shareholder satisfaction and ever-growing profits, regardless of the impact to workers. Today, especially, employees are told to do more with less. It is this relentless pursuit of more that causes employees to be disengaged and results in scandals and embarrassments that seem to have become increasingly prevalent over the past decade. Are the ones at the top, the executive leaders, to blame for enabling work cultures that facilitate these failures? Or has society become so inured to the greedy, unethical behavior typical of corporate life that these leaders are simply enabled by its acceptance?

Here's where I stand. I happen to agree with President Harry S. Truman's philosophy on leadership: "The buck stops here." Leaders are the cultural champions of their respective organizations. They set the tone for what activities and decisions are permissible under their command. Yet, through what seems to be the de facto business model, they shoulder none of the responsibility for wrongdoing and instead enjoy financial success while their employees continue to toil and suffer. They cite global competition and burdensome regulation as the rock and hard place between which they must devise questionable business practices. It's easier for them to scapegoat forces beyond their control and claim innocence (and collect obscene remuneration at the same time) than it is to make ethical decisions in the best interests of their employees. Instead of adopting a servant-leadership mindset and implementing strategies to energize, inspire, and develop employees, these executives sponsor policies—through action or lack thereof—that treat their people as liabilities and greed as an asset.

Organizations today have shed most of their humanity (if they ever had it to begin with) in favor of cold, clinical efficiency protected by devious legal tricks and heartless business discipline designed to serve the bottom line. They pursue results at any cost, and employees are invariably the ones to foot the bill. No wonder today's workforce is so disengaged from their work. The leaders who should be their biggest champions and supporters are too busy devising newer, more creative ways to screw them over.

Unfortunately, the corporate machinery in place to benefit executives and shareholders also has triggers and firewalls set up to intimidate, silence, and punish employees who speak out about mistreatment and malfeasance. Human capital, as employees are referred to by the business-minded, is expected to follow orders and produce, produce, produce, all the while being fully engaged with great big smiles on their faces. If they don't like working for *the man*, then they can leave. It's not until these companies are caught with their pants down that they admit culpability and their inexcusable behavior toward employees is exposed.

Corporate scandals have a funny way of laying bare the ugly truth that hides behind layers of institutional constructs designed to protect and enrich the upper echelon at the expense of those in the bottom ranks. They form cracks and holes in the carefully built edifices surrounding a complex business engine that churns and pollutes the very people being paid to make it run.

In this chapter, we will examine several recent high-profile corporate scandals through the lens of employee engagement. The leaders involved willingly advocated shady policies and procedures, sowing bitter seeds of disengagement among their employees, and harming their customers as a result. We will look at the practices they espoused and discuss how these are sadly all too common in the corporate world today. Even if such transgressions don't technically break the law or rise to the level of a scandal, they still disengage employees. And senior executives need to finally accept full responsibility for their key role in the employee engagement problem.

But before we actually delve into the drama and intrigue of these corporate embarrassments, we will first look at the way business schools haven't been doing their part to prevent unethical, disengaging leadership from taking hold in today's workplaces. After all, institutions of higher learning are supposed to produce the best and brightest minds to ensure a better future for our society, right? If there is any hope of reversing the current employee disengagement epidemic, it lies in the potential of tomorrow's leaders. They require the right guidance and support to prepare them for the responsibility of rescuing the modern workplace from its self-destructive ways.

IT'S NOT PERSONAL, JUST GOOD BUSINESS: MBA PROGRAMS TURN OUT BUSINESSPEOPLE INSTEAD OF PEOPLE LEADERS

Last year there were more than one hundred fifty thousand Master of Business Administration degrees conferred upon U.S. graduate students hungry to make it big in the business world. That number represents roughly a quarter of all master's degrees earned—the largest percentage of any field of study. Enrollment in MBA programs is higher than ever and degree holders enjoy more positive post-graduation employment prospects than law school graduates.[1] The corporate world has long held an MBA from top-tier schools as the gold standard for up-and-coming talent. Freshly-minted MBAs are recruited from their prestigious schools by firms anxious to bring bleeding-edge business thinking into their ranks. These organizations offer handsome salaries, attractive signing bonuses, and fast-track career growth, which make earning the degree all the more appealing for industrious professionals who want a bigger slice of the pie. Older generations of MBA-holding managers recognize the rigor and discipline that goes into earning it. They are more comfortable hiring and working with individuals who think and speak like they do because they've been through business school and believe in its content and instruction. After all, it got them to where they are. Therefore it must be the best way to prepare business leaders for the challenge of running an organization.

An MBA curriculum certainly has tremendous value; I won't argue that point. Unfortunately, business schools have historically focused almost exclusively on building students' so-called hard skills through quantitative, analytical, and strategy-intensive coursework. The human component of business—what I would argue is the biggest and most important part—was mostly ignored. From an employee engagement perspective, therein lies the problem. Allow me to explain.

Financial accounting, advanced macroeconomics, applied statistics, and operations management all teach MBA students to view business through a filter. The emotional, human aspects barely register, because students are taught how to understand and work with numbers, not people. But the numbers don't just happen, so MBA graduates are left unprepared as managers to handle the complex people issues that stand between them and their desired results. They don't realize the business value of empathizing with their employees. To them, it doesn't matter why an employee is disengaged; they're not performing, so they simply need to be fixed (or replaced) like a broken laptop. Get the job done. Meet the KPIs. Efficiency should be paramount. And all decisions are made on the basis of rational, analytical consideration for the bottom line. Anyone who isn't on board or questions the strategy, regardless of the reason, needs to get with the program or get lost. That's how successful businesses operate, isn't it? In a perfect world populated by perfect talent—i.e. Stepford Employees—that would be a viable operating model. But, as I discuss throughout this book, the world simply doesn't work that way. Employees don't work that way.

I believe traditional MBA programs don't prepare students to be the humble, curious, empathetic leaders that the business world needs. It sounds counterintuitive and perhaps even heretical to say that a strictly traditional business administration curriculum isn't the best education for the next generation of leaders. But look through the required courses for a typical business studies program, and you're unlikely to see courses in psychology, philosophy, sociology, or any other soft-skill-centric class. In other words, the people being primed to lead the future of business are, and have historically been, removed from understanding what truly drives, inspires, and engages any business' most critical asset: its people.

In November of 2016, Harvard Business Review published a study on the world's best-performing CEOs in terms of their organizations' financial performance.[2] Researchers gathered data from nearly nine hundred companies and their chief executives and calculated key financial metrics, such as shareholder return, to determine the best performers who had been in their roles for at least two years. The results were interesting. Out of the top twenty-five CEOs listed, only three hold MBAs. Now, that might be because they chose not to go any further than a bachelor's degree with a business focus. Or, it could be that they decided a different master's degree would better suit them. Regardless of the reason, it seems that having MBAs among executive ranks does not necessarily translate to better organizational performance. It also seems that the rational, analytical business maxims taught in MBA programs don't substitute a more human approach to leadership, at least not for the most successful CEOs. As part of his interview for the study, the CEO of Inditex, Pablo Isla, noted the importance of rationality taking a back seat to emotion. He attributes his ability to foster a high-performing work culture to this transformational shift in management thinking. Having an understanding of, and appreciation for, employees as unique, emotional humans creates the kind of engaging environment that yields innovation and amazing results.

Still, there are plenty of organizations that cling to old ways of thinking and reward leaders who care more for financial gains than for their own employees. Business schools, of course, don't advocate or instruct unethical decision-making, but, historically, they have not challenged students to view business or leadership through a humanistic lens.

If there is one teaching all MBA programs should make the focal point of their curricula, it is the need for leaders to consider the human impact of their behaviors, decisions, and interactions. Companies employ and do business with human beings. Ignoring that fact can be seriously hurtful to the bottom line. Refreshingly, there *are* colleges and universities offering business degrees that focus more on effective, engaging leadership—my alma mater, Nichols College, being one of them. And more business schools, like University of Vermont, are starting to break free from the MBA curricula of old, allowing students to concentrate in areas like sustainability and corporate social responsibility. If this trend continues, and tomorrow's leaders learn about business from a people (instead of a profit) perspective, then there is a good chance we will see global employee engagement improve as a result.

BOTTOM LINE CULTURE: GENERAL MOTORS' IGNITION SWITCHES AND VOLKSWAGEN'S DIESEL ENGINES

The automotive industry has always found it difficult to strike a balance between financial discipline and quality engineering. Manufacturers like General Motors and Volkswagen have landed themselves in serious trouble when their bottom-line-focused leaders listened to the number crunchers and MBAs instead of the engineers and designers. In his book, *Car Guys vs. Bean Counters: The Battle for the Soul of American Business*, Bob Lutz shares compelling insights on the U.S. automotive industry as former product development chief at GM during a time when the organization was on the brink of bankruptcy.[3] Lutz blames the near-collapse of the third largest car and truck manufacturer on the cost-cutting, profit-maximizing mentality that became the preferred business model across most industries in the last twenty or so years.

General Motors executives seemingly placed more emphasis on containing costs and following the advice of financial analysts than allowing those with a passion for building great cars to have the final say. This resulted in non-competitive vehicles that couldn't capture buyers' attention the way foreign cars did. Even though Lutz was able to turn GM around with better products, there was still a firmly entrenched hierarchical culture that prevented lower-level employees from truly having their voices heard. The well-publicized ignition switch scandal was a tragic culmination of the decades-old practice of discouraging employees from reporting quality issues or challenging upper management's decisions. When GM engineers and safety inspectors discovered that the ignition switch in certain vehicles could be unintentionally turned to the OFF position while driving, they feared retribution from managers if they didn't simply ignore the problem. One whistleblower was transferred to another department in an apparent effort to silence him. The ignition switch defect caused multiple vehicle crashes—some involving fatalities—and led to current CEO Mary Barra being called before Congress in 2014 to explain what happened. General Motors ultimately paid hundreds of millions of dollars in fines and settlements, making the company a cautionary tale for other doctrinaire, numbers-focused automakers.[4]

Evidently Volkswagen threw out that memo.

Volkswagen's diesel emissions scandal represents another example of a culture focused on unrealistic bottom-line results forcing employees to make impossible decisions. In the case of Volkswagen Group, overly ambitious executives, who were hell-bent on cracking the American diesel market, told their engineers to develop a powerful, clean diesel engine that would meet the United States government's strict emissions standards. Former chairman, Ferdinand Piëch, and former CEO, Martin Winterkorn, envisioned Volkswagen as not only a global leader in diesel vehicle sales, but as the world's largest auto manufacturer, surpassing both General Motors and Toyota for the title.[5] This meant employees faced intense top-down pressure to deliver on these goals with limited time and budget to do so.

Winterkorn was Piech's protégé, and he reportedly had a management mindset that almost matched his mentor's notoriously inflexible, despotic style. As the CEO, he was seen as terrifying and exacting by his direct reports, a man singularly concerned only with perfect results and positioning Volkswagen for great success. That success hinged on VW's ability to increase sales in its most important market, the United States, where regulators had implemented an aggressive cap on acceptable pollutant emissions from diesel engines. So Winterkorn tasked engineers with developing a viable diesel motor that would satisfy both market appetites and government regulations. In Volkswagen's demanding, autocratic work culture, the impossibility of this assignment meant engineers had to devise a way to make the engines appear as though they emitted acceptable levels of pollution when subjected to testing. Software in the engine's computer would detect conditions under which the car was being tested, and lower the emission of nitrogen oxides.[6]

The problem had been solved and Volkswagen enjoyed increased sales and strong brand cachet—until independent researchers began noticing odd results in their emissions testing of certain diesel vehicles. Their findings caught the attention of the U.S. Environmental Protection Agency, and, by the fall of 2016, VW was forced to admit that they had been installing software on millions of cars to circumvent pollution regulations since 2008. Many of the engineers who worked on these vehicles faced disciplinary action from VW's home office, and Martin Winterkorn resigned from his post as chief executive, though he admitted having no knowledge of the issue. The company now faces lawsuits from hundreds of thousands of vehicle owners, along with possible criminal investigations.[7] The scandal has surely affected Volkswagen's public perception and certainly damaged employees' already strained relationship with upper management.

What the General Motors and Volkswagen cases show is the tendency for those in managerial positions to put far too much emphasis on numbers and far too little on trusting their employees' judgment. Steve Jobs once said of Apple's hiring philosophy: "We hire smart people so they can tell us what to do." Though he wasn't known for having a very compassionate leadership style, Jobs was at least right about relying on employees for their ingenuity.

Being conscious of costs and striving to grow profits are both necessary for any business to thrive. However, focusing only on the bottom line is dangerously myopic and can have a chilling effect on employee engagement. The best way to go about executing organizational priorities is to always inspire and engage the employees who are closest to those goals. GM and Volkswagen hoped to claim the hearts of consumers worldwide but failed in a spectacularly dramatic fashion, because they relied solely on numbers to drive their respective strategies. GM focused on cutting costs to the detriment of vehicle quality and safety, while VW saw dollar signs where its engineers saw an impossible (and unethical) decision. They trusted sales forecasts and financial analyses more than they trusted their employees' expertise. For that, they *lost* the trust of those employees and the motoring public.

HOW MANY LAWYERS DOES IT TAKE . . . ? PROTECTING FOX NEWS FROM SEXUAL HARASSMENT LAWSUITS

Fox News found itself on the other side of media scrutiny in 2016 after a former anchor, Gretchen Carlson, filed a sexual harassment lawsuit against the notoriously boorish network chief, Roger Ailes. She alleged that he repeatedly propositioned her and created a work environment where she felt harassed and uncomfortable. Carlson's suit prompted other women at Fox News to come forward with their own harassment allegations against Ailes and his most popular on-screen commentator, Bill O'Reilly.[8] It also started a conversation about just how pervasive sexual harassment continues to be in the workplace. Even relatively immature companies like Uber have been exposed for having cultures that turned a blind eye toward this sort of misbehavior from senior staff.

In an effort to minimize the damage this kind of scandal could cause, Fox News and its lawyers tried to force Ms. Carlson's dispute into arbitration according to the contract she signed when she joined the network.[9] Arbitration is ostensibly an efficient, cost-effective means of alternative dispute resolution. Truth be told, today most organizations include some form of arbitration agreement similar to Fox's as a condition of employment. But mandatory arbitration agreements are of no benefit to employees in the event of a dispute. They deprive employees of their right to sue and have their case heard in court. That's why they are favored by corporate counsel and employer-side attorneys.

Many employers have only recently jumped aboard the arbitration bandwagon and are forcing their current employees to sign an agreement under threat of job loss. This particularly insidious tactic is made worse by the fact that some courts have ruled employees must submit to arbitration even if they only acknowledged receipt of the company's employee handbook but did not sign the agreement. If an employee is wronged during the course of her employment and refuses to sign on the dotted line, she can still be compelled to arbitrate if the company's lawyers prove arbitration language was part of the employee handbook she received.

Disputes that are adjudicated through arbitration tend to result in a favorable outcome for the employer. This could be because arbitrated cases are not decided by juries; an arbitrator reviews the details and makes a binding decision. Arbitrators are typically retired judges who won't be as inclined to side with the wronged employee as would a jury of the employee's peers. And arbitration is a very lucrative business. Arbitrators can make several thousands of dollars in a day, depending on their case load, so it behooves them to side with employers who keep giving them business. The more employers who compel arbitration, the more cases arbitrators hear, the more money they make, the more they rule in favor of employers, the more employers compel arbitration, and the cycle continues to feed on itself.

If an employee (or former employee) somehow beats the odds and succeeds in arbitration, the award is marginal at best and not likely to make a dent in the employer's pocketbook. Moreover, since arbitration is a private method of dispute resolution, the public won't hear the details of the case or its outcome. Businesses have historically been motivated by money, not necessarily by acting in an ethical manner, so large punitive damage awards and public trials are strong deterrents against corporate malfeasance. Losing a lot of money in a lawsuit is pretty compelling motivation not to mistreat employees. Arbitration all but removes a very tangible incentive for employers to treat their employees ethically.

When people are wronged by their employer, it has a real and lasting effect on them mentally, financially, professionally, emotionally, and even physically. Gretchen Carlson earned millions of dollars under her contract with Fox, though she was no less entitled to compensation for the harassment she allegedly suffered. She could go on to write a book or retire or pursue a career in another form of media. But what about a junior staffer making $15 per hour? Even if the staffer wins, she has to pay for half the cost of the arbitrator. And then there's the not-so-small task of finding another job, recovering from all of the anguish caused by this situation, paying her bills, and supporting herself and her family. Even if she wins, there is nothing to stop her employer (or any future employer that mandates arbitration) from wronging her again.

Companies that force employees into arbitration agreements are basically saying, "If we wrong you (not that we'd ever admit it), then we'll settle the matter in private, on our terms, using a method that's guaranteed to work in our favor." It's a perfect system to reinforce bad behavior and prevent employees from asserting their legal rights. These organizations task their legal and HR teams with conceiving policies to take advantage of employees and figuratively beat them into submission. Take a look through any new-hire packet, and you'll see pages of non-disclosure, non-disparagement, non-compete, arbitration, and other restrictive covenants that give the employer seemingly limitless power to mistreat its employees and get away with it. Wronged employees can't sue, can't publicly talk about their experiences, can't go work for a competitor; they essentially sign their lives away when they take a job with employers who are more concerned with protecting their reputations than doing right by the people who make them successful in the first place.

Fox News settled Gretchen Carlson's lawsuit against Roger Ailes—one of several multi-million-dollar payouts to employees claiming sexual harassment—and Bill O'Reilly left the network after allegations of his own inappropriate behavior started to come from more women who worked with him. It's unfortunate that it takes cases like these to demonstrate the kind of toxic work cultures employees endure on a daily basis, ones in which managers can abuse those who are lower on the corporate ladder and hide behind their lawyers to shield them from justice. Instead of promoting fair, compassionate environments where employees feel inspired and safe to work with their leaders, far too many organizations rely on legal traps to keep workers quiet, compliant, and subservient. That's the exact opposite of employee engagement.

GUTLESS LEADERSHIP: THE WELLS FARGO CROSS-SELL FIASCO

John Stumpf must have needed a stiff drink (or several) after his two-hour Senate Banking Committee hearing on Capitol Hill in September of 2016. As CEO of Wells Fargo at the time, he faced a barrage of harsh criticism from Washington lawmakers over the bank's fraudulent opening of roughly two million accounts without customers' knowledge or consent. At one point, he even seemed to shrink under the stone-cold glare and relentlessly savage line of questioning thrown by Massachusetts senator, Elizabeth Warren.[10]

As a fierce advocate for "the little guy" and chief architect of the U.S. Consumer Financial Protection Bureau, Senator Warren was livid with Stumpf and his fellow Wells Fargo executives who had purportedly created a high-pressure sales environment in which employees were forced to meet unrealistic account cross-sale goals. Accusing him of "gutless leadership," Warren lambasted Stumpf for setting such impossible standards.

She also called him out for bragging about the bank's status as a market leader during analyst calls, effectively boosting Wells Fargo share prices and personally reaping tens of millions of dollars from increased investor confidence. It wasn't until the Consumer Financial Protection Bureau uncovered the fraudulent activity that Stumpf and Wells Fargo went public with their admission that it took place and that they had fired more than five thousand employees for opening the fake accounts.

How did this happen? As is the case in so many organizations today, Wells Fargo's senior leaders were too far removed from the day-to-day bank operations and set ridiculous sales quotas for lower-level employees without their involvement or input.

I once worked with a workers compensation insurer where the claims staff was hamstrung by unworkable case loads. Home office management devised standards for claim handling and the number of claims employees could manage on a monthly basis without much interest or insight into the real-world complexities involved in actually being a claims adjuster. It's not fair to say any given adjuster can easily handle two hundred claims per month and should therefore strive to resolve two hundred fifty as a "stretch goal." How did the leadership team devise this metric? They had a finance woman—someone who had never touched a claim in her life—develop models and algorithms to calculate the precise number of claims the adjusters could handle, despite the fact that spreadsheets and management reports only show an extremely narrow view of any organization's productivity and capacity. At least in this case, leaders attempted to support their lofty expectations with empirical data and analyses, however flawed and one-dimensional they were.

John Stumpf's justification for requiring employees to sell customers at least eight bank products was that the number eight rhymed with "great." I'm not kidding. That's it—no statistical analysis, market research, or historical customer audit. Never mind the fact that other large banks, on average, strive to sell their customers only three accounts. He simply thought of an ambitious goal that none of Wells Fargo's competitors had been able to match, and then he succeeded in pushing it down the chain with charismatic CEO-speak that so many executives falsely believe will be enough to garner buy-in from the front lines.

According to current and former Wells Fargo employees, any opposition to the crazy sales target was met with typical management stonewalling and labeling workers who raised concerns as negative or lacking a team-player mentality.[11] Sounds familiar? We've all probably run into this scenario at one point (or many points) in our careers. The last thing managers want to do is entertain critical feedback from employees, so they use corporate control mechanisms to silence agitators and intimidate them into obedience. I'm sure you can imagine how many employees who couldn't (legally) meet the eight-product sales goal were put on performance improvement plans, managed out, or fired "for cause."

The fifty three hundred employees who opened fraudulent accounts for Wells Fargo customers had a choice: try to fight an unwinnable battle against bank leadership and most likely lose their jobs, or find any and every way to meet their sales targets, even if they had to fabricate accounts. They chose the latter and were ultimately punished for it.

And what came of Mr. Stumpf? He retired as CEO amid calls from lawmakers like Elizabeth Warren for him to not only resign, but to become the subject of Securities and Exchange Commission criminal investigation for fraud.[12] Another Wells Fargo executive who left the bank after this whole thing boiled over was Carrie Tolstedt. Tolstedt was a long-time Wells honcho who headed the consumer banking division. She vehemently defended the high-pressure sales model that led to the creation of so many fake accounts. Stumpf enabled her rather than heeding warnings from other executive officers who feared the culture was conducive to misconduct. Wells Fargo's board of directors decided to claw back part of Tolstedt's and Stumpf's compensation as a measure of accountability for the very damaging scandal.[13] That translated to tens of millions of dollars out of the hundreds of millions they received during the years the activity took place, a relatively small fraction of the sizable fortune each executive accumulated during their tenures.

But what about the employees making $30,000 per year who were terminated for struggling to meet impossible sales goals? What about the remaining employees who saw what happened to their colleagues, who watched their greedy executives get off scot-free with more money than most people know what to do with, who probably know how much more of the iceberg there is below the surface, but fear speaking out?

The problem with Wells Fargo is just a prominent example of what goes on in so many organizations today. Selfish, out-of-touch executives force unreasonable expectations upon their employees and squash any dissent, pushback, or criticism, especially if it makes them look bad. They expect a workforce of yes-men and yes-women to outperform any goal put in front of them so they can impress shareholders and line their own pockets. And that is a major contributing factor to the sad state of employee engagement we see today. Workers really don't feel engaged or committed to organizations when their leaders conspire to use them as human batteries, extracting every last bit of energy to generate more profits, all while expecting them to be happy, smiling, and dedicated to the company cause.

LOOKING AHEAD

Each of the shameful examples and missteps discussed here could have been avoided if the leaders involved had put their employees first as discussed in Chapter 2. Most companies don't engage in practices that rise to the level of scandal (or they just don't get caught), but that doesn't mean their employees feel any less disengaged by their leaders' decisions. The corrosive effects of disengagement should not be underestimated; they can be just as damaging as any of these scandals were to an organization's success. However, managers tend to blame employees for their lack of engagement instead of trying to understand the root cause, which, more often than not, relates to putting employees last.

Next, we will move on to Part II where we carefully examine seven unfounded beliefs about employee engagement that enable the kind of organizational dysfunction covered in this chapter. These components of the Stepford Employee Fallacy are each rooted in a fundamental ignorance of, or disregard for, the human condition. Hopefully the companies in this chapter realized just how bad of a business practice that can be.

NOTES

1. Hansen, Drew. "Why MBA Programs Don't Produce Leaders". Forbes. October 4, 2011. https://www.forbes.com/sites/drewhansen/2011/10/04/why-mba-business-school-not-leaders/2/#78daa722559a

2. Harvard Business Review. *The Best Performing CEOs in the World*. November 2016. https://hbr.org/2016/11/the-best-performing-ceos-in-the-world#roundtable

3. Lutz, Robert. "Car Guys vs. Bean Counters: The Battle for the Soul of American Business". New York: *Penguin Group*. 2011.

4. Higgins, Tim and Summers, Nick. "GM Recalls: How General Motors Silenced a Whistle-Blower". *Bloomberg*. June 19, 2014. https://www.bloomberg.com/news/articles/2014-06-18/gm-recalls-whistle-blower-was-ignored-mary-barra-faces-congress

5. Edgers, Jeff. "What the VW Scandal Says about the Hazards of Hyper-Competition". *Fortune*. November 13, 2015. http://fortune.com/2015/11/13/vw-scandal-martin-winterkorn-apple/

6. Bergin, Tom and Cramer, Andreas. "Fear and Respect: VW's Culture under Winterkorn". *Reuters*. October 20, 2015. http://www.reuters.com/article/us-volkswagen-emissions-culture-idUSKCN0S40MT20151010

7. Parlor, Roger and Smith, Geoffrey. "Hoaxwagen: How the Massive Diesel Fraud Incinerated VW's Reputation - and Will Hobble the Company for Years to Come". *Fortune*. March 7, 2016. http://fortune.com/inside-volkswagen-emissions-scandal/

8. Wemple, Erik. "Bill O'Reilly Says Roger Ailes Always Had His Back. And That Was Precisely the Problem". *Washington Post*. May 19, 2017. https://www.washingtonpost.com/blogs/erik-wemple/wp/2017/05/19/bill-oreilly-says-roger-ailes-always-had-his-back-and-that-was-precisely-the-problem/?utm_term=.f0ab7ad2e9f7

9. Stempel, Jonathan. "Fox News' Roger Ailes Demands Arbitration in Gretchen Carlson Harassment Case". *Huffington Post*. July 8, 2016. http://www.huffingtonpost.com/entry/roger-ailes-gretchen-carlson-arbitration_us_578028dae4b0344d514f72a3

10. Merle, Renae. "Wells Fargo CEO Pummelled on Capiol Hill over Multi-Year Scam". *The Washington Post*. September 20, 2016. https://www.washingtonpost.com/news/get-there/wp/2016/09/20/wells-fargo-ceo-to-accept-full-responsibility-before-congress/?utm_term=.ff28dcea2117

11. Levine, Mark. "Tough Targets and Short-Term Projects". *Bloomberg*. September 19, 2016. https://www.bloomberg.com/view/articles/2016-09-19/tough-targets-and-short-term-projects

12. Blake, Paul. "Timeline of the Wells Fargo Account Scandal". *ABC News*. November 3, 2016. http://abcnews.go.com/Business/timeline-wells-fargo-accounts-scandal/story?id=42231128

13. Frost, Wilfred and Giel, Dawn. "Wells Fargo Board Slams Former CEO Stumpf and Tolstedt, Claws Back $75 Million". *CNBC*. April 10, 2017. http://www.cnbc.com/2017/04/10/wells-fargo-board-slams-stumpf-and-tolstedt-claws-back-millions.html

PART II

THE STEPFORD EMPLOYEE FALLACY

Once upon a time, I worked for a company that set out to create a "culture of engagement." One day, my coworkers and I received an e-mail from our CEO explaining that we would be meeting in groups with a consultant who had worked very closely with the senior leadership team to develop the company's mission, vision, and values. We were told that this man would teach us all about our role, as employees, in shaping this new cultural framework for our organization. Everyone seemed a bit confused as to what this meant, and nobody was particularly enthusiastic about having to attend this meeting while work continued to accumulate on their desks. The day of the meeting came and I, along with about twenty-five of my colleagues, cautiously stepped into the conference room waiting to hear what this "engagement" business was all about.

The man introduced himself and gave a brief history of his consultancy's partnership with our company. He then walked us through some exercises that initially seemed to have no point. One involved staring at a PowerPoint slide that looked like one of those Magic Eye posters from the 90's that made you cross-eyed. It had the word "FLY" hidden within colorful dots. I suppose the intent was to get us to practice looking at the bigger picture. Things started to come together when he told us about the importance of being engaged and how our commitment to go above and beyond for the company was our obligation as its employees. Using a four-quadrant infographic, he went on to explain the differences between active engagement, engagement, disengagement, and active disengagement. Each of the quadrants on his presentation slide had cartoons depicting these employee engagement archetypes. He described disengaged employees as "zombies" and actively disengaged employees as "terrorists".

To illustrate what qualifies someone as being disengaged, he relayed a story about another consulting engagement in which one of his client's employees was complaining about his experience working there. He asked the employee what his supervisor's name was while taking out a piece of paper and writing something on it. The employee asked what he was doing, and the consultant said, "Oh, since you aren't too keen on working here, I'm writing your boss a resignation letter. All you need to do is sign it." Of course, the employee didn't want to lose his job. That, the man said, gave the employee a chance to rethink his attitude and raise his level of engagement. The message was pretty clear: We were expected to be positive and engaged. If we didn't like working for our employer, we could leave.

Looking around the room, I could practically see the thought bubbles hovering over each of my colleagues' heads. I'm sure they said something along the lines of, "Are you f—ing kidding me?" These people were overworked, underpaid, under-appreciated, and treated like children by managers whose approach to leadership consisted of factory-era autocracy with a sprinkling of pot lucks, dumb contests, and insulting, feel-good platitudes. The culture was not conducive to engagement, at least not true engagement as I describe it throughout this book. Ultimately, instead of a culture of engagement, our leaders created a culture of obedience. Instead of human beings with needs, limitations, strengths, and expectations, they wanted Stepford Employees who would come skipping into the office every day, ready to give 110 percent with creepy, fake smiles on their faces.

About a week after attending the presentation, I was talking with one of my coworkers outside our office, and I asked her what she thought of it all. She let out a brief sigh and said:

> You know, I've worked here a long time. I've seen leaders come and go, and each of them had a flavor-of-the-month change initiative for the organization. Now this. Engagement? They expect so much from us, and now they want us to be married to the company. I

really don't care anymore. I'm just going to keep my head down and work until I can retire.

As we saw in Chapter 2, managers and HR practitioners would place my coworker toward the disengaged end of the engagement spectrum, while blithely ignoring the reasons why she felt the way she did. Her cynical and jaded sentiments are unfortunately shared by the majority of employees worldwide. And yet, leaders are blissfully unaware of, or arrogantly indifferent about, their responsibility for the lack of engagement within their organizations. They delude themselves with convenient fantasies about how they think employee engagement *should* work.

In Part II, we will look at each of these beliefs in depth and discuss why they do not support true engagement. My hope is that, by disproving the Stepford Employee Fallacy, I can enlighten leaders and show them how the false engagement beliefs we will review in the next chapters are no good for them or for their employees. Each chapter contains examples of its respective belief in action to demonstrate how it affects engagement and hurts the organization. There is also a case study detailing a particular company's subversion of that chapter's belief through effective employee engagement practices. Bear in mind that no company is perfect. An organization might do exceptionally well in one area of employee engagement but not so much in others. My former employer appeared on a prominent Best Places to Work list several years in a row mainly because of its impressive focus on corporate social responsibility and charitable initiatives. That did not necessarily mean the company was an engaging place to work. In fact, during a town hall meeting with the same group of employees that attended the consultant's bizarre presentation, the CEO spent time defending our Best Place to Work ranking because he knew we thought it was a crock. If you have to convince your disengaged employees that they work at a great company because a magazine says so, you've only received a hollow accolade without merit; you haven't truly fostered engagement.

It's been quite a few years since I worked for the company in our story, but I often think of the coworkers I left behind and whether or not things got any better for them. If the sad state of worldwide employee engagement is any indication, I suspect not much. In fact, I learned that, soon after I left, upper management made an especially disturbing change to performance standards for all staff. Not only were employees judged on how well they performed in their roles, but they would also be rated on how engaged they were. In addition to appraising an employee's level of competence, her manager would assess whether or not she acted like a good little corporate sheep. You can probably guess what happened to employees who received low engagement scores on their performance appraisals. For reasons we have explored, and will continue to look at throughout this book, this is evidence of what's wrong with the modern workplace and why disengagement continues to plague our organizations.

CHAPTER 4

BELIEF # 1: ENGAGED EMPLOYEES WILL EXERT DISCRETIONARY EFFORT JUST BECAUSE THEY'RE GETTING A PAYCHECK

Work, when boiled down to its basic definition, is merely an exchange of labor for currency. For centuries, this construct was widely understood to be what it meant to "go to work" or to "be employed." Then the idea of employee engagement was introduced. Well, it wasn't really created by one individual in a single fit of genius. It evolved over the years with various industrial organizational psychologists, HR practitioners, and management experts adding their own spin along the way. William Kahn first used the term "engagement" back in 1990 when he wrote a piece for the *Academy of Management Journal*.[1] In his paper, Kahn proposed that employees engage by bringing their whole, authentic selves to the workplace, which fosters team effectiveness and allows for optimal performance.

It wasn't until 2008 that the concept of discretionary effort became synonymous with employee engagement when William Macey and Benjamin Schneider made their contribution in the *Industrial and Organizational Psychology Journal*.[2] Now the definition has become so muddled, it's almost understandable that business leaders haven't really been able to make noteworthy strides in overall engagement levels. They have hordes of experts giving them different explanations of what employee engagement is and how to achieve it. Still, the central theme of discretionary effort seems to be what has leaders clamoring for an engagement silver bullet. And that's where things start to head south.

Of course executives and managers would want their workers to exert discretionary effort. Labor is the biggest cost for any organization, so it would make good business sense to maximize the benefit derived and squeeze every last ounce of productivity from employees. Discretionary effort, or the extra effort workers could give if they so choose, is what propels innovation, enhances customer experience, and precipitates growth. It's the special talent sauce that differentiates mediocre companies from the most admired and successful.

What actually stimulates discretionary effort is debatable. Some practitioners believe an employee's choice to go above and beyond is totally independent from her experience of working for her employer. In other words, she can still choose to put on a smile, show up to work early, stay late, and give 110 percent toward the company's objectives. Attitude is a choice, as they say. Or is it? As we saw with the Experience-Effort Correlation in Chapter 2, that just isn't realistic. However, that doesn't stop leaders in organizations across the United States and around the world from thinking they can expect discretionary effort from employees in exchange for nothing more than a paycheck. They think to themselves, "Employees have the esteemed privilege of getting paid to work for our fantastic company, so they should be giving us extraordinary performance all day every day." If profit and prosperity are the ends and employee engagement is the means, then these leaders believe they are owed engagement (read: discretionary effort) simply because each employee is cut a check every pay period.

This belief represents the crux of the Stepford Employee Fallacy: that a salary is enough to inspire employees to go above and beyond for your organization. What actually inspires them is a great employee experience, or the combination of factors that make up what it's like to work at your organization. And what tempts them to your company in the first place is an attractive employee value proposition, which we discussed in Part I. If a steady paycheck is the only thing your organization has going for it, if there's nothing that makes you a more valuable employer than your competitors, you won't attract and retain top talent who *want* to go above and beyond.

WHAT DOES DISCRETIONARY EFFORT LOOK LIKE?

I recently changed to a new auto insurance company in search of a better rate, and I was working with both my new insurer and the old one to ensure the process went smoothly. Upon discovering that my old insurer had not yet received the paperwork needed to cancel my policy, and that they had billed me for the next month's premium, I reached out to the new carrier for assistance. The service representative with whom I spoke was helpful in providing information to resolve the problem, but I sensed no genuine desire to provide a great customer experience. I did get what I needed out of the phone call, yet something was missing. It was almost as though I were a nuisance by calling with my issue.

When I worked in customer service what seems like ages ago, I was trained to talk with a smile in my voice, making any interaction feel special for our customers simply by presenting a positive disposition. There were certainly days when doing so wasn't possible because of various factors causing me to feel disengaged, such as being scolded like a child by my micromanaging boss or being overwhelmed with more work than could reasonably be done by one person. I wondered what might have caused the representative from my insurance company to speak with such a flat affect. Having been in the woman's position previously in my career, I had my suspicions. Ironically, when I called my old carrier about the mistake, the customer service representative who helped me was chipper, friendly, and seemed to have a sincere interest in making everything alright.

That's a pretty straightforward and simplistic example of what discretionary effort looks like. I received adequate customer service from my new insurer, but the representative could have made my experience more special by talking with a smile in her voice. The representative at my old insurance company went above and beyond just answering my questions by approaching the interaction with a friendlier temperament. Some would argue that being upbeat is part of the customer service role. But it's hard for employees to be upbeat if they aren't treated well. Sure, they're getting paid, but that doesn't offset mistreatment nor does it inspire them to go above and beyond. Think of it this way: a paycheck is the bare minimum employers trade for just adequate employee effort.

A cashier working for a company that pays $7.50 an hour but does little else by way of inspiring or engaging its employees isn't likely to do any more than what's in his job description. I once bought some office supplies at a Dollar Tree where the cashier who rang me up barely acknowledged me and looked like being there was akin to slow torture. Did that make her a bad employee? Not necessarily. She promptly completed my transaction and I carried on with my day. Did that make her a disengaged employee? You bet. If you were to take a look at Dollar Tree's atrocious Glassdoor ratings, you'd see why. The retailer actually has the distinction of being ranked one of the top ten worst employers to work for.[3] Employees like the customer service representative and the cashier are technically doing their jobs. Their employers just aren't inspiring them to do any more than that.

Discretionary effort manifests in several different ways. We've already looked at how it is demonstrated in an employee's demeanor. It also presents in the way employees manage their time, which we will examine in Chapter 8. For now, let's focus on the customer experience aspect of discretionary effort, because that is what can make or break a company's reputation and, as a result, its financial success. My earlier examples of personal incidents, though pretty basic, illustrate what kind of customer experiences are created when employees exercise discretionary effort and when they withhold it. Having the benefit of context and understanding for what those employees were going through, my experiences did not necessarily affect my desire to patronize their employers. But customers who lack this kind of insight might be turned off by their experiences or, at the very least, be indifferent about continuing to do business with these companies and could easily be lured away by friendlier competitors. Defining moments in the customer relationship are those points of contact when customers form positive or negative impressions about a business, decide whether they will continue to buy its products or services, and share their experience with others.

THE WALT DISNEY COMPANY

A company that excels at creating defining moments for customers is the Walt Disney Company. Every year, millions of people visit Disney theme parks to partake in all the magic and excitement that Mickey and his friends have to offer. What sets Disney's parks and resorts apart from other destination experiences are its employees—or "Cast Members" in Disney-speak—who are the ones making all the magic happen. Sometimes guests don't even have to be on the Disney property to feel touched by the special kind of magic its cast members spread on a daily basis.

One particularly sweet story even made headlines in 2014.[4] A young teen took a very special stuffed bear named Toby with her on a trip to Disney World, but when she returned home to Alabama, she discovered Toby was missing. The bear was a gift from the teen's father who sadly passed away several years prior. When the girl's mother posted their story on social media asking for any leads on the bear's whereabouts, an eagle-eyed Disney employee recognized Toby and made it her mission to reunite him with his family. But first, she enlisted the help of other Disney Cast Members to take photos of Toby visiting various attractions at Magic Kingdom. Toby was returned home along with a photo album of him hanging out with Pooh and Tigger, and riding Dumbo, among other adventures around the park. It was the kind of defining moment that made a lasting impression not only on the young girl who was grateful to be reunited with her venturesome stuffed bear, but one that realized Disney's vision to make people happy.

What makes Disney's employees so willing to go above and beyond for guests (customers), giving them a unique and truly memorable experience? Do they get a fat paycheck to motivate them? No, they aren't paid exceptionally well. Costumed characters, for example, earn only slightly more than minimum wage. So, money definitely isn't the reason why people want to work so hard for the Mouse. That's not to say pay doesn't affect engagement levels. Recall our discussion of the Fair Wage-Effort Hypothesis from Chapter 2. Don't make the mistake of thinking that you can get away with being cheap, unless you also don't mind your employees withholding effort.

Disney Cast Members' jobs aren't just all whimsy and pixie dust. They often work long shifts and must adhere to strict rules of conduct and dress. The reason Disney Cast Members go above and beyond to create defining moments is because they feel a sense of meaning, of purpose, in what they do. Sure, they receive great discounts on merchandise, free park admission, world-class training, and near-limitless career development opportunities, along with tons of other unique perks and benefits. But these folks are dedicated to making sure customers who pay a visit to "The Happiest Place on Earth" have an especially magical experience. They don't do it just because they're getting compensation. Disney empowers and inspires its cast members to create these defining moments and then celebrates their efforts loud and often.

It is important to note that Disney is, first and foremost, in the entertainment business, and Cast Members are required to put on happy performances because that is literally their job. Disney employees are not Stepford Employees. Unless you, too, are in show business, do not expect your workers to emulate the Disney persona with nothing but their wages to motivate them. It takes much more than just a paycheck to engage employees. It takes purpose.

In the next section, we will further explore the power of purpose in engaging employees. We will also take a look at the reasons behind motivation and how different factors in the overall work experience affect employees' inclination to exert discretionary effort.

IF NOT A PAYCHECK, THEN WHAT INSPIRES DISCRETIONARY EFFORT?

If you took any business management courses in college, you might recall Frederick Hertzberg's Two Factor theory.[5] Hertzberg's theory essentially bifurcates employee experience into two sets of factors: hygiene factors and motivation factors. Hygiene factors, as the name implies, refer to the work conditions that will maintain the minimum level of satisfaction for employees. In other words, these factors preserve employees' mental, physical, and emotional health and security. Examples of hygiene factors would be fair pay for work being done, safe and reasonably comfortable working conditions, reliable and efficient technology, and positive relationships with effective leaders. Hertzberg's research showed that, without these factors in place, employees will be dissatisfied and demotivated. And with these factors present, employees will merely be satisfied but not motivated.

Beyond hygiene factors are motivation factors: rewards and recognition, career development and growth, job purpose and meaning, and a sense of achievement in the work accomplished. Note that these motivation factors are mostly intrinsic. This is because extrinsic motivators such as free meals or tuition reimbursement aren't as effective in fostering true, sustained engagement and definitely are not a substitute for any of the hygiene factors. Extrinsic motivators can make employees happy, and they surely have a place in the overall employee experience, but it's important that workers are first engaged.

This theory aligns perfectly with the engagement continuum of actively disengaged → disengaged → engaged. Absent one or more hygiene factors, employees will be actively disengaged as a way to compensate, which we saw in Chapter 2. With all hygiene factors in place, but none or few of the motivating factors, employees will only be satisfied or disengaged. Organizations that have all hygiene and motivating factors in place are far more likely to enjoy the benefits of an engaged workforce. Think of fostering a culture of employee engagement like building a house. Each stage must be completed with care before starting the next. A house first needs a foundation on which to build the structure and a roof covering it before adding fixtures and amenities to make it a home worth living in. An organization needs to have basic elements of employee engagement in place—first hygiene factors, then motivating factors—before considering the fun and fancy benefits and perks. Even the fanciest amenities can't compensate for a poorly built house.

Figure 4.1 Employee Engagement Is Like Building a House

Stage 3: Features and Amenities
Hygiene factors, motivation factors, and extrinsic motivation factors are in place and employees feel satisfied, engaged, and happy.
Stage 2: Framing, Roofing, Plumbing, Electrical
All hygiene factors and motivation factors are in place and employees feel satisfied and engaged.
Stage 1: Foundation
All hygiene factors are in place, and employees feel satisfied.

Many leaders fall into the trap of focusing on the features and amenities aspect of their organization's employee experience while neglecting the foundational and structural elements that are prerequisites to engagement. They think they are at Stage 3 when they're actually stuck at Stage 1. It really doesn't matter that your house has an infinity pool and a wine cellar if the foundation is crumbling and the plumbing leaks. It doesn't matter to employees that they get to wear jeans at the pizza party on Friday if their boss is a jerk, they're paid below average, or the technology needed to do their jobs is woefully inefficient. Get the basics down before moving on to the cool and fun stuff.

Keep in mind, fair pay is fundamental to building engagement, but take care not to assume that increasing pay is a substitute for more thoughtful organizational development. Data from Glassdoor concerning the effects of pay on employee engagement show that higher compensation does not equate to higher levels of engagement.[6] In fact, their research revealed that the more money someone earned, the greater emphasis he or she placed on culture and quality of leadership. What this tells us isn't that low earners are more engaged by money than high earners. Rather, it demonstrates that those who earn less value pay raises and bonuses as hygiene factors to satisfy their basic needs, which we reviewed earlier in this section. Naturally, a raise would mean much more to minimum-wage worker whose rent is about to increase than it would an executive already earning six figures. But that's not to suggest any of the other factors leading to engagement should be ignored with lower-level employees. Compensation is important; it just becomes less so higher up the pay scale. For employees at all levels of pay, the elements that inspire engagement are still critical.

As we saw with the Disney case study, a powerful motivation factor is the sense of meaning employees derive from their work. Now, some might say that meaning is dependent on the individual and an employer cannot *give* its employees meaning in their jobs; they find it on their own. That's not really true because, in taking this stance, one confuses meaning with passion. True, different people have different passions. But passion cannot withstand a disengaging employee experience. Even if an employee were passionate about his job at one point, a lack of meaning can erode engagement to the point where he feels disengaged. Meaningless work does not inspire employees to continue giving discretionary effort. In order for them to feel engaged, they must know that their efforts are not wasted and that their work makes a real difference for the organization and its customers, thus creating purposeful and emotional connection.

Dan Ariely, professor of psychology and behavioral economics at Duke University, gave a TEDTalk in 2012 about the evident power of meaning and purpose in work.[7] He described a series of experiments in which he and his researchers tested their hypothesis that meaning impacts engagement and motivation. Research participants were given LEGO pieces to assemble toys, one after another, being paid a decreasing amount of money until the payment no longer justified the effort. They were told that the toys would later be used with another research group. The next group was similarly paid to assemble the toys, but instead of building one after another, researchers would disassemble their completed toys and hand them back to the participants to build them all over again. Participants in the second group chose to build fewer toys than the first because they perceived no meaning in the task if their work did not amount to any real significance. Even the research subjects in the second scenario who loved to build LEGOs were no more inclined to continue the task than those who felt no emotional attachment to the task. It didn't matter that they would continue to get paid if they built more toys.

That last point perfectly illustrates our earlier discussion of how passion wanes in the presence of disengagement factors, and it further demonstrates that payment alone is not a motivation factor. A separate experiment involved participants filling out pieces of paper and handing them to a researcher. The same descending pay scheme as the LEGO experiment applied. In one subject group, their papers were acknowledged by the researcher when received. In the second group, their papers were unacknowledged upon receipt. The third group saw their submitted papers go directly into a shredder. Participants in the first group—the ones whose work was acknowledged—put forth more effort and continued the experiment longer than the other two groups. The latter quit after approximately the same short period of time, showing that meaningless work, even if the effort just goes unrecognized, is demotivating.

These experiments prove a very salient fact about the nature of motivation in work. Just like the test subjects whose LEGO toys were disassembled and whose papers were ignored or shredded, employees who see their continued inputs as meaningless will eventually lose motivation. In casual parlance, this is known as "shoveling shit against the tide," and it is corrosive to engagement. If employees feel that their contributions have no purpose and that they're just stuck like a hamster running on a wheel, day in and day out, then they will have no reason to put forth discretionary effort. Pointless work is not inspirational.

I once had a boss who insisted that everyone on our team manually create time sheets using Microsoft Excel to show her exactly what tasks we worked on and how much time we dedicated to each. These weren't entry-level, hourly employees, mind you. This was a group of mid-level professionals. One day, I learned that nothing had been done with the data after nearly a year of following this process. It was never reviewed to see where efficiencies could be gained or where we were adding the most value. The time sheets just sat collecting digital dust in our department's shared drive because our boss never once looked at them. Aside from it being a bit of an insult to require professional-level employees to complete time sheets, this also demonstrated that our boss hadn't a clue as to what we did in our jobs, and she would rather weigh us down with fruitless busywork than partner with us to actualize meaning in our jobs.

In order to engage employees, leaders cannot underestimate the power of meaningful work. Deloitte's *Talent 2020* report surveyed over five hundred employees in various industries to determine what work experience factors most inspired employees to stay with their employers and exert discretionary effort in their roles.[8] The majority of respondents (42 percent) indicated meaningful work is what drives them. Leaders can inspire meaning for their employees in several different ways which are discussed throughout this book. For example, in Chapter 6, we will cover what makes meaningful work a major factor influencing employees to act as brand ambassadors. In Chapter 10, we will examine the effects of meaningful work on employee retention and loyalty. It is a powerful motivator that most business leaders have trouble understanding because, like other soft skill topics, it requires a more human-focused comprehension than the modern workplace will allow. Recall from Chapter 3 that business professionals are trained to care about numbers and facts, not feelings. But science does make a strong case.

The human brain is indeed *wired* to seek meaningful tasks and avoid painful or unpleasant ones. Just as extrinsic rewards such as monetary gain will trigger release of the neurotransmitter dopamine in the reward center of the brain, finding meaning and purpose in work will have the same physiological effect. However, research shows that the pleasure gained from financial rewards is fleeting and, therefore, not as effective of a motivating factor as is commonly assumed.[9]

In general, connecting your employees with their work on both an emotional level and a cognitive level is the way to go. That's what employee engagement is really all about: capturing the hearts and minds of talent and harnessing the resultant energy through purposeful work. First, make sure their role is in alignment with their skill set and passions. Ideally, hiring managers will glean this information from candidates when selecting for a specific role. For current employees, leaders should be having frequent conversations to understand how they feel about their roles, what, if anything needs to change, and remove any barriers and motivation-sucking processes that prevent them from adding the most value that they are able. Then, help them envision where their role fits into the overall scheme of things. If they can see how the work they do creates a positive customer experience and is integral to the company's success, then, to them, their efforts are meaningful and valued. If they can't make that connection, show them! Don't just regurgitate the cliché corporate platitude of "our employees are our greatest assets." Every employee has something to contribute toward their organization's goals. It's a leader's job to tease out those strengths and abilities, nurture them, and sustain them with a meaningful, engaging employee experience. A paycheck alone just doesn't cut it.

LOOKING AHEAD

The fatal mistake made by so many people managers today is treating employees like machines and thinking that remuneration is their ON switch. Throughout this chapter, we've examined the relationship between pay and employee engagement, arriving at the conclusion that it takes much more than a paycheck to engage and motivate employees. Believing you are entitled to discretionary effort from workers just because they are being paid represents a gross misunderstanding of how employee engagement really works. Employees are emotional, complicated, multifaceted human beings. If you expect them to somehow suppress their innate, inalienable human qualities, then you will lose any hope of inspiring them to go above and beyond for your organization.

In the next chapter, we will see how leading and engaging people means having to accept their humanity and that they have lives outside of work. Professionalism is often falsely equated with having a robotic drive to serve the organization while ensuring any personal matters do not impede your performance. According to the Stepford Employee Fallacy, engaged employees can and should leave any aspect of their personal lives outside the office. But, as we will discuss, this is simply another foolish premise of the modern workplace.

NOTES

1. Kahn, William. "Psychological Conditions of Personal Engagement and Disengagement at Work." *Academy of Management Journal.* Vol. 33, No. 4. 692-724. December 1, 1990.

2. Macey, William and Schneider, Benjamin. "The Meaning of Employee Engagement." *Industrial and Organizational Psychology, I.* 3-30. 2008.

3. Komen, Evan, Frohlich, Thomas, and Stebbins, Samuel. "The Worst Companies to Work For." *24/7 Wall St.* June 10, 2016. http://247wallst.com/special-report/2016/06/10/the-worst-companies-to-work-for-2/

4. Egan, Nicole W. "Lost Teddy Bear Tours Disney Before Heading Home to Alabama." *People.* February 26, 2014. http://people.com/celebrity/lost-teddy-bear-tours-disney-before-heading-home-to-alabama/

5. Hertzberg, Frederick. "One More Time: How Do You Motivate Employees?" *Harvard Business Review.* January 2003. https://hbr.org/2003/01/one-more-time-how-do-you-motivate-employees

6. Wong, Patrick. "Does Money Change What We Value at Work?" *Glassdoor Economic Research Blog.* January 17, 2017. https://www.glassdoor.com/research/more-money-change-value-at-work/

7. Ariely, Dan. "What Makes Us Feel Good about Our Work?" (Lecture) TEDxRiodelaPlata. October 2012. https://www.ted.com/talks/dan_ariely_what_makes_us_feel_good_about_our_work

8. Erickson, Robin, Kwan, Alice, Nevaras, Neil, Pelster, Bill, Schwartz, Jeff, and Szpaichler, Sarah. *Talent 2020: Surveying the Talent Paradox from the Employee Perspective.* Deloitte University Press. 2012. https://www2.deloitte.com/content/dam/insights/us/articles/talent-2020-surveying-the-talent-paradox-from-the-employee-perspective/DUP194_Talent2020_Employee-Perspective1.pdf

9. Williams, Ray. "Why Financial Incentives Don't Improve Performance." (Blog) *Psychology Today.* November 28, 2015. https://www.psychologytoday.com/blog/wired-success/201511/why-financial-incentives-don-t-improve-performance

BELIEF # 2: ENGAGED EMPLOYEES WILL FORGET ABOUT THEIR PERSONAL PROBLEMS WHEN THEY COME IN TO WORK

The idea and practice of work-life integration is becoming increasingly prevalent in today's demanding and interconnected working world. Rather than treating your job and personal matters as separate and unrelated— never the twain shall meet—integrating both aspects of your life is supposed to create more internal harmony and decrease stress. Essentially, integration of each major life facet—career, family, community, and self—by creating synergy among them leads to greater overall satisfaction without sacrificing one for another.[1] This allows business leaders and HR professionals to make a prima facie case that their employees can succeed in life and at work if they blend the two in service of a *whole self* concept. In theory, work-life integration is a viable model. However, just like work-life balance before it, the nature of the modern workplace stands as a barrier preventing employees from achieving any semblance of equilibrium or maintaining priority for what matters most in their lives. Hint: for the majority of employees, work isn't most important.

Managers don't mind giving their employees company smart phones and expecting them to be available on nights, weekends, and even while on vacation. But when personal issues require employees to put work duties on the back burner, well, that's just unacceptable! It's a classic case of employers wanting to have their employee engagement cake and eat it too. And it points to a much bigger problem in organizations today: businesses refuse to accept that their employees are human beings, personal problems and all. This doesn't just involve time spent working, which we will cover more in Chapter 8. The problem extends to all attributes of employees' lives, from family obligations to financial struggles.

I once worked in a client-facing role for a company that expected employees to deliver what it called "stellar service" to internal and external customers. We were told to act engaged by dedicating extraordinary time and effort toward keeping customers happy and growing the bottom line. The fact that employees actually had lives and concerns outside of work mattered little to management. Our manager placed a sign at the front of the office, which everyone could read as they came into work each morning: "Leave your [personal] problems at the door and drink the Stellar Service Kool-Aid!" They weren't even trying to hide their attempts at building a workforce of Stepford Employees. This was the same company I mentioned in Chapter 1, the one that sacked a woman for taking time off to be with her sick child.

Sadly, this isn't at all uncommon in today's workplace, and it represents a lack of understanding on the part of leaders who fail to see their staff as nothing more than labor machines. If a machine isn't producing at full capacity, then it's clearly defective (read: disengaged) and must be replaced. There's no room for human problems in organizations that apply these kinds of cultural standards. Leaders continue to believe this piece of the Stepford Employee Fallacy while their employees grow more disengaged and disenfranchised from the lack of support. This affects their ability and desire to give a committed effort, causing managers to step in with punitive action, thus creating a vicious cycle. Managers don't care about employees as human beings, so employees don't care about their employer's priorities. In order to break this cycle, leaders need to fully grasp what issues their employees are facing outside of work, how they can overflow *into* work, and how to be empathetic and supportive in addressing them.

THE SPILLOVER EFFECT

Imagine your life as a drinking glass and the water that fills it represents all of the stressors you have to handle every day. Some stressors are small droplets, easy to digest. Other stressors, like major life events, produce a steady deluge that cause your glass to run over before you can even attempt to take a sip. Just when you think you have one area of your life under control, another stressor from a different area comes along and dumps gallons of water into your eight-ounce drinking glass. Stress spills over until you're looking at a flood, paralyzed with no idea about how to make all that water fit in the glass and get back to normal.

The spillover effect basically tells us that stress or emotion in one area of a person's life can spill over into another area. I purposely modified this theory with our drinking glass metaphor to illustrate the work-life integration concept discussed at the beginning of this chapter. If we aren't going to view different aspects of a person's life as distinct and separate from one another, instead going for a *whole self* model, then we must acknowledge that there simply isn't enough capacity for one person to handle the immense stresses that can accumulate. Whether the stress of family life spills into their work and vice versa, or whether the aggregate stress from multiple sources completely overwhelms them, the results for employees are the same: decreased engagement and inability to perform. Of course, the default management attitude equates properly running a business with forsaking anything else that distracts from the organization's objectives.

This goes back to the notion that employees can and will neglect their personal lives as soon as they clock in to work every morning. It just isn't feasible, nor is it very humane for that matter. That's the paradox of employing people in business. Humanity is what turns the gears of enterprise, not cold, cruel efficiency. Whenever managers complain about employees' personal problems, they throw out the standard line, "We have a business to run." My response usually makes them stop and think: "And who's running your business? Human beings!" The robots haven't taken over, yet, so employers will have to accept the very human nature of their workforce.

Stress outside of work can and does spill over into employees' performance, costing companies billions of dollars each year due to absenteeism, errors, and lost productivity among other outcomes. One particularly exhausting source of personal stress among employees is caregiving. As the population ages, there will be a greater demand for elder care, with few options available to those who can't balance the demands of caring for loved ones with the expectations of their employers. Costs associated with caregiving stress alone set employers back almost $38 billion per annum, and one in six Americans have some kind of caregiving role.[2] That number jumps to nearly 50 percent for middle-aged employees in the so-called "sandwich generation"—those who provide support to aging parents and young or even grown children at the same time.[3] So there are a lot of people in the workforce who are stretched pretty thin.

Caring for an elderly or sick parent, as an example, carries with it a laundry list of responsibilities, from coordinating doctor's visits, to feeding, to mobility assistance. The physical and psychological toll for those in care-taking roles can be harrowing, while the out-of-pocket financial expenses can easily reach thousands of dollars. Most companies do not allow for additional paid time off above and beyond regular vacation or sick time. The Family Medical Leave Act (FMLA) affords eligible workers up to twelve weeks of leave to deal with their own or a relative's healthcare. But employers aren't required to pay them during their absence. Even if an employee manages to get by without a paycheck during FMLA leave, she still has to worry about whether being away from work makes her look unreliable or uncommitted. In fact, employees with caregiving duties typically do not divulge this information to their managers for fear of it negatively affecting their career or their employment status. They feel trapped. Of course, it's illegal for an employer to retaliate against employees protected under FMLA. However, as we saw in Chapter 3, corporate lawyers have plenty of tricks up their sleeves to mitigate or even circumvent justice for people who've been wronged by their employers. If a company or any of its managers deem an employee to be a problem, they are often very good at finding ways to get rid of him.

In my prior corporate life, I worked with a woman—let's call her Lydia—who had the unfortunate burden of taking family leave to travel across the country so she could declutter her elderly parents' home, prepare it for sale, and move them into assisted living. This came at a critical time for the project we were working on, but of course her family should have taken priority. As the key member of our team, she was certainly missed and the project suffered during her absence. Returning to work brought her no respite from the personal stress back home because she had to work twice as hard to catch up. Our VP was displeased with the state of the project and blamed Lydia since she was the project lead. He was the type of manager who decided, once he didn't like someone, there was no hope of getting back in his good graces. So, he found fault in almost everything Lydia did and grew even less patient when she dared to raise concerns about his lack of support. That led to a closed-door meeting in which he threatened Lydia with a performance improvement plan as she sat hyperventilating from the relentless emotional pressure. Luckily, she found a better job several months later. This is just one example of what employees experience when their personal matters conflict with company needs.

Employees dealing with personal stressors are far more likely to experience burnout, which puts them at much greater risk of physical conditions like hypertension and mental illnesses such as depression and anxiety.[4] Lack of support from employers can aggravate these issues, resulting in higher insurance premiums to cover the healthcare cost of employees seeking treatment. Still, too many business leaders fail to appreciate the business case for offering assistance to workers struggling with issues like elder care. They want to pretend that engaged employees don't have personal problems or, if they do, that they're willing and able to keep those challenges from impacting their level of engagement. If someone needs to take time off and tend to a personal matter—like their own health or the death of a loved one—then they are eyed with suspicion, regarded as disruptive, and subjected to intrusive policies that make them feel like criminals.

There are still companies today that require employees to bring in a doctor's note after taking a sick day. There are still managers and HR folks who think it's perfectly okay to demand proof of death when an employee's loved one passes away. What a callous, merciless mindset for relating to the people who make their businesses successful. Instead of being empathetic toward employees and supporting them when personal stress spills over into their work, leaders continue to put their faith in the Stepford Employee Fallacy while engagement plummets.

NO MONEY, MO' PROBLEMS

Remember the 2008 recession? Most people would prefer to forget it. After the housing bubble burst and financial markets tanked, many were left bankrupt, unemployed, underemployed, or in otherwise dire straits. That did little to dissuade millions of young people from making what they were told was a smart investment and taking out loans to go to college. As of today, the student loan bubble has ballooned to almost $1.5 trillion, and many economists worry it will cause a repeat of the 2008 financial crisis when it deflates.[5] Obtaining a college degree is still touted as the sure path toward career success and increased lifetime earnings, despite graduates' inability to secure jobs that pay enough to cover their loan installments and other basic costs. Real wages for most Americans have barely moved in over thirty years, while an increasing number of graduates with baccalaureate degrees flood the job market. You would think that the optimistic estimates for college graduates' earning power indicate some positive trend for overall income levels. Universities report that the average bachelor's program graduate earns about $51,000 per year which, at first glance, is quite a bit more than one might expect 20 years ago.[6] But the numbers university administrators share about the average starting salary for their graduates only tell part of the story. When we talk about real wages, we are taking inflation into account, so that gives a better representation of people's purchasing power. And, unfortunately, they can't purchase much. Experts fear student loan defaults will have the same crippling economic impact as the Great Recession.

This all ties in with a larger issue with the modern business world. While recent graduates struggle to pay their loans as the college debt bubble is fixing to pop, and tenured employees haven't seen their take-home pay increase in years, executive compensation has grown exponentially. In 1965, CEOs were paid twenty times more than the average worker. By 1995, the ratio widened to 123:1. As of 2017, typical chief executive pay was about 274 times that of their employees[7]. Let's put that into perspective. If the median salary for US workers is just over $44,000 per year[8], then CEOs rake in, on average, $12,056,000 each year. Are the companies these executives run doing so well as to justify such obscene pay? It doesn't appear that way, given the amount of cost-cutting that goes on these days. Go out to eat at your local chain restaurant and you'll probably notice the meal portions are conspicuously smaller than they used to be. The next time you buy a jar of peanut butter, look at the bottom of the container. There's an indent where it used to be flat, leaving you with less creamy goodness for your money.

More troubling and audacious than the companies cheating customers with downsized products are the decision makers who terminate scores of workers in the name of cost savings while paying themselves eight-figure salaries. Actually, that's not fair. Executives can be let go just like any other employee. I remember one senior executive at a former employer leaving with nothing but a $17 million golden parachute to break his fall, the poor thing. At the same time, a co-worker also lost the layoff lottery as she was caring for her pneumonic husband, raising her autistic son, and living in a hotel because a leaking septic tank rendered her home untenable. Reductions in force affect employees at all levels, albeit unequally. People at that company lived in constant fear of getting *RIFfed* while the top brass enjoyed the comfort and security of being multi-millionaires, job or no job.

Employees' money problems might seem like they are personal and separate from their employer's own financial health, but business leaders should really reconsider this assumption. It's dreadfully short-sighted. Going back to my earlier point about the student loan crisis, there is much to be said about the fact that, for the first time in history, younger generations are financially worse off than their parents were at the same age. Unable to find employment commensurate with their education and saddled with trillions of dollars in debt, Generation Y is generally delaying major milestones like buying a home and getting married. At this point, they're just trying to make ends meet. This doesn't bode well for the economy at large, but employers should be especially concerned because of the deleterious effect on engagement.

Some organizations are responding by including student loan debt assistance as part of their employee benefits packages, which is smart. It's one way to attract and retain talent but should be applied in conjunction with other policies that demonstrate an employer's overall commitment to treating employees fairly and caring for them as people. Does that mean paying off their mortgages, student loans, credit cards, and grocery bills? Of course not. It simply means not being cheap, greedy, or insensitive. If you can afford to dole out millions of dollars for your executive team's lavish compensation, but freeze everyone else's pay, take away their jobs, or start your lowest ranks at poverty-level wages, don't expect engagement within your organization.

HEALTH MATTERS

Take a look at any major company's careers web page, and you'll find lots of flowery language about workers being their greatest assets and that they offer competitive health benefits in support of employees' wellbeing. Just ignore the extra fine print about punishing employees who have the audacity to ever get sick or require professional assistance. The underlying culture that continues to infect the modern workplace is one of disdain toward the inconvenience of illness. It's simply not conducive to efficient business operations for employees to be unhealthy. Sure, companies talk a big game about wellness initiatives and industry-leading health insurance plans, but those mean nothing when employees can't take time off because they need emergency surgery or because their panic attacks are flaring up again. Unfortunately for managers who have no interest in being sensitive to employees' health matters, the total cost of disengagement will far exceed any loss in productivity from a few sick days. It just doesn't pay to disregard the human needs and limitations of your workforce. People fall ill. They require help. Being an employer of choice means supporting workers when their health is at stake and giving them peace of mind so they can focus on getting better. Kindness, not apathy, drives engagement.

The Mental Struggle is Real

Putting up an out-of-office e-mail message that lets your coworkers (including the CEO) know you are taking a couple days off to restore your mental health seems like it wouldn't be the best idea. But that's just what one web developer at Olark Live Chat did, and her CEO's response was so pleasantly surprising that it went viral.[9] Rather than denigrate, roll his eyes, or chastise his employee for frivolous dereliction, Olark's chief executive responded to her message with an e-mail of his own. He praised her for being authentic and thanked her for doing her part to break down the stigma of mental health issues, especially in the workplace. The developer ended up sharing the e-mail exchange on Twitter where it garnered broad attention with over twelve thousand re-tweets.

Mental health is still fairly taboo in our society. Whether they are suffering from bipolar disorder or postpartum depression, people living with psychiatric conditions often feel isolated because there is such a lack of understanding among the general population. They are reluctant to share their experiences and struggles for fear of being judged. It's natural to be afraid of others' judgment, particularly within a professional setting. At work, there is an unspoken rule to not share personal health issues because of the perception that it might portray someone as weak or problematic. True, there are legal protections for anyone with a handicap or illness covered under the Americans with Disabilities Act. But that doesn't help with the feelings of shame and loneliness people with mental illnesses internalize as they go about navigating daily life, including the demands of the modern workplace. Also, the burden of proof for bringing action under the

ADA rests on the plaintiff's shoulders, making it difficult to show that there was a clear case of illegal discrimination.

Making accommodations for someone with anxiety to take breaks throughout the day might become irksome for less-empathetic managers, so they'll find a way to document other performance issues and "manage the employee out" by making work so miserable that the employee quits. This particular tactic, known as constructive discharge, is considered tantamount to wrongful termination. But again, the bar for employees to prove mistreatment is fairly high. It's just safer and easier from a job security standpoint for mentally ill employees to keep quiet. After all, they are expected to be fully engaged, so they should just pretend their conditions don't exist while they are at work.

According to the National Alliance on Mental Illness, a non-profit community of mental health providers and volunteers, nearly 20 percent of adults in the United States experience some form of mental disorder, 9.8 million of whom are limited or handicapped in some way by their conditions.[10] The prevalence of particularly severe psychiatric illnesses like chronic depression has coincided with an increase in suicidality for all age groups over the last ten years. Suicide among young Americans in their twenties is on the rise, but older adults actually succumb at a higher rate of ten to fifteen per hundred thousand.[11] There is a mental illness epidemic of troubling proportions, and those who need the most help are least likely to access or receive the necessary treatment. At least some medical afflictions present with obvious symptoms that are taken seriously by most reasonable managers. Psychiatric disorders are like invisible chains that too many employees wear as they suffer in silence while indifferent employers regard them with scorn or as liabilities. Eventually, the weight of those chains become too much to bear and sufferers lose their jobs and, in the most tragic cases, their lives.

Working in a management position grants the ability to create an engaging work environment simply by making it safe for employees to candidly share their mental health stories, as the CEO of Olark Live Chat did. For so many people, their careers are tightly bound to their identities and sense of purpose. Feeling unable or unsafe to live and work authentically can compound the effects of psychiatric conditions, thus rendering scores of valuable employees unproductive and disengaged. If only all employers would give the mental health of their employees the level of concern Olark does, we would see much better workforce engagement, lower turnover, less absenteeism, and greater innovation. That's because we currently work in a knowledge economy where our brains are the means of production and ideas are the output. The best companies don't punish or cull employees who have mental illnesses. They foster empathy and authenticity in the workplace to draw out the best thinking from every one of their employees, no matter what their struggle happens to be.

The Real Sickness

As the healthcare debate in the United States rages on, millions of Americans wait and wonder what the future holds for them and their families. Healthcare costs have grown unmanageable in many respects and, as of this publication, our branches of government continue to bicker over the best solution. A discussion of the broken U.S. healthcare system is, of course, well beyond the scope of this book. However, the topic of healthcare in general is inseparable from employee engagement because caring for one's health has become something of a catch twenty-two in today's working world: Employees need to work in order to afford health insurance and pay any out-of-pocket costs associated with treatment they need, but getting sick and losing time at work jeopardizes their employment. They either tough it out and work through an illness or injury, or they take the time they need to seek treatment and get well, thereby running the risk that doing so will affect their standing with the boss. When workers face such a tough decision every time they or their loved ones get sick, is it really any wonder that global employee engagement is so dismally low?

The Centers for Disease Control estimate that there were over 141 million emergency room visits last year, roughly 8 percent of which required hospital admission.[12] Those were just the ones who made it to the hospital. Surely people avoid going to the doctor because they can't afford healthcare services, or they are afraid of losing their jobs if they miss work. I consider that the real sickness afflicting today's workplace. When employees lose their sense of safety and security, it's impossible for them to feel truly engaged and committed. Recall Maslow's hierarchy of needs. Near the very bottom of the hierarchy sit safety and security. Leaving these needs unfulfilled puts an individual in a constant state of stress—also known as a reactive state—which prevents higher-level thought processes and motivation that are absolutely necessary for engagement.

I've worked at companies where the running joke was, "Unless you're on your death bed, you're expected to show up at work." It would be funny if it weren't actually true. That management mentality is sadly commonplace, particularly in the private sector where time equals money and employees taking time off are treated as though they are robbing their employers blind. What utter, hypocritical nonsense. Employers want their talent to be fully engaged and constantly going the extra mile but can't excuse, much less show concern for, employees who take sick.

Family Values at Work, a national coalition advocating for worker's rights, recently reported that nearly a quarter of American workers were either threatened with termination or outright fired for being absent due to illness.[13] When you think of the sheer size of the U.S. workforce, it gives you a fairly clear indication of just how extensive this problem is. The worst offenders are usually the companies big enough to think that they can get away with it.

A recent report published by the legal advocacy group A Better Balance exposed Walmart's (alleged) unfair treatment of employees with health issues. In partnership with OUR Walmart, a worker support center founded by United Food & Commercial Workers, A Better Balance surveyed over one thousand retail workers from Walmart stores across the United States, and what they found was pretty disturbing.[14] Based on accounts from the workers they spoke with, researchers learned that Walmart has a disciplinary system wherein an employee can receive points for unexcused absences. If someone gets too many points, they're out of a job. Managers have total discretion for administering the policy, and they seem to commonly punish employees even when medical emergencies require time away from work. One employee's appendix ruptured during his shift and he was told by a manager that if he went to the emergency room, he would reach his point quota and be terminated. Another's daughter attempted suicide, and she received points for staying by her side in the ICU. Even documented illnesses are subject to the point system. Diabetics with kidney disease or chronic migraine sufferers can expect their conditions to be held against them.

Store managers also have a practice of refusing doctors' notes, presumably to give Walmart plausible deniability should the Department of Labor come snooping around. A worker in Kentucky spent two days in the emergency room vomiting blood, but her supervisor would not accept the hospital's admission notes and so she received a point for each day.

Walmart is the world's largest retailer with almost $496.9 billion in revenues for the 2017 fiscal year[15]. That's billion with a B. And the Walton family, Walmart's controlling dynasty, is one of the wealthiest in the world. You'd think they could afford a relatively minuscule dip in productivity if an employee, say, had to spend several days in the hospital because she almost bled to death from a hemorrhaging ovarian cyst. But no, that woman was written up for her absences, as well. If the allegations are true, Walmart isn't just violating established labor law, it's validating the company's reputation for being an evil employer. Thankfully, there *are* organizations that don't kick their "greatest assets" when they're down and instead opt for a refreshingly human employee engagement tack.

SAS

As the dark cloud of recession hovered over the late 2000s, most, if not all, large employers looked to their headcounts for opportunities to save money. Mass layoffs left departed workers reeling. Survivors wondered if they would be next as they did their best to pick up the slack without succumbing to burnout. One company bucked the trend and refused to shore up its bottom line at the expense of its employees' livelihoods. Jim Goodnight, CEO and co-founder of analytics firm SAS, pledged in 2009 that none of the thirteen-thousand-employee workforce would lose his or her job because of a layoff. He kept his promise and the company even turned a profit that year. SAS has the lowest turnover rate in the tech industry—about 3 percent—and continues Goodnight's no-layoffs policy to this day.[16] It is interesting that similarly sized corporations viewed their employees as burdensome expenditures, yet they couldn't match SAS in terms of performance or survivorship during the recession. SAS is a perennial appointment to various Best Place to Work lists, and for good reason. In 2017, People Magazine awarded the company fifth place on its list of 50 Companies That Care.

The culture at SAS is what makes it such a phenomenal employer. When you think of large technology conglomerates, fancy perks and benefits like free meals, on-site child care, and a state-of-the art fitness center, probably come to mind. SAS does provide these and then some. But those are really just superficial trappings, though they certainly have value for employees. What makes SAS's culture so unique is the emphasis it puts on caring for those who work there. Work-life balance is taken very seriously, with employees at all levels strongly encouraged to give priority to family needs. They can still get their work done by taking advantage of the company's flexible working arrangements instead of adhering to a strict schedule or being physically present in the office.

Jim Goodnight gave an interview with the Huffington Post, in which he quite succinctly laid out his leadership philosophy: He expects employees to be there for their families, whether that means going to a child's sporting event or taking a loved one to a medical appointment. It doesn't matter where or when work gets done, as long as the output is there. Employees can take several weeks of paid leave for maternity, paternity, adoption, or elder care. The focus on employees' total well-being is almost unbelievable. At SAS corporate headquarters, there's a meditation space, forty miles of jogging trails, a pharmacy, and a Work-Life Center that offers free counseling services on topics ranging from personal finance to mental health. They even lend out medical assistance equipment like crutches, wheelchairs, and walkers on a short-term basis, so employees don't have to spend the money or go through insurance. Who *does* that? A company that actually cares does it.

Plenty of leaders will likely complain that they don't have the massive budgets that tech companies like SAS or Google do to craft such robust benefit menus. They're missing the point, though. When it comes to its employees, SAS's guiding principle is to care for them so well that they will take great care of customers. Care doesn't necessarily equate to free haircuts and M&Ms (the latter an SAS staple since its inception). It comes from leadership's genuine desire to do the right thing for employees and afford them the time and support to not only enjoy their lives outside of work, but to make the most of their experience *at* work. Caring for employees means lifting them up when they're about to fall under the weight of life's challenges, instead of dismissing their personal issues as inconsequential to the company's goals.

Organizations like SAS know and appreciate the value of supporting employees because that's what it takes to drive success. Starting with a caring leadership mindset will inspire more engagement from employees. This, in turn, results in better business outcomes and generates more money to spend on both the organization and its workforce. The mindset precedes the money.

LOOKING AHEAD

When people find themselves in difficult or even life-changing circumstances—whether for family, financial, or health reasons—their employers can either ease their worry with empathetic leadership and compassionate policies, or they can add to their stress with typical, unfeeling corporate insouciance. Which do you reckon is more likely to engage employees and inspire them to bring their A game? Going even further, which prompts employees to act as brand ambassadors, as committed advocates for the organization? That's what we will be exploring in Chapter 6.

The kind, humane quality of an organization's employee experience is, in large part, what drives engagement as well as brand ambassadorship. In addition to caring about workers' personal lives, what else inspires them to become brand ambassadors? What turns employees into unofficial marketers who are so enthusiastic about their employer that they go out of their way to draw in customers and job candidates through social networking and other means? We will discuss the components of an attractive employee value proposition and how they translate to powerful brand advocacy. An organization's current state, culture, and product lineup all have tremendous influence over employees' sense of pride and will affect their willingness to preach about its value relative to competitors. Developing and improving each of these areas is certainly no small task but ultimately pays off big time in terms of employee engagement, reputational capital, and profits.

NOTES

1. Berdahl, Jennifer, Vandello, Joseph, and Williams, Joan. "Beyond Work-Life 'Integration.'" Annual Review of Psychology. Volume 67. 515-539. January 2016. http://www.annualreviews.org/doi/pdf/10.1146/annurev-psych-122414-033710#article-denial

2. Nobel, Jeremy, Pickering, Laurel, Sasser, Emily, Sherman, Candice, and Weiss, Jennifer. Northeast Business Group on Health. *The Caregiving Landscape: Challenges and Opportunities for Employers*. March 2017. http://nebgh.org/wp-content/uploads/2017/03/NEBGH-CaregivingLandscape-FINAL-web.pdf

3. Parker, Kim and Patten, Eileen. "The Sandwich Generation: Rising Financial Burdens for Middle-Aged Americans." Pew Research Center. January 30, 2013. http://www.pewsocialtrends.org/files/2013/01/Sandwich_Generation_Report_FINAL_1-29.pdf

4. Duxbury, Linda and Higgins, Christopher. *Balancing Work, Childcare, and Eldercare: A View from the Trenches*. Carleton University. 2012. https://sprott.carleton.ca/wp-content/uploads/Duxbury-BalancingWorkChildcareEldercare-ENG-1.pdf

5. Kantrowitz, Mark. "Why the Student Loan Crisis Is Even Worse Than People Think." *Time*. January 11, 2016. http://time.com/money/4168510/why-student-loan-crisis-is-worse-than-people-think/

6. National Association of Colleges and Employers. *Compensation*. NACE Center for Career Development and Talent Acquisition. Retrieved January 7, 2018. http://www.naceweb.org/job-market/compensation/

7. Mishel, Lawrence and Schieder, Jessica. Economic Policy Institute. *CEO Pay Remains High Relative to the Pay of Typical Workers and High-Wage Earners*. July 20, 2017. http://www.epi.org/publication/ceo-pay-remains-high-relative-to-the-pay-of-typical-workers-and-high-wage-earners/

8. Bureau of Labor Statistics. *Usual Weekly Earnings of Wage and Salary Workers Third Quarter 2017*. October 18, 2017. https://www.bls.gov/news.release/pdf/wkyeng.pdf

9. Stahl, Ashley. "Why Companies Should Care about Employees' Mental Health." *Forbes*. July 14, 2017.

https://www.forbes.com/sites/ashleystahl/2017/07/14/why-employers-should-care-about-our-mental-health/#72e191023c84

10. National Alliance on Mental Illness. *Mental Health by the Numbers.* October 2015. https://www.nami.org/Learn-More/Mental-Health-By-the-Numbers

11. Annest, Joseph, Dahlberg, Linda, Luo, Feijun, Simon, Thomas, and Sullivan, Erin. "Suicide Trends among Persons Aged 10-24 Years — United States, 1994-2012." Centers for Disease Control and Prevention: Morbidity and Mortality Weekly Report. Volume 64. Number 8. March 6, 2015. https://www.cdc.gov/mmwr/pdf/wk/mm6408.pdf

12. Centers for Disease Control. *National Hospital Ambulatory Medical Care Survey: 2014 Emergency Department Summary Tables.* 2014. https://www.cdc.gov/nchs/data/nhamcs/web_tables/2014_ed_web_tables.pdf

13. Family Values @ Work. *Sick and Fired: Why We Need Earned Sick Days to Boost the Economy.* 2011. http://familyvaluesatwork.org/wp-content/uploads/2011/10/FVAW_SickAndFired_Online.pdf

14. Bakst, Dina, Gedmark, Elizabeth, and Suvall Cara. A Better Balance. *PointingOut: How Wal-Mart Unlawfully Punishes Workers for Medical Absences.* 2017. https://www.abetterbalance.org/wp-content/uploads/2017/05/Pointing-Out-Walmart-Report-FINAL.pdf

15. "Walmart U.S. Q4 comps grew 1.8% and Walmart U.S. eCommerce GMV grew 36.1%." 2017. https://news.walmart.com/2017/02/21/walmart-us-q4-comps-grew-18-and-walmart-us-ecommerce-gmv-grew-361

16. Brenoff, Ann. "What We Can Learn from the Man Who Runs The 'World's Happiest Company.'" *Huffington Post.* January 29, 2014. https://www.huffingtonpost.com/2014/01/29/worlds-best-company_n_4655292.html

CHAPTER 6

BELIEF # 3: ENGAGED EMPLOYEES WILL ACT AS BRAND AMBASSADORS REGARDLESS OF THE COMPANY'S CURRENT STATE, ITS CULTURE, OR THE QUALITY OF ITS PRODUCTS

There's a famous quote from the American author and motivational speaker Zig Ziglar that perfectly sums up people's affinity for one brand over another: "People don't buy for logical reasons. They buy for emotional reasons." A fairly obvious example would be consumers' obsession with Apple products. Apple's computers and mobile devices have a devout following even though competitors like Samsung offer more sophisticated alternatives. The overall feeling and experience of owning an Apple product is enough to retain buyers who swear that their device is the best on the market. Steve Jobs, despite his flaws as a manager, was a brilliant marketer who understood that the key to staying relevant and dominant is to design with the customer in mind. The same could be said of engaging employees to act as brand ambassadors.

A brand ambassador or advocate is an employee who speaks positively about the company to her network and to the public, recommending it as an employer of choice and an exceptional business that provides quality products and services. But just like an Apple fan won't endorse the iPhone solely because it can make calls and take photos, employees won't behave as brand ambassadors without an emotional reason. Unless they genuinely feel that connection and think to themselves, "Wow, this really is a terrific company and I want to tell everyone how much I love it," they aren't likely to sing their employer's praises for the world to hear. Could we follow Mr. Ziglar's logic and conclude that, while emotions are what make consumers loyal to certain brands, they are *also* what motivate employees to be brand ambassadors? Yes, indeed! And neuroscience can tell us why.

If there were a switch you could flip to simultaneously engage both customers and your employees, wouldn't that simplify and streamline your organization's path to success? It probably sounds too good to be true. In a way, it is. Because, if it were that easy, we would see a perfect global economy full of happy customers and engaged employees. We, of course, know that is not the case. Consumer preferences and employee motivations are driven by complex neurological processes, thus pointing to one universal truth: all human behavior can be linked to specific activity in certain areas of the brain. There are physiological reasons behind a person's fondness (or disdain) for a particular brand or employer. So, in order to influence stakeholder behavior, one would need to identify the brain region linked to a desired response and find a way to trigger it, in essence, flipping the engagement switch.

Located within the reward center of the brain is a small collection of gray and white matter called the ventral striatum. This area is responsible for feelings like trust, pride, desire, and even love. Each of these feelings is directly related to the concept of engagement. We consumers choose to purchase certain products because of their desirability, their manufacturer's trustworthiness, and the sense of pride we can derive from ownership. Essentially, our brains are pre-wired with the circuitry for engagement as customers or employees, requiring the right stimulation to activate it. Studies involving functional magnetic resonance imaging (fMRI) brain scans have produced evidence that the ventral striatum in participants' brains showed higher levels of activity—that is, greater dopamine release— when each of them viewed advertisements for brands they felt most likely to patronize.[1] This same part of the brain produces dopamine in response to receiving recognition, when developing a mutually trusting relationship with a supervisor, or when feeling proud to work for one's employer.

Brand ambassadorship, like customer loyalty, depends upon and is driven by the overall experience with the organization. That's why I stress the importance of creating an attractive employee value proposition and a phenomenal employee experience. You've probably heard the phrase "feeling the love." It is quite literally possible to *feel the love* when an employer or service provider creates such a positive experience that it activates your ventral striatum. What happens after that? You're much more likely to show some love in return, right? It's the difference between feeling just "meh" about an employer versus being so proud to work there that you choose to engage as a partner in action through brand ambassadorship. Yet subscribers of the Stepford Employee Fallacy don't understand this process and expect their workers to idolize the organization even when they have little reason to.

As mentioned earlier, trust is one of the primary feelings triggered when the ventral striatum is active. According to Nielsen's *Global Trust in Advertising* report, people trust their peers and those they know far more than any other source of advertising.[2] With the omnipresent nature of social media, organizations have a substantial opportunity to reach existing and potential customers through peer-to-peer marketing, which is where brand ambassadors come into play. Engaged employees share news, updates, and recommendations about employers with their social networks and potentially maximize customer outreach with a level of efficacy that other advertising methods can't touch. That explains the popularity of websites like Yelp and Glassdoor where users can rate their experiences with businesses and employers respectively.

Glassdoor is an especially useful tool to gauge not only the quality of an organization's employee experience, but also the degree to which its employees act as brand ambassadors. I often hear managers and HR dismiss Glassdoor as a place for unhappy employees to gripe. They try to say that negative reviews are part of a new Internet trend called "employer shaming." I'm not sure which is worse: a company's leaders burying their heads in the sand because they don't want to hear criticism, or playing the victim card as if they were totally innocent and vengeful employees with axes to grind are just out to get them.

No company is perfect. And many have serious cultural or operational problems that employees are too afraid to discuss with management, so they resort to anonymous forums like Glassdoor to vent their frustrations. There's a difference between a review written by someone who simply says "this place sucks," but leaves no other details about their function or experience, and a reviewer who cites specific examples of why working for their employer is/was so awful. The latter review is more credible, even if its content makes the organization look bad. Just because you don't like what someone has to say about your company, doesn't mean it's not the truth. Take the feedback as a generous gift and use it to improve. Until leaders begin listening to what their employees have to say and then make substantive changes, brand ambassadorship will remain more wishful thinking than measurable reality.

What makes employees *want* to take on a brand ambassador role? More importantly, what has the opposite effect? In this chapter, we will look at three facets of an organization's existence that, when mismanaged, will actually discourage ambassadorship and sabotage engagement.

CURRENT STATE OF AFFAIRS

Change is a part of life and should be embraced, or so they say. But change can be frightening, especially if it has a negative effect on our lives. It represents a threat to our sense of stability. Organizations undergoing change need to understand that instability, whether perceived or not, is preclusive to employee engagement. Even if change occurs as a natural response to market demands and is carefully planned and executed, it still raises a scary question in every employee's mind: "How will this affect me?"

I worked with one large financial services company that was constantly making changes to its structure and headcount, leaving employees both exhausted and constantly on edge. Whole departments were eliminated in a matter of days, culling hundreds of jobs in the process. Divisions were sold and restructured. Nobody felt safe. They wondered whether today would be the day a manager taps them on the shoulder and brings them to meet with HR and learn how little severance they'd be getting. Of course upper management couched the changes as necessary to ensure the organization's success, but that did nothing to comfort a change-fatigued workforce whose CEO literally told them not to count on long-term employment there. Engagement suffered, and the common refrain among the rank and file became "I really don't care anymore." That sure doesn't sound like a workforce of engaged brand ambassadors. Can you really blame them, though? Uncertainty can kill any motivation employees have to go the extra mile through brand ambassadorship and advocacy.

With the ever-changing nature of the global economy, organizations *do* need to be agile and responsive. The saying "adapt or die" has never been truer than it is today. Change for its own sake is certainly not an effective strategy. But organizations like Blockbuster and Kodak were knocked flat by a massive tidal wave of change. They were caught unawares, resting on their laurels as Netflix and the Digital Revolution swiftly disrupted them into irrelevance. It is therefore critical for the strategists and visionaries leading an organization to be able to quickly implement change. This puts leaders in a precarious position when dealing with employees who are resistant to change. They know that their organization needs to anticipate, acclimate, and innovate if it is to survive.

Organizational development practitioners will say it takes careful and disciplined change management to guide a company through any transition. What exactly does that mean? Telling employees that change is coming and they need to either hop aboard the train or they'll be left at the station? Even if your organization isn't in apparent disarray as with the earlier finance company example, forcing change is a sure-fire way to stir up dissension, making things unnecessarily difficult. Add in the expectation that employees should remain engaged advocates for your brand, and you've doomed your change effort before it even gets off the ground. Employees won't be willing to recommend customers or job candidates if they are too busy stressing about a merger, layoffs, loss of benefits, new job requirements, or any other changes that could negatively affect them. When they feel as though management is inflicting these changes upon them, they withhold discretionary effort out of fear, resentment, or apathy. It turns out we can once again look to the human brain for an explanation as to why.

Dr. David Rock, co-founder of the NeuroLeadership Institute, developed an acronym to describe five dimensions of an employee's identity that, when subject to change, can activate areas of the brain responsible for pain, pleasure, and fear: SCARF, which stands for status, certainty, autonomy, relatedness, and fairness.[3] Status refers to one's place of importance within a social structure. Certainty is in reference to one's confidence in the future. Autonomy is the degree of control over one's environment. Relatedness has to do with a sense of belonging or one's social safety. Finally, fairness is what one would perceive as justice.

A change—or the potential for change—to one or more of these dimensions can trigger a threat response in the amygdala which tells the body to fight, flee, or freeze. For example, reorganization, though necessary from a purely business standpoint, can undermine an employee's certainty and autonomy. This will activate her brain's limbic system, where the amygdala is housed, and hinder her ability or desire to accept the change, much less engage in any kind of marketing on the company's behalf.

Change management is a complicated discipline; one could fill an entire book on that topic alone. My take, as it relates to employee engagement and ambassadorship, can be summed up thusly: the key with any organizational change is to plan activities and transition steps in such a way that they don't trigger a limbic response in employees' brains. Put another way, manage change so that employees want to lean in and be part of something special, rather than run away from it or try to fight it. This is accomplished by having candid, frequent, multidirectional communication to clarify your course and hear what people at all levels are thinking. Involvement is also critical. When people feel that they are part of a change—giving input on what will or won't work—and are therefore responsible for its success, they experience feelings of achievement, which quells their fear. Change doesn't have to be frightening, so don't give employees *reason* to be afraid.

Another factor that can affect employees' sense of esteem toward your brand is meaning. Recall our discussion of meaningful work in Chapter 4. The more meaning or purpose an employee derives from his or her work, the greater is the potential for engagement and, by extension, brand ambassadorship. An organization's current state has a direct relationship to employees' sense of meaning and purpose. Will employees be brand ambassadors if the company is circling the drain or they might be laid off? Not if they feel their work has no meaning. There really isn't a point to putting in the effort to benefit your employer if you have no idea which direction the company is headed or whether you'll have a job tomorrow. Wasted efforts lose any meaning they did have or could have had for those who made them. Conversely, when a workforce feels confident and optimistic about their organization's current state—or *can* feel excited about future prospects—they will be in a state of mind to do more than the bare minimum.

CASE STUDY

STARBUCKS

It's hard to remember a time when Starbucks wasn't on top of the world as the dominant and ubiquitous purveyor of coffee enjoyment we now know it to be. But during the mid-to-late 2000s, Starbucks looked like a much different company. Focus had shifted away from its core coffee business toward music and entertainment, much to the detriment of financial performance, customer experience, and employee morale. Competition from McDonald's and Dunkin' Donuts stole customers away with cheaper prices, making a sizable dent in Starbucks' profits. By 2008, the company's stock price dropped to a record low of just under $8 per share, and the following year thousands of employees were laid off with the closure of over six hundred stores. Around that time, Howard Schultz returned to his position as the CEO of the company he helped build after an eight-year appointment to the board of directors. His mission was to reinvigorate and refocus the brand; to infuse a double-shot of espresso into a struggling multinational corporation, which was certainly a tall order (or rather, a Trenta order).

To start, Schultz closed all seventy-one hundred U.S. stores for one February evening in 2008 so employees—Starbucks calls them "partners"—could be trained on pouring the perfect espresso. As a gesture of transparency and collaboration, he told employees to e-mail him directly with their concerns or suggestions, and he called stores all over the country to ask how they were doing. He also mandated that stores should grind their own coffee beans and hired a new store design chief to bring back the coffeehouse vibe that had been lost in expansion over the years. Customers once again enjoyed the unique feel of being served quality coffee by knowledgeable baristas in a cafe setting.

Next, the CEO turned his attention to employee engagement through leadership development in the form of a $35 million four- hundred-thousand-square-foot Leadership Lab. Part experiential learning center, part brand exhibition space with live coffee trees and theatrical presentations, Starbucks' Leadership Lab exposed store managers to the company's best practices and rich history as they immersed themselves in a one-of-a-kind training venue.

Even as the organization was slogging along on a difficult comeback journey during the Great Recession, Schultz prioritized investment in people over cutting costs. An aggressive shareholder tried persuading him to cut healthcare benefits for employees—$300 million in potential savings—but he refused. Schultz knew the long-term cost of disengaging Starbucks' partners, whether part-time or full-time employees, would far outstrip the immediate benefits of spoiling any aspect of their employee experience. He believed employees' faith in the company mission was the key to a successful turnaround. From this premise, Starbucks was able to reinvent itself with the help of its brand ambassador partners. Howard Schultz wrote a book about this endeavor, *Onward: How Starbucks Fought for Its Life without Losing Its Soul* [4], in which he noted:

> [Employees] are the true ambassadors of our brand, the real merchants of romance and theater, and as such the primary catalysts for delighting customers.

Today, with a market cap of close to $85 billion [5], Starbucks is one of the top fifty most valued companies in the world because of Howard Schultz's determined leadership and concentration on employee engagement. He transformed the company from a state of decline into a cultural staple by capturing employees' enthusiasm for the Starbucks brand. Recognizing that employees would not advocate for the company when it was in a slump and their jobs were in jeopardy, Schultz took decisive action to shape Starbucks into an employer they could be proud of.

Now, the combination of a phenomenal employee experience, model corporate citizenship, and streamlined operations has created a powerful brand that excites its partners to evangelize on its behalf. Employees are even encouraged to share their stories and thoughts about the organization on their social media channels. A barista started Starbucks' official Twitter account in 2008 and has been the company's social media envoy ever since. With almost 12 million Twitter followers and 35 million on Facebook, Starbucks has a massive social media footprint thanks in no small part to the involvement and engagement of its workforce.

When an organization is in turmoil, the last thing its employees will be thinking about is spreading the good word through brand advocacy. They need a leader who will reassure them through the difficult times, one who has a vision to move forward and will address their concerns along the way. How an employer treats its workers during a tough period speaks volumes about its understanding of employee engagement. Leaders like Howard Schultz recognize the correlation between engagement and ambassadorship, and they capitalize on this relationship, especially in economic downturns. Companies that think they can afford to burn their employees when a recession hits are sorely mistaken. Starbucks went with a completely different strategy and engaged its employees even as industry observers wondered whether the company could survive the 2008 financial crisis. It turned out to be the right play.

CULTURAL ABSOLUTION

Culture is often referred to as the soul of an organization. Ideally, culture forms the *esprit de corps* among employees and unifies them in achieving company goals. Peter Drucker once said that "culture eats strategy for breakfast." That's very true. A strategy is useless without execution. Common values, behaviors, and expectations are what guide and drive an organization's workforce to perform as a cohesive team. However, it only works that way if the culture is healthy and engaging. Toxic work cultures marked by bullying, harassment, perfectionism, unrealistic expectations, and discrimination eventually become unsustainable. Ultra-successful companies that are exceptions to this rule unfortunately serve as inspiration to leaders who wish to mimic what they perceive to be the magic formula.

Amazon is a prime (pardon the pun) example. The online retailer famous for completely revolutionizing how people purchase and receive goods has a notoriously savage corporate culture, according to current and former employees. Surely, Amazon's hard-driving, borderline-sadistic (or perhaps masochistic?) operating model is the platform from which its massive success sprung. Or is it because founder Jeff Bezos came up with a radical idea for disrupting commerce just as the Internet was becoming widely accepted and utilized? He captured lightning in a bottle and his idea for an online bookstore grew into the multi-billion-dollar e-merchant it is today. Amazon is now one of the most valuable companies in the world because it *changed* the world, not necessarily because it is a highly demanding employer.

The New York Times published an exposé[6] in 2015 giving the public an inside look at Amazon's brutal culture, and the article's contents made it quite clear that the company is proud of its reputation for chewing up talent and spitting them out. One of Amazon's former HR executives described the company's talent management philosophy as "purposeful Darwinism." Speaking on the condition of anonymity, employees past and present told the authors about grueling work hours, vicious management, forced ranking, back-stabbing coworkers, and rapid turnover. The average tenure for Amazon employees is just one year, and yet it's a top-choice employer among job applicants. That's because ambitious would-be Amazonians hope to make a small fortune by developing the next big innovation, until they realize the commitment required is more than most people can handle. And Amazon makes no secret of the fact that it pushes employees to their breaking points by squeezing every last drop of productivity from them, claiming this separates the wheat from the chaff.

For all its success and acclaim, Amazon must be doing something right with its insane culture, yes? No. Amazon is a global household name in spite of how it allegedly treats its employees, not because of it. The company simply has much more notoriety given its undeniable economic significance. But just because something is done doesn't mean it should be done. Just because Amazon can force warehouse employees to work in one-hundred-plus-degree heat to fulfill customer orders doesn't mean your company should follow its example. Just because Amazon's employees suffer emotional breakdowns caused by stress or humiliation doesn't mean you can crank up the pressure on your workforce and expect revenues to soar. Toxic cultures are not viable, despite what a mammoth success story like Amazon might lead you to believe.

Another company famous for disrupting an entire industry, Uber, faced a public relations meltdown once the world saw all of the cultural skeletons in its closet. In February of 2017, a former engineer at the multinational ride-sharing giant wrote a blog post detailing her experiences working there.[7] The claims of sexual harassment, gender bias, complicit management, and a culture of covering up the truth set off a firestorm that then CEO, Travis Kalanick, could barely contain. A few days later, media outlets blew the story of Uber's dysfunctional culture wide open.

Interviews with dozens of Uber employees confirmed what the engineer revealed in her blog: a frat house meritocracy on steroids where female staffers were sexually assaulted by senior employees, managers blocked promotions or transfers to keep their teams competitive and make themselves look good, under-performers were threatened with physical violence, and Human Resources enabled bad behavior by protecting superstars who contributed most to the bottom line.[8]

This kind of behavior isn't indicative of a company that values its talent by treating them with humility and respect. And it definitely isn't limited to these companies or the industries in which they operate. During my time in the financial services industry, executives would say to us that they cared nothing for morale and only numbers mattered to them. I heard stories of sexual harassment being swept under the rug because the perpetrator's father sat on the board of directors. The difference between these organizations and Uber is the latter offers a strong combination of desirability, utility, and convenience that is unique to the tech space and accounts for its monumental prosperity. Engagement and a toxic work culture are mutually exclusive. Success and toxicity, sadly, are not.

Of all the poisonous, disengaging organizations I have worked with and researched, there is a popular mindset among leaders who vehemently defend their malignant cultures and refuse to acknowledge anything is wrong. Managers and their HR enablers at all levels are indoctrinated with this same mentality so as to maintain cultural congruence. They mistakenly believe a harmonious workplace, where everyone is smiling and in agreement with whatever management wants, is indicative of a healthy culture. To maintain the illusion that the company is a great place to work, they root out dissenters, blacklist them, or simply tell them, "If you don't like it here, then leave." It's as though they read Jim Collins' *Good to Great* and took the idea of "getting the wrong people off the bus" to mean ridding their organization of anybody who disagrees with decisions or objects to mistreatment. There's nothing wrong with the culture as long as someone with a fancy title thinks it's A-OK. The emperor's clothes look just splendid, thank you very much. And if the peasants don't think so, then they can take up residence in another kingdom! I would be willing to bet most managers who have spent any substantial period of time in the modern workplace have uttered something similar.

But let me ask you, would you post "If you don't like working here, take a hike" on your company's Careers web page? Would you say it when trying to recruit the perfect job candidate? Would you write it on your company's marketing collateral for a career fair? I suspect not. Then why say it to the people who already work for you? The arrogance of this sentiment would be comical if it were not predicated on the same attitude that Uber's managers had when dealing with the sexual harassment complaints. If only there were a group of people whose job it was to foster a healthy, engaging organizational culture and prevent employee maltreatment from happening.

Human Resources: Cultural Sherpa

HR has a pretty unsavory reputation. Employees consider them to be mostly duplicitous corporate shills; management's goon squad sporting fake smiles and spouting feel-good bromides as they plot your downfall should you find yourself on the company black list. The Human Resources department at Uber was no help to the engineer who alleged harassment and mistreatment during her time there. When presented with the woman's grievances, HR's reactions ranged from indifference to victim blaming. They protected the guilty and flipped the situation by telling the engineer that she was not a "team player" and perhaps she should ask herself whether she was the problem. Now there's an oft-utilized Human Resources tactic, especially in toxic cultures: turn a negative scenario around on the employee and tell her to think about how she might be causing it.

In HR's defense, they spend much of their time trying to justify their existence by adding value for senior management however they can. Since they are a cost center, they have to prove their worth, and often that means running interference when employees pose a threat to the organization (i.e. when they won't take abuse lying down). They serve a purpose when they administer nefarious tools and policies like performance improvement plans or progressive discipline. Ask any honest HR practitioner about a PIP's true purpose, and they'll tell you it has nothing to do with rehabilitating a struggling employee and instead starts a paper trail—in many cases, for bogus reasons—laying the groundwork for that person's demise. But Human Resources has a very important role to play within an organization, and it doesn't involve concocting ways to punish or restrict employees.

The term cultural steward is often applied to HR as an explanation for their job of preserving the norms and values of an organization. Depending on the culture, this could be a good or bad thing. At Uber, the Human Resources department ignored complaints of sexual harassment and protected the guilty parties because they were top performers or members of management. Since the engineer published her story, dozens more women have come forward with their own disturbing tales of mistreatment met with Human Resources' indifferent or even antagonistic response. As cultural stewards, the people in HR were technically fulfilling their function within the organization. But as catalysts of engagement, they failed miserably.

Within any company, the personnel department, HR, people operations—whatever they call themselves—are capable of informing and shaping a culture that inspires employees to engage and become brand ambassadors. Instead of reinforcing a broken or poisonous organizational culture through idle stewardship, HR should be a proactive, benefi-cent sherpa.

A sherpa is a highly skilled climber who safely guides explorers as they scale the world's highest mountains from base to peak. Tenzing Norgay became perhaps the most famous sherpa in history when he brought Sir Edmund Hillary to the summit of Mount Everest in 1953, earning both men the distinction of being first to ever do so. Norgay was selected to lead the expedition team because of his familiarity with Everest's treacherous terrains and slopes. But it wasn't just mountaineering expertise that carried his team to the highest peak; his incorruptible good nature was what made him such an effective sherpa. Speaking on his experience, Norgay said:

> You do not climb a mountain like Everest by trying to race ahead on your own, or by competing with your comrades. You do it slowly and carefully, by unselfish teamwork.[9]

To reach the highest peak of employee engagement and enjoy the resulting brand ambassadorship, leaders must follow the guidance of their Human Resources professionals. HR can advise on the best cultural prac-tices, steer managers away from disengaging behaviors, and advocate for a collaborative, not competitive or militaristic, work model. And those in HR need to hone their knowledge of what fosters a truly engaged work-force. They can start by listening to employees, taking their feedback or concerns seriously, and teaching leaders how to do the same. Here are four hallmarks of a healthy organizational culture:

1. Constructive, respectful debate is expected for developing the best ideas, practices, and products.

2. Employees share candid feedback anytime (instead of during a yearly survey) and their leaders act on it.

3. There is zero tolerance for bullying, retaliation, or discrimi-nation; bullies are fired without prejudice and without regard for their titles.

4. Leaders treat employees as valuable partners in action, not children, criminals, or disposable office equipment.

Had Uber's HR managers striven to implement and enforce these cultural tenets, it would not have found itself in the mess it did. Amazon might be able to get away with similar treatment of its employees—for now. However, as we saw in Chapter 3, cultural malignancy begets unethical behavior, and scandal won't be too far behind. In the business world, slow and steady might not win the race, but a high-performance culture can't maintain its stamina if employees are not treated like your first and most valued customers.

QUALITY IS A HABIT

If a company's reputation is built on the quality of its products, then it stands to reason that management would expect employees to report defects or safety issues so they can be corrected. As brand ambassadors, employees should *want* to ensure the products and services they recommend are not harmful, faulty, useless, illegal, unethical, unhealthy, or otherwise unfit for consumption. Having a genuine sense of pride in your employer's offerings is integral to the brand ambassador concept. The modern workplace reflects a much different standard for managing a brand's reputation, however. Companies today amass and maintain reputational capital through the control of information about their products and services. In other words, a bad product alone doesn't damage a brand; the negative exposure and resulting loss in sales are what really bother head honchos. So they carefully regulate consumer perceptions of the brand through various means, one of which is the power they hold over their employees. Unless a worker has something nice to say about his employer or its products, he best not say anything at all (or else the company will enforce the non-disparagement agreement he signed to get a job there).

According to the Stepford Employee Fallacy, engaged employees will worship the brand whether or not product quality is up to snuff.

Employees who can think for themselves or, heaven forbid, raise concerns that something isn't right are not welcome in companies that subscribe to this hogwash.

A Golden Corral employee in Ohio learned this the hard way when he reported several health code violations while being trained on the job.[10] The woman training him demonstrated their practice of switching preparation and expiration labels on food trays to ensure nothing went unused, even if it had gone bad. He took it upon himself to check the temperature of food being served to their customers and remarked that it was undercooked. All along, he had been secretly recording these egregious food safety infractions to substantiate his claims. His manager caught wind of the young man's actions and called him on the carpet for it, advising him that he had no business inspecting the meat and warning him that the company would take legal action. Upon turning in the video evidence to health inspectors, he was fired after only a week of employment at the restaurant. A subsequent lawsuit led to Golden Corral paying an undisclosed settlement to the former employee in an attempt to buy his silence. Whether he and his legal team pursued remedy under whistleblower protection laws is unknown, but the company's misdeeds are reflective of habitual malefaction that runs throughout the corporate world.

Even non-profit organizations aren't above letting service quality slip if it leads to better short-term financial outcomes. In 2017, nurses at Boston Tufts Medical Center went on strike for the first time in thirty years to protest management refusing to keep the hospital's nursing headcount at safe levels.[11] Although members of the Massachusetts Nurses Association were also negotiating for higher wages and better pension benefits, adequate staffing was their first and primary goal in the interest of patient safety. The strike lasted a day, and hospital administrators hired replacement staff to ensure uninterrupted care. After the staff made their point and picket lines dispersed, Tufts senior executives decided to enforce a consequential four-day lockout as punishment. In response, the affected nurses marched outside the hospital as security blocked their entry, creating an even bigger spectacle of the proceedings.

This wasn't the first time hospital administrators and union representatives clashed over Tufts being understaffed. A 2011 labor dispute nearly led to nurses striking, but tensions settled when both sides came to a barely satisfactory agreement at the eleventh hour. Compared to other Boston-area hospitals, nurses at Tufts Medical Center historically spend less time with each patient because they are assigned a higher case load as a result of insufficient staffing.[12] We'll talk in-depth about the effect unrealistic workloads have on employee engagement in Chapter 9. As far as brand ambassadorship goes, workers who can't meet service level expectations because they are overworked will not speak highly of their employers. In the worst scenarios, this disconnect is made public as with the Tufts example. Leaders felt the need to posture and stonewall, damaging the hospital's brand image in the process.

Lousy quality might not be detrimental to customers' health and safety in every industry, but it is nevertheless unacceptable. Not only does it sour your brand's reputation, it puts employees in the very uncomfortable position of having to defend something they know is indefensible. Strong-arming employees to either stand behind a weak product or keep their mouths shut about it is demoralizing and unethical. It's also counterproductive. Managers often assume their staff lack the interest or the smarts to make useful suggestions for improvement or that they don't even care to do good work in the first place. That's not exactly the best attitude if you aspire toward having an engaged workforce.

Imagine giving front-line employees ownership of the products and services you offer. Think of how much more engaged they would be if they had a say in refining your brand's product and service lineup. As your closest connection to customers, doesn't it make sense to heed their recommendations? Naturally, employees who feel they are partners in creating a superior product will take on brand ambassador duty with zeal. R&D

might have responsibility for devising the newest and hottest ideas to bring to market, but the people who can make the greatest impact on your brand are the ones down in the trenches every day. Make a habit of listening to them as you would a trusted advisor. After all, you hired them to be the experts at what they do.

LOOKING AHEAD

The immense potential for brand ambassadorship to elevate a company's reputation—and thus profits—makes it a desirable outcome of employee engagement. What many executives fail to realize is that advocacy doesn't come automatically as a condition of employment. Employees will not engage as brand ambassadors without the kind of inspiration that's derived from working for a great organization with superior products and services. *Leaders* are responsible for fostering an inspirational employee experience through their decisions, behaviors, and interactions. That isn't the typical mindset of today's management professionals, however. They believe their management title grants them infallibility and deity, that it somehow elevates them to a higher stratum than their subordinates, and therefore they are owed respect and engagement.

In the next chapter, we will delve into the topic of leadership and how being a true leader transcends command, control, and hierarchy. A leader is a coach and a mentor, not a slave driver. We will look at which modern management paradigms are engagement blockers and which lead to more effort from a galvanized (as opposed to disenfranchised) workforce. As we saw in this chapter, ineffective leadership can cost companies some serious brand credibility in the eyes of their employees. They are indeed the first ones you need to convince that your organization is something special before your customers start to believe it.

NOTES

1. Lieberman, Matthew. "Social: Why Our Brains Are Wired to Connect." New York: *Broadway Books*. 2014.

2. Nielsen. *Global Trust in Advertising: Winning Strategies for an Evolving Media Landscape*. September 2015. https://www.nielsen.com/content/dam/nielsenglobal/apac/docs/reports/2015/nielsen-global-trust-in-advertising-report-september-2015.pdf

3. Rock, David. "Managing with the Brain in Mind." *Strategy+Business*. Issue 56. Fall 2009. http://2uxlo5u7jf11pm3f36oan8d6-wpengine.netdna-ssl.com/wp-content/uploads/2016/06/ManagingWBrainInMind.pdf

4. Schultz, Howard. "Onward: How Starbucks Fought for Its Life without Losing Its Soul." New York: *Rodale Books*. 2011.

5. "The World's Most Valuable Brands." *Forbes*. 2017. https://www.forbes.com/powerful-brands/list/#tab:rank

6. Kantor, Jodi and Streitfeld, David. "Inside Amazon: Wrestling Big Ideas in a Bruising Workplace." *The New York Times*. August 15, 2015. https://www.nytimes.com/2015/08/16/technology/inside-amazon-wrestling-big-ideas-in-a-bruising-workplace.html

7. Fowler, Susan. "Reflecting on One Very, Very Strange Year at Uber." (Blog). February 19, 2017. https://www.susanjfowler.com/blog/2017/2/19/reflecting-on-one-very-strange-year-at-uber

8. Isaac, Mike. "Inside Uber's Aggressive, Unrestrained Work Culture." *The New York Times*. February 22, 2017. https://www.nytimes.com/2017/02/22/technology/uber-workplace-culture.html

9. "10 Awe-Inspiring Quotes about Mount Everest: 'Because It's There'." *The Inertia*. September 18, 2015. http://www.theinertia.com/mountain/10-awe-inspiring-quotes-about-mount-everest-because-its-there/

10. Phillips, Josh. "Golden Corral Paid Fired Employee Just to Keep Quiet about This Disgusting Reality." *Elite Readers*. 2014. https://www.elitereaders.com/employee-exposes-golden-corral-disgusting-reality/

11. Lehrenbaum, Sophie. "Tufts Medical Center Nurses Back at Negotiating Table." *The Tufts Daily*. January 8, 2018. https://tuftsdaily.com/news/2017/10/04/tufts-medical-center-nurses-back-negotiating-table/

12. Zimmerman, Rachel. "CommonHealth Analysis: Nursing Staff Levels At Tufts Medical Center Trail Competitors, Data Suggest." *WBUR*. March 11, 2011. http://commonhealth.legacy.wbur.org/2011/03/hospital-staffing-levels-tufts

CHAPTER 7

BELIEF # 4: ENGAGED EMPLOYEES WILL LISTEN TO AND RESPECT YOU JUST BECAUSE YOU HAVE A TITLE

What is a job title? Is it simply a descriptor of someone's role in an organization based on the tasks he or she performs? Or is it something more, depending on the title itself? Leaders come in many forms and with many different titles. A leader doesn't necessarily need to have a certain title in order to influence those around her. By the same token, a prestigious title doesn't automatically engender sway over those on the lower rungs of the ladder. Sure, the chain of command assures stability and accountability. But what about engagement? Will employees go the distance for a leader just because that individual holds a certain position in the corporate hierarchy? Based on my research and experience, the answer is a resounding "no." It takes more to make a leader than his or her office. And it takes more to engage employees than waving your rank over their heads. This chapter will explain the leadership behaviors that catalyze workforce engagement versus those that have the opposite effect, as well as propose a different way of looking at the relationship between leaders and those who follow them.

FELLOWSHIP AND FOLLOWERSHIP

The Fellowship of the Ring, the first movie in Peter Jackson's wildly popular *The Lord of The Rings* epic fantasy adventure trilogy, was an amazing film-making achievement, both in terms of its ambition and its impact on cinema. But the film adaptation, like its source material, also delves into some pretty heavy themes: leadership, faith, and sacrifice. A group of unlikely comrades embark on a mission to destroy a powerful ring that could spell certain doom for all inhabitants of the fictional land of Middle Earth should it fall back into the hands of its master and creator, Sauron.

One of the group, Boromir, succumbs to the ring's lure of granting its wearer immense power and tries to take it from Frodo, the young hobbit burdened with carrying it. His intentions were not evil. He merely hoped to use the ring to defeat Sauron and return Gondor, his home, to its former glory as mankind's greatest kingdom. Still, Boromir's lust for power causes a chain of events that fracture the party—the Fellowship of the Ring, as they were called—and sadly leads to his downfall.

The word fellowship, meaning a company of equals working toward a common goal, aptly describes the characters who set out on this grave journey with the fate of their people at stake. Boromir, who thought himself a distinguished leader, jeopardized the mission and broke the Fellowship when his egotism got the better of him. He went against what the group agreed to be the best course in favor of his own interests. Contrast that with two more leaders in the Fellowship, Gandalf and Aragon. The former sacrificed himself to save the others from a cave monster in his iconic "You shall not pass!" scene, while the latter refused the ring's temptations because he knew taking it for himself would ensure catastrophe for others, making these characters exemplars of both leadership and fellowship.

Managers often don't think of themselves as having equal footing with their employees. They see their titles as badges of honor that set them apart from those further down on the organizational chart, anointing them the right to act in any way they please. They reinforce the distinction and privilege afforded by their position through their words, their actions, and even their body language. I worked with an extremely strong-willed executive who would use overt and subtle cues to maintain an air of superiority and separation when interacting with her staff. During meetings around a conference table, she would sit a few seats away from the rest of the team. Or she would stand to take part in the conversation when everyone else was seated, although there were still plenty of chairs available, as though she wanted to make sure employees knew she stood above them both literally and figuratively. She also wasn't open to dissenting viewpoints in her department and would grow visibly agitated if anyone questioned her. It was her way or the highway, a stance she made crystal clear when, in one instance, she declared "This isn't a democracy!"

The problem with this management approach is it undercuts the sense of fellowship necessary for teams (and, on a larger scale, organizations) to foster trust and work together toward their objectives. A team cannot perform if it is divided by mistrust because of one member's hubris. Whether front-line employee or senior executive, hobbit or Captain of Gondor, no one in a fellowship is any better than another. In *The Fellowship of the Ring*, Boromir broke his companions' trust, and it cost the group time and effort trying to make it right.

Fellowship in organizations requires leaders to adopt a selfless mindset and place their team's needs ahead of their own. A leader who acts out of selfishness to further his own career or financial success will use employees as pawns in any agenda or campaign. The thing is, workers are much smarter than their managers give them credit for. They can recognize when a manager is protecting himself at the expense of employee engagement. In the interest of driving engagement, it is imperative that every one of an organization's management staff act in a manner that builds trusting relationships with their employees. Establishing trust doesn't even have to involve overtures or extravagant gestures; just be a decent human being.

I interviewed one woman, Sarah, who worked in software development overseeing client implementations, and her new boss displayed some baffling passive aggressive behavior in the office. Sarah injured her leg playing tennis requiring her to wear a cast and the new manager never once showed concern or asked what happened. After Sarah gave an important presentation one day, her boss said to her in front of colleagues, "Well that didn't completely suck." Basic kindness and recognition go a long way toward laying the groundwork for trusting employment relationships, but it would seem a lot of managers are failing in this area.

Recent research on more than two hundred companies showed that 60 percent of employees do not trust their leaders, yet 82 percent reported trust in management was necessary for job effectiveness.[1] These findings don't really come as a surprise given what we know about the poor state of employee engagement today. Clearly, there is a trust deficit in the modern workplace, and it is causing many companies to lose more than just the goodwill of their workers. Adopting a fellowship framework to sincerely win employees' trust will yield meaningful gains in most every metric that demonstrates an organization's financial health. Businesses with high levels of trust between employees and managers earn higher profits, see increased customer loyalty, and perform better in their respective markets.

What does a fellowship model look like? In a word: democracy. There is a business philosophy that has slowly gained traction and attention in the corporate world and I see it as the basis for establishing fellowship between employees and their leaders. Workplace democratization, as opposed to the more popular autocratic model, creates a sense of equity within participating companies by giving workers greater say and stake in their employers' operations. This isn't quite the kind of democratic construct we see in systems of government with elected officials and drawn-out bureaucratic processes. It is participatory in nature, yes, but it still utilizes effective leadership at its core. Employees have the ability to participate in decision making, especially for matters that will directly affect them and their coworkers. Their leaders usher the entire organization toward its larger goals while collaborating with them along the way.

For example, IBM recently overhauled its entire performance review program by crowdsourcing recommendations from its three hundred eighty thousand employees and implementing substantial changes based on their feedback.[2] They wanted to do away with relative performance scores (forced ranking) and self-appraisals as well as stretch the review process into a series of regular conversations with their direct managers. The result was a more cohesive work environment with a much more engaging employee experience and stronger relationships at all levels. In Europe, employees elect representatives to sit on their company's board of directors, giving them a seat at the table and a voice in deciding what is best for the organization and the people who work in it. Other businesses supporting a fellowship model offer employee stock ownership plans (ESOPs) as part of their total compensation packages which gives employees direct ownership and accountability for their employer's performance.

Though it is certainly appealing to employees, a democratized workplace does not negate the need for leaders who can inspire followership among their staff. During times of crisis, employees look to their leaders for reassurance and guidance. When faced with unfamiliar or challenging circumstances, they seek out leadership to help them navigate and succeed. In order for employees to even care enough to make their organization a better place to work and serve customers, they first need competent leaders to galvanize and motivate them.

The notion of followership refers to a set of desirable traits that manifest in what would be considered good employees. Qualities like a strong work ethic, ability and willingness to meet reasonable requests, loyalty, and being a team player would of course make any employee easier to lead. The trap managers fall into when they expect their workers to possess these attributes is they assume each characteristic is fixed and cannot be influenced by employee experience. Said a different way, managers think their staff should be perfect followers independent of what it is like to work for them. That's the Stepford Employee Fallacy right there. Don't confuse engaged followers with brown-nosing sycophants. Ineffective leaders might have dedicated followers who try to do their best in spite of management failures, but they eventually burn out and disengage or quit in frustration. Leaders can cultivate genuine followership if they clearly communicate a compelling vision for the company or team, exhibit integrity in their words and actions, and guide all members of the organization with compassion. Figure 7.1 shows all three of these conditions have to be met for followers to feel inspired and engaged.

Figure 7.1 Leadership Conditions for True Followership

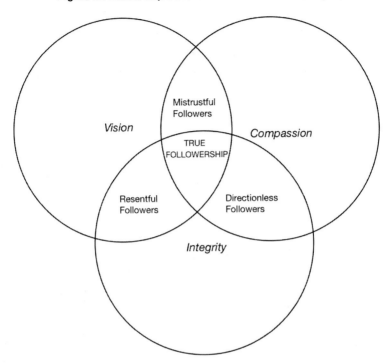

<u>Vision</u>

Visionary leaders have the ability to see and articulate a better state for their people. They have strong conviction and an unflappable sense of direction toward ambitious goals. They use stirring language to shake the apathetic and provoke determined action. Recall the "Today is our Independence Day!" monologue in the film *Independence Day.* Or, for a more historic and significant example, think of Martin Luther King Jr.'s "I have a dream" speech. In an organizational setting, vision alone does not spark followership. Vision without integrity begets mistrusting followers who question their leader's motives. Similarly, a lack of compassion will not engage employees as true followers no matter how mind-blowingly fantastic their leader's vision is; they will absolutely resent being mistreated or spurned.

Integrity

Leaders who act with integrity are honest and honorable, keeping their word and never misleading or manipulating their followers. It speaks to their character. They give credit for successes and take ownership for failures. A strong set of values inform their actions and they concern themselves with always doing the right thing for the right reasons without ever stooping to petty political warfare. They lead by example, holding everyone in the organization, especially themselves, to high standards of righteous, ethical conduct. Marcus Aurelius once said, "A man should be upright, not kept upright." Taken in the context of great leadership, this means true followers extol those who lead with integrity, rather than support those who do not.

Compassion

Compassionate leadership might strike some as being indecisive or coddling. But when leading other human beings, it is critical to take care and do no harm. Showing concern and watchful benevolence toward followers does not make one a gutless doormat. On the contrary, leaders who are courageous enough to care for employees when cold-hearted business sense would dictate otherwise are better suited to guide their organizations. Looking at the word "compassion," we see there are actually two more words that can help us grasp its true meaning. A compass is an instrument used to find direction. Passion is an intense feeling of emotion. Leaders who practice compassion are deeply invested in and passionate about the wellbeing of their followers. It serves as an internal compass pointing them toward decisions that will not injure or abandon those who place their trust in them. That's not to say one should forsake business strategy and leave followers to their own devices. Employees without direction will not feel engaged or inspired. However, having a bold vision does not (and should not) preclude compassionate execution.

RESPECT MY AUTHORITY: THE HAZARDS OF FEAR-BASED MANAGEMENT

In the fall of 2017, Harvey Weinstein, Hollywood mogul, co-founder of Miramax films, and former co-chairman of the Weinstein Company, became the focal point of scalding disapproval from basically anyone with half a conscience after dozens of women came forward with claims he sexually harassed and assaulted them. Weinstein apparently had a reputation in Tinseltown for being a bit of a creep with the ladies, but there were never formal investigations by authorities until 2015 when the NYPD had one of his accusers confront him while wearing a wire. That woman's story was just one of many similar accounts detailed in a devastating New Yorker article that led to Weinstein's firing from his own company and expulsion from the Academy of Motion Pictures Arts and Sciences.[3]

As a film producer and businessman, Harvey Weinstein was wildly successful and carried tremendous clout within the Hollywood community. He was instrumental in the creation of such movies as *Good Will Hunting*, *Silver Linings Playbook*, *Gangs of New York*, and *Chicago*. While he may not have made inappropriate advances toward everyone he employed or cast in his movies, he was allegedly a notorious thug who used his physical and professional stature to intimidate and bulldoze people around him. Former employees have recounted instances of Weinstein's verbal abuse, physical bullying, and his general propensity for raging outbursts. He could get away with this behavior because his production company's reputation for churning out hit movies gave him an enormous degree of power and influence in the industry.

The modern workplace tends to excuse (or even encourage) bad bosses like Harvey Weinstein because they produce such stellar results. Brilliant jerks are tolerated despite the grievous toll their antics take on morale and employee engagement. Even if a manager isn't necessarily adding any extraordinary value to the bottom line, it seems that he or she can still mistreat employees with little to no consequence for such behavior.

But there are repercussions; they just aren't always as obvious as, say, civil lawsuits, criminal investigations, or public relations fallout. There's a hidden cost in the form of disengagement. Actually, it's an opportunity cost. Leaving talented bullies to their own devices might generate impressive revenues, but it deprives an organization of the full potential its employees could bring if they were so inspired.

The quality of leadership from an employee's manager has a direct impact on his or her level of engagement. Robert Sutton, author and professor of management at Stanford University, gained attention with an eye-catching article he published for Harvard Business Review, called *The No Asshole Rule*. The article and subsequent book of the same name explained how rude, hostile, abusive managers poison the climate within their organizations and should therefore be removed.[4] Unfortunately, senior executives permit these "assholes" to remain in positions of power (or they are, themselves, the problem) without grasping the virulent effect they are having on employee experience. Believers of the Stepford Employee Fallacy think they can insist on seeing full engagement from their workforce even if they have heinous tyrants running amok, making everyone hate their jobs.

Last year, I gave a talk about employee engagement and leadership for a group of Boston-area professionals. After the presentation, one of the audience members approached me to discuss a point I made about inspirational relationships between leaders and employees positively affecting engagement levels. He quoted Machiavelli, who once wrote that "It is better to be feared than loved," and said he felt that mindset was conducive to better business results. I told him it's important to understand what drives that fear. If it's a worry about disappointing your boss because you and she have a mutually respectful, trusting relationship—and disappointing her would be just as bad as disappointing yourself—then that makes more sense than fearing your boss' wrath because she's a terrifying dictator. And even if you fall short of her expectations, her job is to compassionately help you learn from the mistake and coach you toward becoming your best self.

Leadership is about being human and relating to employees *as* humans, rather than bullying or intimidating them to perform. So I most certainly disagree with Signore Machiavelli. Remember what he said about the ends justifying the means? Despite what plenty of business big shots might think, the means of strong-arming people are not excusable even when they produce short-term gains. Not if you want real, long-term employee engagement. Good business results don't justify terrorizing your employees. Fear and engagement are mutually exclusive.

Respect is often confused with obedience, especially in the context of managerial influence. Back in the days of nascent industrialization when factory employees were quite literally a dime a dozen and work was akin to paid slavery, the prevailing management archetype was one of despotism. Managers ruled over the shop floor with an iron fist, using fear tactics to drive productivity, while unions formed in response to negotiate better wages and working conditions. Of course, the modern workplace looks much different from its Industrial Revolution predecessor with protections in place to guarantee fair pay and safe work environments. There does, however, seem to be a carryover from the dark ages in the form of fear-based management.

Abraham Kaplan, professor of philosophy at UCLA, famously said that if you "give a boy a hammer . . . everything he meets has to be pounded." As applied to the management profession, leaders today—be they supervisors, middle managers, or executives—still believe the most effective and efficient way to motivate employees is to bring the proverbial hammer down. Any situation involving labor issues can be resolved through force. They assume that their titles grant them infallibility. The only way employees will respect them is if they are militant control freaks, using their position power to punish anybody who steps out of line or messes up. That is not how respect works, though. It doesn't even meet the definition of respect, which is a feeling of deep admiration for someone. We humans are not programmed to admire that which causes fear; we run from it or fight it. In the case of fear-based management, we'll do what is expected of us because we are conditioned from childhood to comply with authority figures, but only to avoid pain or immediate danger (i.e. losing a job, getting yelled at, or being humiliated).

Proponents of fear and intimidation as leadership tools will surely say that their efficacy can't be denied. They're right. If someone were to put a gun to your head and demand your wallet, you would most definitely comply. But you wouldn't trust or respect a gun-toting mugger, so why would it be any different with a fear-wielding manager? Engagement is basically impossible when fear is present. Again, we'll see it's a brain science thing.

Deep within the human brain lies its emotion center, the limbic system, with its almond-sized alarm switch, the amygdala. We talked about the amygdala and its function in the previous chapter. As the primary actuator for our fight-or-flight response, the amygdala helps us identify threat from safety and friend from foe. When a person registers in the amygdala as someone to be afraid of, he is automatically remembered that way: someone who should be avoided at all costs. This makes a positive relationship very unlikely, which we know is not a solid foundation for employee engagement. For such a small part of human anatomy, the amygdala sure does control a lot of our behavior. The fight-or-flight reflex does much more than prime our bodies to duck and cover or start swinging.

In addition to causing a surge of the stress hormone cortisol, when the amygdala perceives a threat, it can shut down our cerebrum, which is the part of the brain responsible for logic, reasoning, and creativity. For example, when a manager sends an e-mail to one of her employees harshly criticizing his work and then follows up with a calendar invite to further discuss in her office the next day, his amygdala is activated by the initial pain of her rebuke along with the fear of facing her disapproval again. With his limbic system on high alert, functions controlled by the cerebrum—problem solving, innovation, information processing—are all offline. For the rest of the day, he will be unproductive and unable to engage as a partner in action because all he'll be focusing on is his manager's admonishment.

Employees who work in high-conflict, fear-driven environments are constantly in a tense state, only able to accomplish enough work to avoid being chewed out by the boss. They report taking more sick days, being less invested in the organization's success, intending to look for a new job, and feeling overall disengaged in their role.[5] That is why we can safely say employees' relationships with their direct managers have the greatest influence on their engagement.

As we saw in Chapter 6, the brain's engagement button is the ventral striatum, which activates when we feel trust, recognition, and social connection. It is, therefore, essential that managers understand what behaviors, decisions, and interactions on their part will trigger engagement in the striatum versus the ones that cause disengagement when the amygdala is tripped. Here are some common bad manager tactics intended to ensure control but invariably end up disengaging staff:

Yelling

This one should be a pretty obvious no-no, but still there are managers who think it's perfectly acceptable to angrily raise their voices to command attention or reprimand subordinates. Beyond the fact that you lose credibility when you lose your temper, yelling can activate the same region of recipients' brains that processes physical pain. In other words, screaming "How the !@#$ could you miss that deadline?" at an employee has the same neurological effect as beaning him with a stapler.

Glaring

There's nothing like a death stare from your boss to send icy beads of sweat running down your back and make you start updating your resume right quick. As a form of intimidation, glaring only has the effect of making someone believe they are in danger. It does little to foster a productive relationship. Instead, it reinforces an unequal power dynamic and makes the user out to be a bully.

Humiliating

Shame is another emotion processed through the amygdala. Humiliating employees in front of their peers or customers triggers the same limbic response that shuts down higher-level cognition and thought. This is why, when we feel ashamed, all we want to do is find a place to hide. I knew a project manager who constantly, albeit unintentionally, humiliated her employees with some seriously cringeworthy faux pas. For example, she would stomp over to one employee's cubicle and dramatically question her judgment in front of the entire work group. Unless you want your staff to hate you, don't do that.

Threatening

Issuing threats to employees is never okay. "You better not do X or I'll do Y to you" isn't exactly the best way to maintain a positive work environment nor does it inspire employees to go above and beyond in their jobs. And, again, it will trigger the brain's fight-or-flight reflex, which inhibits engagement. There's a difference between setting clear performance expectations with employees and just throwing your weight around to show who's the boss.

Browbeating

Relentless criticism might seem like a method for promoting excellence among employees, but it really only makes them want to stay out of trouble. This goes back to what happens when the amygdala is triggered. Continually telling an employee how much he is screwing up doesn't help him or inspire his engagement as a partner in action. At best, it discourages him from reporting mistakes for fear that they will be held against him. Framing errors as learning experiences while taking care to frequently recognize successes will motivate workers to own the work they do. That's why coaching and recognition are vastly more effective at cultivating excellence.

Stonewalling

Managers in the corporate world seem to go through the same training that tells them the boss is always right, even when she's in the wrong. It's a way of preserving the unequal power dynamic between them and their staff. One technique, the deflect-and-pivot maneuver, is used to shut down an employee's argument when she is making a valid point but the manager just doesn't want to admit defeat. Rather than conceding the employee's position, the manager ignores what she says and pivots to another topic that provides a tactical advantage. Picture a manager sitting behind her desk with her hands folded and a blank look on her face who, after listening to you lay out specific documented grievances, tells you that you have an attitude problem and are being put on probation.

Condescending

Condescension makes it nearly impossible to have constructive, engaging conversations because it drives a wedge between you and your employees. Examples include the exasperated tone, the downward vocal inflection, or just repeatedly using their name when you're looking right at them. These mannerisms sound like a parent chiding her toddler for drawing on the wall with crayon. You hired adults. Talk to them like adults. Treat employees as business partners whose expertise and contributions are just as valuable to the organization as yours. Use the same tone and demeanor as you would if you were speaking to the CEO.

Here's the thing about respect: it is earned from employees, not demanded from them by using the scary boss shtick or hiding behind a title. Back in my 9-to-5 days, I had a supervisor—we'll call her Martha—who thought leadership was synonymous with coercion. She micromanaged, nitpicked, and used fear and intimidation to manage our team. A co-worker had one of those talking greeting cards with the pink and green cartoon animals on the front. And whenever Martha was out of the office, we'd open the card and hear it go: "It's Boss Free Day! Oh I love Boss Free Day; it's the best day of the year. I can actually get my work done! Every day should be Boss Free Day!" That's pretty bad if your employees literally celebrate the fact that you're gone.

One time I met with Martha to share some observations on her management style and said, "I can't remember the last time you told me I did good work on something." She responded with a patronizing smile as though she were speaking to a preschooler: "Jonathan, that's not my job. I'm not your mother." Sadly, a lot of managers these days have the same disposition. But a leader's job *is* to inspire her employees as a coach, mentor, and cheerleader if she thinks they are ever going to be engaged.

GET OVER YOURSELF: CURIOSITY AND HUMILITY ARE LEADERSHIP VIRTUES

In my coaching practice, I ask a lot of questions. It's something all leaders should learn to do better. I teach leaders to be more curious by guiding them through the processes of exploration, reflection, and invitation. As a people manager, when you dare to explore new and more enlightening sources of truth, you gain invaluable knowledge that will help you to lead exceptionally well and to make more informed leadership decisions. When you question yourself on your motivations, assumptions, plans, and choices, you hone your ability for self-examination. And when you invite those around you—especially your followers—to share candid thoughts while graciously listening, you open your mind to beneficial information about areas for growth. Being a curious leader requires a willingness, even a desire, to hear positions other than your own. Doing so gives you an opportunity to build stronger relationships with employees. By asking them for their views, their feedback, their stories, and then listening without judgment or interruption, you are positioning yourself as a leader who wants to collaborate on solutions, instead of just bark orders. Woodrow

Wilson notably said, "The ear of the leader must ring with the voices of the people." When leaders curiously listen, they are indicating that they wish to co-create a positive and engaging employee experience.

Disinterest and indifference toward employees' experience of working for you create a mirror effect. They will reflect whatever their experience is through their level of engagement, as we saw with the Experience-Effort Correlation in Chapter 2. Practicing curiosity by asking employees what they think will pay off big time. Moreover, when an employee shares a critique that doesn't exactly make you or the organization out to be paragons of propriety, saying "Tell me more" can help you get to the root of problems that are actually causing disengagement and friction. I once heard a manager tell her team of professional-level IT specialists to "drop the drama" in response to their vehement warnings that the system they purchased from an outside vendor was causing a suboptimal customer experience. By not listening to understand, she basically destroyed her chances of having meaningful, collaborative discussions that could improve both the quality of their service and her relationship with the team.

Managers typically (and wrongly) assume a leadership style of steadfast dominance, thinking they should never give their employees an inch. I interviewed one leader, Danielle, who received a sobering dose of reality shortly after she started off her management career with this disengaging mindset. At just twenty three, she landed a supervisory role with a Fortune 500 healthcare company. Determined not to let her employees believe they could walk all over her because of her age, she adopted a strict, no-nonsense attitude that was at odds with her normally genial disposition. Unfortunately, Danielle's stern boss persona did not win the trust or engagement of her staff, as she learned from her poor employee survey results. Compared to other managers in the organization, she scored lower in every engagement category related to how employees perceived their leaders. "It broke my heart," she told me. She decided to hold a focus group and ask her team what she could do to be more trustworthy. Based on their responses, she grew into a more curious, humble, and authentic leader.

Two years later, she won an award for being in the top 10 percent of managers with the highest employee engagement scores. Danielle now teaches graduate-level leadership courses and is a strong proponent of being curious and authentic about how you are seen by your employees.

Curiosity takes a high degree of emotional intelligence that comes from being humble. Humility allows us to challenge the ego and make decisions that are more effective in the long run, as opposed to satisfying our own immediate need to feel important. Many people, when given power over others, tend to let it go to their heads at the expense of the relationships with those in their charge. But hierarchy does not equate to deity for those with fancy titles, even though many think it does. We are all flesh and blood. None of us is any better than the rest. What makes a leader is not her status, nor her ability to control and punish. The measure of a great leader is seen through the eyes of people whose lives are better for having followed her. A humble leader believes employees are the ones who make an organization great. This goes far beyond spouting the cliché platitude that "employees are our greatest assets." It takes servant leadership.

Servant leaders use their eminence for the benefit of others, not as a cudgel to subdue and discipline their underlings. For a servant leader, there is no need for carrots or sticks. They are in service of the people they lead, whether that involves developing an employee in her current role or helping her find another one that better suits her skill set and interests. Someone who practices servant leadership understands that the position they hold is a privilege and an honor, and they derive satisfaction from seeing team members succeed. They strive to lift others up while removing any obstacles for them along the way. Sometimes that means having to get your hands dirty and helping your employees if they are experiencing productivity or efficiency bottlenecks.

I am always impressed when I go to a restaurant and I see the manager bussing tables, or dropping off orders, or mopping up a spill. Picking up the slack when there is simply too much work to be done sounds simple enough, but it sends a powerful message to employees. They won't think that you see yourself as too important to carry out the more menial organizational tasks; they'll see you as a member of their team who is willing and able to pitch in when needed. They will also be much more likely to return the favor.

Servant leadership should not be confused with weakness or tolerance for neglect. One can be a servant leader and still call on followers to perform. This deviates from traditional management in that a leader who serves her followers goes to great lengths to create and sustain engaging work conditions. Compare a servant leader to a farmer tilling his land to make it arable so crops will grow. He plants seeds and tends to the vegetation, thus ensuring healthy fruit and a bountiful harvest. The farmer who nurtures his crop most attentively will reap the greatest rewards. Servant leaders see the success and welfare of their employees as prerequisite to the organization's prosperity. Leaders serving their workforce might seem as backwards as farmers serving their vegetable crops, but doing both will guarantee fruitful outcomes.

CASE STUDY

POPEYES LOUISIANA KITCHEN

Cheryl Bachelder, former CEO of Popeyes, grew up in a family environment that taught her the value of true leadership. Her father, a successful manufacturing executive, would share his leadership stories and philosophies with his children during dinner every evening, even admitting the sheer turmoil he felt when agonizing over tough personnel decisions. Bachelder and her three siblings each went on to lead companies in chief executive roles, carrying with them the invaluable lessons their father instilled starting when they were very young. Following an ascent through the ranks of companies like P&G, Nabisco, and Dominos Pizza, she landed a role as President and Chief Concept Officer at KFC in 2001, with responsibility over all of the chain's U.S. stores. Up to that point, her marketing acumen and management discipline had carried her success. But, after two years at the top, she learned the hard way that business savvy is not enough to inspire performance.

Dwindling sales over the course of Bachelder's tenure disappointed YUM! Brands board members and she was fired. The experience was humbling and gave her the opportunity to reexamine her own leadership philosophy after spending so long conforming to the more traditional command-and-control management style that had seemed to work well enough for other executives. It was this experience that prompted her to adopt a servant leader mentality and commit to treating employees as her first customers so they would go on to engage as partners in action. After taking a few years to spend more time with her children, Bachelder stepped back into an executive leadership role when, in 2007, Popeyes Louisiana Kitchen's board of directors asked her to fill their suddenly vacant CEO position.[6] This was her chance to put into practice her newfound passion for servant leadership and use it to rescue the struggling restaurant chain from its own financial woes.

Around the time Bachelder was named Popeyes new CEO, company stocks were trading at an all-time low of $14 per share and its market position was also in the teens, not a good place to start for an incoming chief executive. The first step in righting the ship was to meet with Popeyes' top franchisees and get a reading on their experiences. Bachelder decided to attend and present at a franchisee conference in her first public address to the company, which turned out to be a bit of a wake-up call. Franchisees represented a growing frustration with the brand that had grown stale and lacked the national recognition of more prominent fast food chains. They felt downtrodden and abandoned without much support from Popeyes corporate, so they had little reason to trust Cheryl Bachelder when she came in and promised positive change; just as her predecessors had done and failed to execute.

After an eye-opening summit with the franchisees, Bachelder gathered her executive team together so they could brainstorm a new strategy for rescuing Popeyes from the brink. The conversation turned toward whom they, as Popeyes' leadership, served. Conventional business thinking would name consumers as a company's most important and first-served stakeholder. Popeyes' leaders arrived at a different conclusion, however. They determined that, by better serving their franchisees, they could reinvigorate the brand and claim a larger slice of the quick-serve restaurant market. That meant they would have to listen to franchisees' pain points and cooperate with them on making Popeyes stores more profitable and employee-friendly.

The first major initiative under Bachelder's purview was the launch of a national advertisement campaign to raise brand awareness and draw more customers into franchisees' stores. The franchisees asked Bachelder and her team to front the cost of extended advertising—$6 million—which would reflect poorly on the company's financial statement and possibly spook investors. Believing it was the right thing to help her franchisees attract more business, she secured approval from the board of directors and moved forward. It was a risky move for a new CEO with a lot riding on her shoulders, but she knew it would pay off. And it eventually did. With increased recognition among diners, Popeyes saw more foot traffic in its stores nationwide. It expanded its menu with fresh products and saw rapid expansion as new restaurants opened at a rate of two hundred every year, grabbing market share and reaping big revenues.

The franchise model is unique in that franchisees are essentially starting their own businesses with an established brand as their product. They contract with franchisors and pay them a fee either up front or through installments with a percentage of their store profits. Contracts typically designate a partnership term of twenty years, so franchisees are indeed making a major life choice in opening a franchise. Before Cheryl Bachelder took the reins, Popeyes' short-term strategy was in conflict with the franchisees' long-term interests, causing agitation and hostility. Even while she was taking steps toward assuaging her franchisees' grievances, she had to bring in a facilitator to ease tensions and open a dialogue during their meetings.

It would have been much easier to make a top-down decree that underperforming franchises either shape up or their contracts would be terminated. Bachelder recognized how that would only drive a larger, more splintery wedge between her and the franchisees, further disengaging them and hurting the brand. Throughout this book, I talk about the need to first engage employees before focusing on customers. But in the case of franchises, the franchisee is a filter between a corporation and front-line employees who interact with consumers and, for better or worse, ultimately create its customer experience. If franchisees are not being engaged by their partner franchisor, then there will undoubtedly be a lack of employee engagement.

Starting with her franchisees' engagement, Bachelder orchestrated a dramatic turnaround for the Popeyes brand and infused her servant leadership doctrine throughout the entire organization. This creed became the basis for Popeyes' culture under Bachelder's supervision. She codified its function as the company's heart and soul with six principles that she called Popeyes' Purpose: passion, listening, planning, coaching, accountability, and humility. You'll recall two of these principles—listening and humility—align with the leadership virtues discussed in the previous section. I believe these are the foundation of servant leadership because, together, they guide leaders toward decisions that will best serve their followers. One cannot understand how to serve without being curious and listening to others. And one will not serve others without being humble.

The service industry is driven by the idea that the customer—or, more accurately, customer's money—is an organization's first concern, leaving workers underserved and disengaged by their leaders. Serve your employees well, and they will return the favor. Popeyes was recently acquired by Restaurant Brands, the company that owns Burger King, and it seems that they have forsaken Cheryl Bachelder's servant leadership tenets. She stepped down from her CEO post in March of 2017, and morale appears to have suffered. Popeyes' Glassdoor page is littered with comments lamenting Bachelder's departure and noting that her servant leadership style is sorely missed.[7] Even the president of the Popeyes International Franchisee Association acknowledged her as the chief architect of Popeyes's success by saying, "Her leadership approach was a welcome one and led to an exciting and profitable ten years for the Popeyes brand."[8] We can see from the Popeyes story that servant leadership is truly the winning recipe, one that leaders in any industry and at any level can adopt to engage their workforce.

LOOKING AHEAD

Leadership is much more than just a title and the power that comes with it. Leaders aren't defined by their ability to control or punish. They listen, inspire, and derive their power from earning their followers' trust. One of the ways leaders can build trusting relationships with employees is to lead by positive example. Engaging leaders don't expect their teams to dedicate every waking hour (and certainly not every hour meant for rest) to the business, so they make time for recharging and for personal development, and they encourage employees to do the same. Unfortunately, that is not the norm in today's workplace.

Workaholic managers set an unhealthy example, creating an expectation for workers to prioritize business needs over their own. Worse still are the managers who sit back and force employees to do all the heavy lifting, then take the spoils of their labor for themselves. In the next chapter, we will look at the crisis of work martyrdom and how companies are perpetuating the myth that engaged employees will sacrifice personal time to meet any and all job demands. One could blame technology and other external forces for disrupting the modern workplace to such a degree that employers must be ruthless in order to compete. I say that is a cop out, an excuse to take advantage of the rank and file. Employees cannot and will not engage as partners in action without time to recuperate and continuously develop as their best selves outside of the office. It is unrealistic to think that they will. Accepting that reality will take you one step closer to shedding the Stepford Employee Fallacy once and for all.

NOTES

1. Atkins, Andy. Interaction Associates. *Building Workplace Trust: Trends and High Performance*. 2014. http://interactionassociates.com/sites/default/files/research_items/Trust%20Report_2014_15IA_0.pdf

2. Gallup. *State of the American Manager: Analytics and Advice for Leaders*. May 2015. http://www.gallup.com/file/services/182216/StateOfAmericanManager_0515_mh_LR.pdf

3. Zillman, Claire. "IBM Is Blowing Up Its Annual Performance Review." *Fortune*. February 1, 2016. http://fortune.com/2016/02/01/ibm-employee-performance-reviews/

4. Farrow, Ronan. "From Aggressive Overtures to Sexual Assault: Harvey Weinstein's Accusers Tell Their Stories." *The New Yorker*. October 23, 2017. https://www.newyorker.com/news/news-desk/from-aggressive-overtures-to-sexual-assault-harvey-weinsteins-accusers-tell-their-stories?mbid=social_twitter

5. Sutton, Robert. "The No Asshole Rule: Building a Civilized Workplace and Surviving One That Isn't." New York: *Hachette Book Group*. 2010.

6. Bachelder, Cheryl. "Dare to Serve: How to Drive Superior Results by Serving Others." Oakland: *Berrett-Koehler Publishers*. 2015.

7. *Glassdoor*. "Popeyes Louisiana Kitchen." Retrieved January 8, 2018. https://www.glassdoor.com/Reviews/Popeyes-Reviews-E14706.htm

8. Maze, Jonathan. "Cheryl Bachelder to Step Down at Popeyes." *Nation's Restaurant News*. March 2, 2017. http://www.nrn.com/people/cheryl-bachelder-step-down-popeyes

BELIEF # 5: ENGAGED EMPLOYEES WILL SACRIFICE PERSONAL TIME IN FAVOR OF COMPANY NEEDS

"All hard work brings a profit, but mere talk leads only to poverty."
Proverbs 14:23

The Protestant work ethic teaches that hard work is its own reward and idleness goes against God's command. Back in the seventeenth century, the Protestant movement spread the idea that people were predestined to salvation or damnation and there was little they could do to change their lot. Then came a new twist on this concept that gave hope to the faithful. Sustained labor and toil in one's trade would earn God's favor and increase the chances of being saved from perdition. Unemployment meant your soul would be doomed for eternity, so hard work became heavenly mandate. This belief system carried through generations of entrepreneurs and laborers who slogged from dawn until dusk in the hope that it would please the Almighty. Fast-forward a few hundred years and the workforce is still called to worship at the same altar in service of a new God: the company. The "saved" are now the "engaged" and their hard work continues to bring a profit, but not for themselves.

As per the common understanding of employee engagement, employees will put in discretionary effort by working long hours and forgoing hiatus. Work itself is the religion with managers acting as clerics preaching and enforcing the dogma of engagement. The real difference now is there is no guarantee of continued employment or career growth, much less salvation from endless suffering in the afterlife. The modern workplace has very much become its own purgatory where hard work has no reward for the workers, only for those whom they oblige. Paradoxically, the more time employees spend growing the profits of their employers, the more their work ethic wears away until they revert to simply doing just enough to keep their jobs. As we've discussed throughout this book, that is the exact opposite of what true employee engagement looks like. Most organizations still adhere to the religion of hard labor without any regard for the everyday parishioners, the ones who pay tribute to the company cause with their time. But work is not the reward. Life is the reward. Leaders need to accept that an absolute claim on employees' time affects the *quality* of their lives and, consequently, their engagement.

GIVE ME A BREAK

Imagine having to choose between your most basic physiological needs as a human being and your job security. Truth be told, it's not much of a choice because job security translates to an income, which allows you to pay for food, shelter, and other base necessities. Still, millions of workers have to choose every day. And, invariably, they end up choosing job security. They forsake sleep and catch a red-eye flight for the work trip their boss insisted was so important. They eat lunch at their desks or skip meals altogether because they need to be available for customer support. They can't remember the last time they had a real vacation because just the thought of being away from work fills them with anxiety that they will fall behind. Leaving the office on time seems like a quaint fantasy and they're lucky if they can disconnect long enough to visit the restroom.

Actually, that last part isn't even a reality for many employees who work on processing lines in the poultry industry. A two-year study conducted by Oxfam America and its affiliates exposed unbelievably humiliating workplace conditions at some of the world's largest chicken producers.[1] The report, published in 2016, shared stories from dozens of line workers at Sanderson Farms, Tyson Foods, Pilgrim's, and Perdue. Something so simple that most people take for granted—using the bathroom when the need arises—can allegedly get poultry workers disciplined or even fired.

Speaking with researchers on the condition of anonymity, employees at Tyson's Arkansas plant recounted the heartbreakingly cruel treatment inflicted by managers and the shocking sacrifices they have to make in order to avoid termination. They reportedly stand on a production line processing chickens for hours at a time with no rest breaks allowed unless a replacement worker is available to insure uninterrupted operations. If no relief comes (which is almost always the case), then they have to wait to use the lavatory, leaving them no choice. Managers are said to mock and threaten employees for asking to leave the line and relieve themselves. Even when they are finally given permission for a bathroom break, they have anywhere from one to ten minutes to finish and return to work. These exceedingly short breaks are closely monitored by management, and anyone who takes more than the allotted time will face disciplinary action. Given that plant workers must wear protective gear while on the production line and it takes at least a minute to remove it all, in addition to the time it takes to walk to and from the restroom, most never even take their breaks. They urinate and defecate on themselves as they stand at their work stations or as they run to the bathroom but don't make it in time. Some have resorted to wearing diapers in anticipation of not getting a rest break.

Employee complaints to management about these situations are met with snide suggestions to stop eating or drinking so much. Bringing concerns to HR just inflames the situation and puts a target on the back of anyone who speaks up. Pregnant women who require more frequent breaks are denied accommodation. Unable to urinate, they develop urinary tract or kidney infections, which put their babies' health at risk as well as their own. Similarly, menstruating women cannot request bathroom breaks without being intimidated, humiliated, or bullied. These aren't isolated incidents. A survey of low-income Alabama workers revealed that the vast majority—80 percent—cannot take bathroom breaks. There is no explicit statute, not even the Fair Labor Standards Act, stating an employer must allow for breaks of any kind. The Occupational Health and Safety Act (OSHA) requires that work sites must have bathroom facilities available, but does not dictate the frequency or duration of use, leaving employers broad leeway to establish and enforce policies as they see fit.

While these seem like extreme examples and most reasonable managers would never subject their people to such humiliation (at least one would hope not), the modern workplace is indeed one where employees' needs carry no weight unless otherwise protected by law. Even when employers break the law, they have substantial means to silence victims and avoid repercussions as we saw in Chapter 3. More often, companies operate in the vast legal gray area where they can wring every last drop of productivity from workers and make as much money as possible in the process.

The year after Oxfam America released its disturbing report on the poultry industry's bathroom problem, Tyson Foods announced it had earned record-high revenues of $10.15 billion and expected to rake in even more in 2018. Their stock price also soared to new heights, trading at over $82 per share as of January 2018.[2] Clearly efficiencies gained by restricting restroom breaks have paid off big time for Tyson. Perhaps a more ethical and engaging business model would be to invest profits in new hires so the employees responsible for those gains would not have to soil themselves at their workstations. But that is expecting too much in today's cutthroat corporate world. Time is money for businesses, and any time employees spend not working is money stolen from the company coffer.

Considering the importance employers put on productivity and efficiency, it seems surprising that they offer vacation and paid time off benefits. Maybe they do support employees' needs after all. Bureau of Labor Statistics research shows that 76 percent of private industry workers have access to paid time off benefits.[3] That's not the entire private sector workforce, but it's still most. However, as we are seeing with the debate on the U.S. healthcare system, access to something is not the same as actually being able to use it. A food service worker might have *access* to a $300,000 loan for purchasing a Lamborghini, but he really can't afford to make the payments. Vacation time, like an exotic sports car, might seem like a luxury and employers offering it tend to pride themselves on having "competitive" benefits packages. But, by and large, these benefits aren't being used. A preponderance of the workforce in every sector is allowed paid vacation time, but only 23 percent of employees actually take full advantage of it. Another 23 percent report using one quarter (or less) of their vacation time allotment.[4] They simply can't afford to be away from work, either because they fear falling behind or because their bosses will frown upon it.

We will talk about the effects of an unreasonable workload in the next chapter, but I can attest that managerial influence is definitely at play in this trend. When I worked in an IT role, my manager asked me to reschedule a vacation I had already planned and paid for, basically laying a guilt trip because my absence would prolong testing of our upcoming software release. One day, she and I met with our department executive to discuss resource allocation for our teams. She grew frustrated that another one of my colleagues was taking a family trip and said it was "disruptive," turning the conversation to whether or not this employee was adding enough value. Managers do hold employees' time off against them. Compounding this issue is the propensity for managers to work even when they, themselves, are on vacation, setting the expectation for their team that the company's needs take precedence. In fact, 80 percent of U.S. workers report feeling uncomfortable requesting more time off because their bosses are not supportive of them doing so.[5]

If relaxing, week-long vacations totally disconnected from the office are out of reach for most employees, then surely they can at least find respite in taking a lunch break. Sadly, that isn't a reality for many Americans, either. Roughly 62 percent of employees eat lunch at their desks to keep pace with tasks, read and respond to e-mails, or to attend conference calls.[6] There are myriad negative health effects associated with sitting for extended periods of time, including diabetes and cardiovascular disease, making this form of inactivity just as dangerous as smoking.[7]

Of course, the demanding nature of the modern workplace makes stepping away from your desk a difficult proposition. There is always some pressing matter, some raging fire that needs to be put out. As a manager, I introduced the idea of "walking meetings" to get my employees up and moving while we talked shop. We may or may not have stopped to get Ghirardelli ice cream on the way back to the office, but that is neither here nor there. The point is: seeing people seated at their workspaces at all times should not send delusions of employee engagement dancing through your head. It's more likely that they feel obligated to work through lunch because of the taxing culture or the overzealous example you set. Make time to take a breather, and encourage your employees to do the same.

Mental recess from work should not be confused with laziness or poor performance, and certainly not with theft. The human brain can only concentrate for so long before it becomes depleted and needs to recharge. This is important to note because we are now working in a knowledge economy where productivity is achieved through intellectual capacity and performance is measured by our ability to reason and problem-solve. It might seem counterproductive, then, to allow employees time to rest and take their minds off job-related tasks. If all of their attention is focused on work, then it should stand to reason that they can accomplish more and generate greater output, right? Not so fast.

Scientists have studied fMRI scans of individuals engaged in tasks requiring intense concentration and saw that when participants were told to rest, several areas of their brains activated at once.[8] They found that these particular regions are linked to memory formation and recall, idea generation, social cognition, and self-development. Additional studies and peer review have confirmed these findings. This system of the brain, called the "default mode network" gives a person time to collect and reflect. It is also responsible for committing newly learned information to memory.

The Pixar movie *Inside Out* depicts the anthropomorphic inner workings of a twelve-year-old girl named Riley. Specifically, the film's focus is what goes on inside Riley's brain, and it's pretty scientifically accurate. As Riley drifts off to sleep one evening, her dominant emotion, Joy, sends all of the memories formed from the day's events down to long-term memory. This is actually what happens during the restful periods before we lose consciousness. We technically learn not when engaged in activity, but when we rest and our default mode network activates, allowing the brain to deposit important data into its memory bank for later recall and application. We also are more creative when not actively engaged in completing tasks. Do you ever wonder why your best ideas come to you in the shower? That's a time when you aren't focused on much else besides the relaxing hot water. This stimulates your default mode network, causing a meditative state that is perfect for ideation. If leaders want an engaged workforce, they need to make it safe for employees to take short mental breaks (or even a nap) throughout the day to increase productivity and spark innovation.

YOUR TIME IS VALUABLE . . . WE EXPECT MORE OF IT

Apple has the distinction of being named a perennial employer of choice on various Best Place to Work lists like the Fortune 100. As the world's most valuable and recognizable brand, Apple should have the financial capital to create a truly one-of-a-kind employee experience. Indeed, employees at its new ring-shaped headquarters in Cupertino, California enjoy a campus equipped with bicycles, golf carts, running tracks, a massive fitness center, and a private orchard.[9] Current and former employees at Apple's retail stores throughout California aren't as thrilled with their experience, however. They filed a class action lawsuit against the tech giant for requiring them to submit to unpaid security checks that can last up to twenty minutes. Apple argued that it needed to prevent employee theft by checking its workers' belongings for stolen inventory, and the inspections were optional for anyone who chose not to bring a bag to work. A California district court made a summary judgment in favor of the defendant, Apple, but the plaintiffs appealed. An appellate court asked the Supreme Court of California to review the case and make a decision.[10]

Apple's defense that the security checks are optional doesn't exactly hold water. Employees need to bring bags with them to carry their lunches or medications or feminine hygiene products or extra clothes or any number of other personal items. But that isn't the point. Apple is (allegedly) stealing wages from its retail workers twenty minutes at a time by forcing them to stay at work after their shifts end. The time might not seem like much, but it's the principle. If an employee showed up twenty minutes late for work and demanded to be paid for time she wasn't even there, she'd be laughed out of the store, pink slip in hand. It's a double standard that pervades the modern workplace: When it comes to time, "What's mine is mine, and what's yours is also mine."

Wage theft is more of a problem than any employer would be willing to admit. That is, they'd never say it's happening. But it is, to the tune of $8 billion annually. American low-wage earners in the ten most populous states lose an average of $64 per week, $3,300 each year. Companies steal from their workers' paychecks in many ways, with employees who receive tips being especially vulnerable because their employers are legally allowed to pay them below minimum wage. However, the most egregious (and most common) wage theft comes in the form of unpaid overtime or when employees work outside their normally scheduled hours. Over one-fifth of minimum-wage workers find themselves in poverty because of wage theft, requiring them to obtain some type of public assistance.[11] So taxpayers also end up footing the bill when companies decide to stiff their talent. Some employers also misclassify full-time employees as independent contractors to avoid overtime requirements. Not cool.

Unfortunately federal and state regulators are inadequately staffed to investigate every instance of wage theft, so enforcement of the Fair Labor Standards Act and minimum wage laws is meager at best. Still, documentation of hours worked can support claims of wage theft for non-exempt workers, even if they invariably prove to be uphill battles. It's hard for employees not to believe that the deck is stacked against them, which has a considerable impact on engagement. Employers might think they are saving money with these practices, but they are, in fact, paying a hefty price on the back end.

Recall our discussion of the brain's reward center and how the ventral striatum is effectively our engagement switch. Researchers at UCLA scanned the brains of participants who were asked to share a sum of money. One participant was given the total sum and instructed to offer the other a certain amount. Offers that the recipient perceived as fair triggered a striatic response in his or her brain. However, when offered an amount deemed unfair—less than 30 percent of the money—researchers saw increased activity in the recipient's anterior insula, which is the region associated with feelings of disgust or contempt.[12] The same brain regions activate when you taste or smell something pleasant versus something off-putting. The next time you experience injustice and exclaim "This is bullshit!", know that the anterior insula region of your brain is quite literally reacting the same way as it would if you were smelling cow manure. When children cry that something is unfair, their parents will usually tell them "Life isn't fair." It's not that life isn't fair; *people* are unfair. People make decisions that negatively affect others and naturally cause them to experience feelings of outrage. Human beings are wired to feel aversion toward someone who treats them unjustly. Therefore, employers cannot expect engagement from workers if they are claiming their time without paying them for it.

Salaried employees face a more blatant disregard for their time, because they aren't protected by overtime laws. The forty-hour workweek famously touted by Henry Ford as the standard for his factory workers, has slowly disappeared over the years. Now the standard is "work however long it takes to get the job done." With exempt employees—specifically knowledge workers—the job is never done because they constantly collate, analyze, manipulate, and act upon information. And there is always more work to do. This poses a challenge for anyone who has a life outside the office. It's not unheard of for professionals to work sixty, seventy, or eighty hours in a week just so they can keep up with the unending demands of their roles.

The former CEO of Yahoo, Marissa Mayer, spoke about her dedication and work ethic, claiming she regularly worked an incredible one hundred thirty hours per week.[13] Even if that were true, and she left herself only five hours each day for sleeping and eating, that is a terribly irresponsible example to set for employees. It establishes an unrealistic and unhealthy expectation that employees who *don't* happen to take home multi-million-dollar annual salaries should also give such high priority to their jobs. It goes back to the basic assumption that more hours spent working will produce greater results.

John Pencavel, a Stanford University expert on economics, recently conducted a review of research done by the British Health of Munitions Workers Committee during World War I.[14] The British Government commissioned the Committee to measure the output and efficiency of munitions plant workers and recommend changes in work policy that would increase productivity. Researchers found, and Pencavel affirmed, that worker productivity started to fall after fifty hours. More interesting was the discovery that there was no difference in output at seventy hours. In other words, not only did productivity decline after a certain amount of time, it actually reached a level where it stagnated. A worker who produced, say, one hundred shell casings in a forty-hour week might have been able to crank out one hundred ten at fifty hours. But at seventy hours she would still have only made one hundred ten casings.

The conclusions were twofold: First, overworking employees produced diminishing returns, and, after a certain point, no further returns. Second, reducing hours actually increased output, especially when there was a day of rest in between. For hourly or piece-rate employees, it might be easier to calculate the benefits of having them work fewer hours. However, the same principle demonstrated by this study applies to all workers regardless of their pay scheme. After working a certain number of hours, employees become more fatigued, more prone to accidents or errors, and more susceptible to stress and the multitude of health problems that accompany it. Based on an abundance of data collected from the aforementioned study along with many others over the years, it is clear that any gains from forcing employees to work long hours are marginal to nonexistent. On the other hand, costs from disengagement and burnout are much heavier as we've seen in earlier chapters.

CASE STUDY

TOWER PADDLE BOARDS

When people think of California and surfing, they most likely envision a carefree, laid-back lifestyle, the very antithesis of the churn- and-burn office culture that epitomizes the modern workplace. Business, as we've come to know it, is about no-nonsense discipline and relentless dedication. Work martyrs who sacrifice everything for their jobs are idolized for their refusal to let such insignificant things as sleep, family, or spirituality get in the way of business needs.

The notion of spending any less than eight hours each day at one's desk is heretical to adherents of the Protestant work ethic. Our life purpose is to serve in a vocation for the majority of our waking hours over the course of forty or fifty years. And then, if we're lucky to finally escape the daily grind, we can retire after decades of stress and labor have robbed us of precious time for what's truly important—time that we will not get back. For Stephan Aarstol, founder and CEO of San-Diego-based Tower Paddle Boards, that was not how he wanted to live or do business. He built a company that caters to active clients who put a premium on having a healthy mind, body, and spirit, and who enjoy time out on the ocean as part of their lifestyle, not just an occasional hobby. This passion for living life to its fullest runs throughout Tower's corporate culture, with the most prominent aspect being a five-hour workday for every employee.[15]

Stephen Aarstol always knew he wanted to be an entrepreneur. His father was a doctor who owned a vision care practice. Although he worked very hard to make his business successful, Aarstol's father never neglected his passion for the great outdoors or reneged on the precious time he had with his family. He would take Aarstol and his brother on long fishing trips, forming cherished memories of their father that they would not have been able to if he had focused solely on his optometry business. Growing up, Aarstol had a friend who had been diagnosed with leukemia. Even though the boy knew his quality of life would never be the same with this disease, he still made the best of the relatively short life it was, refusing to miss out on playing games with the other children. From his father, Aarstol learned that even ambitious entrepreneurs protect time with their loved ones and do not put work before life. From his friend, he learned that the time we are given is not infinite, that it can be cut short at any point, so we must make the most of life and put our energy in activities that nourish the soul. Aarstol took these lessons about work and life from his childhood and let them guide his business philosophy when he later became the successful founder of one of Inc.'s Top 500 Fastest Growing Companies and the top growth company in San Diego.

In 2010, Aarstol decided to partially liquidate a company he had previously founded and used the proceeds to start up Tower Paddle Boards. He got the idea after a friend introduced him to the sport one day and he was amazed at the ease with which he learned how to do it. The following week, he brought his son to La Jolla beach for some paddle boarding and saw how quickly even a five-year-old could balance himself and eventually master it on his own. It seemed shocking that such an easy and fun way to get exercise off California's beautiful shoreline was so unknown in a location famous for surfing. He recognized an opportunity in the fairly untapped paddle boarding industry, pivoting toward a new business venture that would turn out to be more than just a surf company; it became a new paradigm in working for him and his team.

Aarstol's efforts caught the attention of billionaire venture capitalist Mark Cuban on the television show *Shark Tank* where the investor committed $150,000 in exchange for a 30-percent stake in Tower. This capital investment, combined with a customer-friendly direct distribution model that cut out wholesalers and retailers, helped catapult the company to a new level as an internationally recognized beach lifestyle brand. However, Aarstol credits his success to the focus and productivity fostered by fewer work hours—what he calls his "Five Hour Workday" model.

Back when he was still running his old business selling poker chips, Aarstol was spending all of his time answering customer inquiries and fulfilling orders in addition to the other major responsibilities that come with owning a company. He then found ways to gain efficiency (and regain hours in his day) without harming customer experience. He shipped products every other day instead of daily and limited phone calls to certain hours, freeing up time to spend on other professional endeavors. There were no customer complaints, so he kept this approach in mind when he set about scaling Tower Paddle Boards into a viable company with a growing team of employees. Tower had been doing well in its first few years after Aarstol's appearance on *Shark Tank* with nearly $5 million in sales. But he had great ambitions for even more. Given what he knew about efficiencies in the sales pipeline as well as the importance he put on maximizing personal time, he decided to try an experiment: implement a five-hour workday for the entire company and see what effect that had on productivity. What he witnessed in terms of output from his team and the resulting financial gains for the company solidified his belief in this "less is more" strategy.

After permanently adopting five-hour workdays in 2015, Tower Paddle Boards pulled in $7.2 million. The following year, sales reached over $10 million, and performance continues to defy expectations today. How is this possible? Shouldn't Tower employees be accomplishing less in fewer hours, therefore generating lower revenues? Even though his employees work from 8:00 a.m. to 1:00 p.m., Stephan Aarstol still expects them to be at least as productive as someone working eight hours or longer. Because the team has no time to waste, their focus is entirely on work, innovation, and customer attention. They take no lunch breaks, working straight through until they leave the office and spend the rest of the day enriching their lives in ways other than a paycheck. They are paid no less for the time spent not working because Aarstol cares about output, and his people have consistently rewarded his "work to live, not live to work" philosophy with effort and engagement. The Five Hour Workday prompts a company and its employees to be operationally creative, finding new and different ways to achieve more without wasting time, like automating less-critical tasks. The idea is not to take time away from customers, but to give time back to employees who will be more rested, more balanced, and ultimately better able to *care* for customers.

LOOKING AHEAD

In this chapter, we saw the kinds of sacrifices employers are expecting their workers to make for the good of the company. Not only are these expectations unrealistic, they have a negative impact on both employees and the organization overall. The cost might not be immediately apparent on an annual financial statement, but the penalty takes a toll one way or another as we will see in the coming pages. We will continue the discussion of workload in Chapter 9 as we look at the effects of stress and burnout in light of the present business mantra, "Do more with less."

As we saw with Tower Paddle Boards, the company was able to shift toward a productivity ideal that emphasized results generated over hours worked. It should be understood that this case was not espousing a leadership mindset of resource scarcity. Tower employees are not restricted to five-hour workdays. Rather, they are given more time and opportunity to enjoy abundance in their personal lives, and they can work longer hours for the same pay if the need arises. Subscribers of the Stepford Employee Fallacy believe in scarcity for employees and abundance for those at the top. To them, engaged employees produce stellar results with less support and fewer resources. The next chapter will break down this myth by examining the ways employers are gutting elements of their employee experience, eroding morale and engagement in the process.

NOTES

1. Oxfam America. *No Relief: Denial of Bathroom Breaks in the Poultry Industry*. 2016. https://www.oxfamamerica.org/static/media/files/No_Relief_Embargo.pdf

2. Reuters. "Tyson Foods Tops Profit Estimates As Low-Cost Feed Provides Boost."CNBC. November 13, 2017. https://www.cnbc.com/2017/11/13/tyson-foods-tops-profit-estimates-as-low-cost-feed-provides-boost.html

3. Bureau of Labor Statistics. *Employee Benefits in the United States*. March 2017. https://www.bls.gov/news.release/pdf/ebs2.pdf

4. "Glassdoor Survey Finds Americans Forfeit Half of Their Earned Vacation/Paid Time Off." May 24, 2017. https://www.glassdoor.com/press/glassdoor-survey-finds-americans-forfeit-earned-vacationpaid-time/

5. Project: Time Off. *The Hidden Costs of Unused Leave: Balancing Employee Needs with Business Liabilities*. March 2015. https://www.projecttimeoff.com/sites/default/files/PTO_HiddenCosts_Report.pdf

6. Wollan, Malia. "Failure to Lunch: The Lamentable Rise of Desktop Dining." *The New York Times*. February 25, 2016. https://www.nytimes.com/2016/02/28/magazine/failure-to-lunch.html?_r=0

7. Kulinski, Jacqueline. "Is Sitting the New Smoking." *Journal Sentinel*. June 2, 2017. https://www.jsonline.com/story/sponsor-story/froedtert/2017/06/02/sitting-new-smoking/102438354/

8. Jabr, Ferris. "Why Your Brain Needs More Downtime." *Scientific American*. October 15, 2013. https://www.scientificamerican.com/article/mental-downtime/

9. Moore, Amy. "Complete Guide to Apple Park." *Macworld*. September 25, 2017. https://www.macworld.co.uk/feature/apple/complete-guide-apple-park-3489704/

10. Lebel, Philippe. "The Ninth Circuit Asks the California Supreme Court to Weigh in on Bag Checks." *Lexology*. August 18, 2017. https://www.lexology.com/library/detail.aspx?g=63717321-9d74-45ce-a757-3fac4880b130

11. Cooper, David and Kroeger, Teresa. Economic Policy Institute. *Employers Steal Billions from Employees' Paychecks Each Year*. May 10, 2017. http://www.epi.org/files/pdf/125116.pdf

12. Lieberman, Matthew and Tabibnia, Golnaz. "Fairness and Cooperation Are Rewarding: Evidence from Social Cognitive Neuroscience." New York Academy of Sciences. Volume 1,118. 90-101. November 2007. http://onlinelibrary.wiley.com/doi/10.1111/nyas.2007.1118.issue-1/issuetoc

13. Chafkin, Max. "Yahoo's Marissa Mayer on Selling a Company While Trying to Turn It Around." *Bloomberg Businessweek*. August 4, 2016. https://www.bloomberg.com/features/2016-marissa-mayer-interview-issue/

14. Pencavel, John. Institute for the Study of Labor. *The Productivity of Working Hours*. April 2014. http://ftp.iza.org/dp8129.pdf

15. Aarstol, Stephan. "The Five Hour Workday: Live Differently, Unlock Productivity, and Find Happiness." Austin: *Lioncrest Publishing*. 2016.

CHAPTER 9

BELIEF # 6: ENGAGED EMPLOYEES CAN HANDLE STRESSFUL WORKLOADS WITHOUT ADEQUATE SUPPORT, RESOURCES, OR TRAINING

The Great Recession that started in 2008 brought about a harrowing period of unemployment for American workers, one which had not been experienced since World War II. Between the end of 2007 and early months of 2010, roughly 8 million U.S. employees lost their jobs, leaving those who survived the axe stuck with a double workload.[1] This became the new normal for working professionals as their employers realized significant cost savings with this two-for-one deal even after the economy picked up in the early 2010s.

Throughout my career, I've worked and spoken with people who have been in the workforce long enough to remember the "good old days" when companies took care of their employees from recruitment to retirement. The companies they work in today are a far cry from the safe, supportive places they once were. Now the corporate machine is on its churn-and-burn setting, chewing up, burning out, and laying off employees with such speed and efficiency that the workforce has soured with feelings of disillusionment and disengagement. University of Virginia sociologist, Theresa Sullivan, named these organizations "greedy institutions" for their relentless pursuit of productivity at the lowest possible cost.[2]

There is a cost, and employees are bearing the brunt of it in the form of greater stress, compromised mental and physical health, and increased risk of suicide. And an unmanageable workload is to blame. Over 80 percent of employees report feeling unbearable amounts of stress at work, with a large number attributing it to the unreasonable demands put upon them.[3]

Moderate levels of stress aren't necessarily undesirable when it comes to accomplishing objectives. Eustress, or a state of optimal mental focus that enhances productivity, comes from having aggressive but realistic goals and the inspiration and resources to meet them. Employees positively stimulated by eustress are more likely to feel engaged in their work, because it keeps them in a constructive, energetic state. However, when pushed too far by excessive demands, they will begin to experience higher stress that actually inhibits productivity and has some serious effects on their health. Extreme stress presents with elevated levels of cortisol and adrenaline, inability to focus, muscle tension, high blood pressure, and insomnia. Prolonged periods of high stress lead to burnout, which is characterized as a state of feeling cynical, dissatisfied, and utterly exhausted in one's job.

Most companies do not take the problem of employee burnout very seriously, offering only perfunctory solutions like the occasional stress management seminar. Some more progressive firms will include benefits like yoga classes and meditation spaces, but these fail to address the underlying issue of overwork. An hour of meditative Sukhasana won't make the hundreds of urgent e-mails magically disappear from a burnt-out employee's inbox, nor will it stop her impatient boss from breathing down her neck about impossible project deadlines.

UNDER PRESSURE, OVER-PRESSURED

A 2017 report published in Elsevier's *Burnout Research Journal* involved researchers studying the burnout and engagement levels of fourteen hundred employees when controlled for their managers' leadership styles (servant leadership versus autocratic leadership).[4] The results confirmed what previous studies have already shown about the relationship between engagement and burnout: there is a negative association between these two states. In other words, a higher level of one will negatively affect the other. Figures 9.1 and 9.2 illustrate this relationship. We already covered the benefits of servant leadership in Chapter 7. Here, we see how greater servant leadership can reduce burnout, whereas autocratic leaders who care nothing for the effects that overwork have on their workers are actually lowering employee engagement. Bear in mind that we are referring to burnout as extreme, protracted stress. Any amount of burnout will affect an employee's engagement to some degree. It is important, however, to note that healthy stress in the form of challenging work is beneficial and can serve as an engagement factor. Participants with autocratic or even indifferent leaders experienced burnout due to an enormous workload and scant resources. On the other hand, employees felt no burnout and were highly engaged when servant leaders supported their need for more resources and a reasonable workload.

Figure 9.1 Low Engagement and High Burnout Enabled by Autocratic Leadership

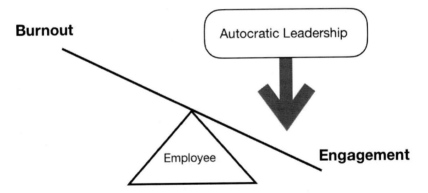

Figure 9.2 High Engagement and Low Burnout Enabled by Servant Leadership

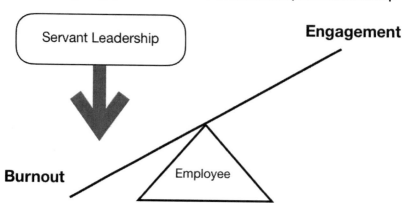

Examples of autocratic leadership quashing engagement can be found in any sector these days. Employees at a Silicon Valley startup were forced to work around the clock by a manager who carried a baseball bat through the office in a display of intimidation. Not only did engagement tank, but employees started making errors that cost the firm customers, all because their boss treated them like slaves and denied them respite from a grueling work schedule.[5]

Given the negatively-associated relationship between engagement and burnout, and the improved state of the worldwide economy, it would seem that we should be seeing less stressed, more engaged employees. That isn't the case. With the 2008 financial crisis behind us and the stock market in dramatically better shape, companies are putting even more pressure on their employees to perform.

A survey of over six hundred Human Resources leaders showed that even HR recognizes the dramatic impact burnout is having on the workforce. Roughly half of respondents reported employee burnout due to workload causing between 20 and 50 percent of turnover in their organizations.[6] And the issue is not unique to the U.S. economy. There is a burnout epidemic sweeping across industrialized nations. In Japan, young men and women are literally working themselves to death. *Karoshi*, as the

Japanese call it, is death caused directly or indirectly by overwork. A quick Internet search of this term will produce photos of young Japanese businessmen passed out or even lifeless in streets and other public spaces, having collapsed from exhaustion. In 2015, a twenty-four-year-old employee of advertising agency Dentsu jumped to her death on Christmas Day after working more than one hundred hours of overtime in a month.[7]

Burnout-related suicide is on the rise, not only in Asia, but in North America and Europe as well. There were 4,750 "economic suicides" between 2007 and 2010 in the United States, an increase of nearly 5 percent from prior years. Canada has experienced a similar trend, and it's been even worse for Europe—7,950 suicides between 2009 and 2011.[8] In 2016, following a seven-year investigation into the suicides of thirty-five France Telecom workers, French prosecutors recommended that the company's former chief executive should be tried for causing their deaths. According to investigators, the CEO instructed his managers to drive down costs by cutting twenty-two thousand jobs through any means necessary. His specific directive was allegedly to psychologically destabilize employees and force the weakest out "through the window or the door."[9]

No one should lose his or her life because of a job. Nobody should lose *anything* because of a job, but the corporate world has become a place where one must give *everything* in order to survive. Ironically, an employee's survival in the modern workplace comes at the expense of his overall well-being. Companies seem to have found their sweet spot in the inconvenient gap between the limitations of a human workforce and the desire for maximum profits. Unfortunately, the gap is widening on the latter end, putting more stress on employees and perpetuating the problem of burnout.

The human body goes through myriad harmful physiological and neurological changes when it experiences burnout. We've discussed the amygdala's fight-or-flight response in previous chapters and learned what happens when employees feel unhealthy stress or fear. With burnout, activity in the amygdala triggers chain reactions in the medial prefrontal cortex—the brain region responsible for executive function (i.e. decision making and emotional regulation). The constant stress from overwork continues to tax both the amygdala and medial prefrontal cortex like a passenger car being continuously driven like a Formula One racer. Eventually, with all of the moving parts being pushed beyond their normal operating parameters for extended periods, breakdown is inevitable. Wear and tear from an unmanageable workload cause damage to the brain's structures much quicker than the natural aging process, resulting in poor memory and emotional dysfunction. Burnout, in fact, shrinks areas of the brain needed for optimal work performance.[10] Amygdala response also prompts release of the so-called stress hormone, cortisol, which precipitates a variety of physical changes once it enters the bloodstream.

If you've ever been home alone and were startled by a loud noise or a strange shadow, you probably felt a sudden rush of adrenaline as your heart began to race, your muscles tensed, and your vision narrowed. Your body perceived a potential threat in the form of a phantom intruder and primed itself for defense or speedy departure. After a few moments, the feeling would pass (assuming there was no real danger). The cortisol that had been coursing through your veins would have dissipated. Your heart rate slowed and your higher-level cognitive processes came back online allowing you to process complex thoughts beyond "Ahh! What was that?"

Work stressors that lead to burnout essentially put the brain on high alert as though it were under constant attack, producing a steady flow of cortisol that never has time to properly run its course. Excess cortisol production inflames tissues and organs, including the heart. Burnout from work stress can lead to coronary heart disease and substantially raise the risk of having a heart attack. The Centers for Disease Control estimate coronary heart disease claims more than three hundred seventy thousand lives per year.[11] One has to wonder how many of those deaths could have been prevented by employers stepping in to lighten the workload of their chronically burnt-out workforce.

Elevated cortisol levels also interfere with sleep quality. When our brains go into a hyper-vigilant state, it becomes extremely difficult to fall or stay asleep. Sleep, as we know, is the body's recharge and repair mechanism. Losing sleep has a litany of consequences for your health and wellbeing, but those that relate closely to employee engagement and productivity include inability to concentrate, irritability, and a compromised immune system (the latter resulting in more absenteeism and higher health insurance premiums). There is no shortcut to earning a workforce of highly engaged and productive employees. Until business leaders either invest in hiring more employees to provide current staff some relief or temper their unreasonable expectations, the burnout epidemic will continue to grow while disengagement consumes the modern workplace. Either spend more money on staffing, or scale back your unfeasible ambitions. When it comes to employee engagement and workload, there is no third option.

CTRL+ALT+DELIVER ME A DAMN COMPUTER THAT ACTUALLY WORKS

Technology is supposed to be the great enabler, helping mankind reach historic milestones like the first manned space flight or the first surgery performed by a robot. Over the last fifty years, technology has transformed the modern workplace by giving employees and managers tools to create, connect, and do work more efficiently. Personal computers, networks, and more recently, the Internet of Things, smart phones, and augmented reality have made it easier to accomplish more at work, thus raising the bar for everyone.

In the insurance industry, for example, predictive modeling and analytics streamlined the underwriting process to such a degree that underwriters can assess and price risks in a fraction of the time it took decades ago. Heck, even e-mail has made an underwriter's job less time-consuming, allowing for higher productivity standards to meet the demands of agents and customers, as well as beat the competition at the fast-service game. But what happens when technology fails and employees are left struggling to reach aggressive goals set by upper management? What if they never even had the right tools in the first place and the C-suite still decides that the organization needs to do more, produce more, respond quicker, and innovate faster?

I worked with a company that forced its employees to change over to remote desktops using what are called "thin client" terminals. For the first year, there were reliability problems that left employees dead in the water as work continued to accumulate on their desks. I witnessed an exhausting confrontation between a supervisor, Tina, and one of her employees over the woman's phone call to their IT help desk. Her remote desktop was totally inaccessible after conversion, preventing her from getting any work done. She opened a help desk ticket and told the technician on the phone that the issue was causing a total work stoppage for her. That prompted Tina, who was sitting nearby, to stand up and tell the woman that she could not refer to the outage as a "work stoppage." The woman was already on edge because of her useless terminal, and Tina's unhelpful interjection only exacerbated the situation.

Given the help desk's typical poor response and resolution track record, it seemed unlikely that functionality would be restored in a quick turnaround. Tina kept repeating the same thing over and over—that the employee could not call her issue a work stoppage—which spiked the woman's stress level as she fumed that not meeting her daily production goals would be held against her whether she had a working computer or not. Still, Tina only reiterated that it wasn't a work stoppage. On a purely semantic level, it wasn't. Work stoppages are when employees intentionally cease operations in protest of an employer's policies. This was a system outage stopping an employee from doing her work. After listening to this exchange for about ten minutes, I felt like saying to Tina "For crying out loud, what difference does it make what you call it? She can't work! Stop arguing with her and try to help her!"

It isn't at all uncommon in the modern workplace for employees to face situations like the one above and receive little to no sympathy from management. Oracle and Kantar TNS recently surveyed close to five thousand employees in twenty countries and their findings showed that digital technology represents a top engagement driver in the workplace today, yet only 44 percent of respondents reported that they had the tools needed to be effective in their roles.[12] More than half of employees are working without the technology necessary to help their employers succeed. Something is very wrong with this picture, especially considering what we know about the high expectations leaders now have for their workers. They want peak performance from employees, but the majority isn't providing adequate resources to get the job done. Imagine a track and field coach telling his team that they need to improve their times for the hundred-meter sprint but forces them to run in flip flops. It seems absurd when put in these terms, but this is what many business leaders are doing to their teams, and it is causing disengagement.

In Chapter 2, we discussed the factors that lead to disengagement at work, with broken or deficient technology being among the biggest culprits. Yes, it does cost money to purchase software and hardware, hire developers and database administrators, and pay for licenses and maintenance. A lack of useful tools and resources isn't an inexpensive disengagement factor to correct. But it is actually costlier to ignore, particularly when technology stops working. We already established that disengagement in general is financially draining for businesses, but there is also a price to pay for malfunctioning software and system downtime. Large companies lose on average $686,000 per hour when technology fails.[13] Even if the impact on engagement weren't a concern, there is still a cost in terms of customer experience and subsequent lost revenues that cannot be ignored. The same can be said for the systems development lifecycle.

In my years working on software implementation projects, I saw that the primary reason for failure was not poor planning or underfunding (though both do contribute). The best way to guarantee a system will disappoint is to exclude its end users from the early stages of development. When it comes to your organization's technology, as with all areas of your employee experience, involve employees from the outset when planning a system change, because they are the ones who will have to live and work with it. A discussion of software coding and testing best practices would venture well beyond the scope of this book, but suffice it to say that things don't turn out well when employees have no voice in building the tools they need to do their work. It's not about letting them dictate or derail IT strategy. It's about letting them co-own the outcome. We will discuss co-ownership of the employee experience in detail in Chapter 11.

There are some organizational development practitioners who believe workers are accountable for their own engagement, the quality of their employee experience notwithstanding. They profess that leaders should not strive to perfect employees' circumstances, that they instead ask their teams what they are doing to accept the reality of their situation and work within those parameters. Heeding employees' complaints and perfecting their circumstances breed entitlement, according to this philosophy. Employees should be resilient and adaptive when technology fails; they shouldn't whine or complain about it. On the surface, it simply sounds like having high expectations as a leader. Calling employees to greatness will lead to great results, right? No. Not if you expect them to process the hundreds of customer invoices sitting on their desks when the infernal accounting system you've saddled them with can only put through one invoice per hour.

Employees will not engage as partners in action if the tools they need to *act* are defective junk or not even available. There is a vast difference between solving your employees' problems when they could truly handle them on their own and creating an engaging work experience that inspires them to produce amazing results. What is an employee supposed to do when the software she needs to use is defect-ridden and handicaps her work performance? Must she shell out some of her own money to have it fixed? Of course not! That would be ridiculous. The obligation falls on an organization's leaders to responsibly budget for and select technology solutions that actually work. Having the right tools to do one's job is not a product of entitlement. It's a basic element of your company's employee experience that must be in place before you can even think about employee engagement and accountability.

SINK OR SWIM

The saying goes that you only have one chance to make a good first impression. In terms of an employment relationship, the time for first impressions is usually the job interview and the onus is traditionally on the candidate to make a good one. But organizations also need to put their best foot forward by preparing new hires for the demands and challenges of their roles. In today's knowledge economy where employers compete for the best talent to fill open requisitions (and keep them filled), one might think an exceptional onboarding experience would be standard practice. However, studies show that nearly 35 percent of companies spend nothing on their onboarding programs, with a quarter failing to include any training whatsoever for new hires. These statistics are worrisome, but also consider that the remaining percentage of companies might only provide marginally better onboarding experiences. This is illustrated by the fact that companies report losing 25 percent of new hires in their first year of service.[14] Clearly many employers are doing a bad job of making a good impression.

What does this have to do with productivity? Everything, actually. Roughly the same number of companies that reported having ineffective onboarding programs indicated that it takes at least a year for their new hires to be fully productive. Surely every organization aspires to create a culture of excellence where high-performing employees contribute steady effort toward achieving company goals. There's nothing inherently wrong with striving for greatness. The problem lies in setting such high expectations for new employees when they were never given a platform to spring from potential to performance. A strong onboarding process starts new employees on their journey with the organization by giving them a historical perspective of where their employer started and where it is headed. They are given a thorough introduction to the company's mission, vision, and values with leaders at all levels being involved.

Early in my career, I worked with an organization whose onboarding program focused on immersing employees in its customer-oriented culture and featured regular, in-person presentations from the executive team to welcome and educate the fresh recruits. Most importantly, it also had a robust training curriculum, something that is critical for equipping new employees with the skills and knowledge they need to be productive. Again, that's where many employers fall short.

One of the most frustrating aspects of a poor employee experience is a lack of practical training, especially for new hires. The sink-or-swim method of onboarding is terribly ineffective and only ends up wasting time as employees struggle to succeed. Throwing new hires into their jobs without any support in the form of structured training with agreed upon goals and milestones hurts both employees and the organization. Without set standards or even clearly communicated cultural norms, untrained employees left to their own devices will do what makes sense to them, which might not be the correct or the most efficient way to execute their duties. They demonstrate limited productivity against growing workloads, potentially leading to failure and the need to recruit and rehire for their positions. Yes, training does have a cost, and that's unavoidable. But it's much more expensive to eschew methodical training in favor of a "set it and forget it" approach.

Human Resources recognizes the need for training probably more than anyone in an organization, but, in a recent survey of HR executives, roughly a quarter said they had no training budget to work with. Worse, over 70 percent of HR leaders report that their employees do not have the job-related skills they need to make them successful.[15] What leaders must recognize is their employees' success is integral to that of the organization. If employees are floundering, the company will start to sink soon after.

As I mentioned before, there's nothing untoward about having high expectations for employees. Mediocrity does not win the hearts and minds of consumers. But if you expect peak performance and engagement from your team, you have to ensure they are properly and sufficiently trained. A demanding workload sans the skills or knowledge to handle it is a recipe for disengagement and burnout, with customers receiving much poorer service than they should.

In most every profession, failing to meet customers' needs can have real consequences for both the employee and organization to at least some degree. But when a customer—especially one who is physically or mentally vulnerable—is actually harmed because of an employee's lack of training, the failure becomes one that can irreparably tarnish the employer's reputation. Such is the case with untrained nursing home staff. The elderly, those with dementia or Alzheimer's disease, the weakest and most indigent members of our society rely on the care of strangers when their families are unable to do so. We've all heard the hidden-camera nursing home horror stories of wonton abuse and neglect at the hands of staff, making it evident that there need to be reforms to the elder healthcare system and severe penalties for errant facilities that ignore or even try to cover up staff misconduct.

There are also those nursing home employees who genuinely *want* to give residents the best care possible, but they are overwhelmed by a skills gap along with deficient support from their employers. Sadly many nursing assistants do not have the requisite training to handle patients with special needs and disabilities. Nursing homes struggle to attract and retain qualified staff, forcing them to hire low-skilled workers whom they pay barely more than minimum wage and skimp on their training. Moreover, budget constraints and attrition cause staff shortages which ultimately create dangerous conditions for patients. Bedsores, bacterial infections, broken bones, malnutrition, and over-/under-medication can be attributed to staff being overburdened and under-trained.

In the summer of 2017, the New York attorney general conducted a raid of a Syracuse nursing home and found evidence of patient neglect by the employees.[16] One worker used improper, unsterile procedures to unclog a resident's feeding tube with a cotton swab, which became stuck, and then used a paper clip to try to fix her mistake. Two others broke a fragile dementia patient's leg when adjusting her position as they put her to bed. A blind resident was left unattended; she fell out of her wheelchair hitting her head, and was later found under her bed by the nursing staff. She died a week after the incident. This facility and others with similarly lax employee training programs could face sanctions in the form of lawsuits and government intervention.

Yet as disturbing as these stories of neglect are, one must also consider the impact of working conditions on nursing home employees, themselves, who are susceptible to on-the-job injuries as well as disengagement, depression, and burnout.[17] At the very least, nursing home administrators, like any employer, could avoid some of the situations described here if they invest in effective training so workers are able to meet the demands of their roles and provide compassionate care to those who need it most. The majority of employees in the modern workplace truly want to perform well in their jobs, but they cannot actualize that goal without their employers giving them ongoing training and reinforcement.

CASE STUDY

EDWARD JONES

Edward "Ted" D. Jones believed very strongly in the value of treating employees well and founded his company on this principle after he quit his job as an advisor with financial services broker Blair & Co in 1922.[18] He managed to sustain Edward D. Jones & Co. through the 1929 stock market crash and grow it into one of the most respected firms in its industry. Today, the company, now known simply as Edward Jones, maintains the same partnership model as it did back when Ted Jones opened the first branch in St. Louis.

Edward Jones' managing partner, Jim Weddle, credits a private partnership model for both the company's success and its frequent recognition as a Best Place to Work. Each of Edward Jones' financial advisors—called associates—has the opportunity to earn a partnership stake in the company and manages his or her own book of business. The close relationship associates have with their clients is reflected in the way Edward Jones has structured its branch network. Multiple branches service a particular market with a single financial advisor at each location. This is done to provide clients with geographic convenience for selecting a branch and to give them a sole point of contact for the duration of their relationship with the firm. Other investment firms might do things differently, but Edward Jones sticks to a framework that works for its customers and, more importantly, for its employees.

As a private firm that's not beholden to the whims and pressures of shareholders, Edward Jones has the flexibility to put its associates first and create an employee experience that undercuts stress while enabling productivity. It starts at the hiring and onboarding process, with selective recruitment—only a small percentage of applicants are chosen to move forward in becoming advisor trainees—and a comprehensive training program that prepares employees for their roles. Edward Jones boasts twice the industry retention rate for new recruits going through financial advisor training, which speaks to both the quality of instruction and the level of importance senior leadership places upon it. The multi-year training program that started in 1978 pairs trainees with mentors and focuses on experiential learning, giving them a practical foundation to grow and thrive as advisors in their own branch offices. *Training Magazine* has consistently recognized Edward Jones for having best-in-class training and awarded the firm with a spot on their Training Top 125 list for 2017.[19]

Recently, Edward Jones enriched its training program with elective course offerings. Advisors learn more about areas of interest so they can use this specialized knowledge to build more trusting relationships with their clients. Additionally, each financial advisor is assigned an on-location branch office administrator to oversee scheduling, client communication, document management, and other tasks, thus freeing up the associate's time to better serve his or her client base.

One of the most significant employee experience differentiators at Edward Jones is its integrated technology platform. Advisors can rely on a suite of proprietary tools designed for ease of use in building and maintaining their clients' investment portfolios. As with their training program, Edward Jones has been recognized in industry publications for the digital tools that make advisors' lives much easier. A 2014 *REP. Magazine* comparison of overall advisor satisfaction with employer technology put Edward Jones well ahead of every other competitor.[20] The firm uses proprietary software to give advisors a guided pathway for building a client's portfolio by assessing financial goals, risk tolerance, and growth strategies. Once a client's unique investment profile is created, the software offers tailored portfolio options with investments that align with his or her needs and preferences. This opens up time for the advisor to do more advising and less research, something both clients and advisors appreciate.

Additionally, Edward Jones' mobile applications provide advisors with the flexibility to serve clients from anywhere using the same patented technology as in their branches. They even have internal social media to connect them with other advisors across the country, as well as data-driven sales tools to help them locate prospective clients. It's another piece of Edward Jones' employee experience that sets itself apart from other firms that do not take such great care to smooth their employees' work experience.

The financial advisory business has traditionally been a tough one, with high average turnover and burnout rates among advisors. However,

Edward Jones has a remarkably low voluntary turnover rate of 7 percent for full-time employees.[21] One can safely attribute this to the company's focus on retaining talent with various work-life balance programs, generous paid time off, telecommuting options, flexible schedules, and even reduced hours for branch office administrators. The 2008 financial crisis hit the investment community hard, with many firms laying off large segments of their workforce. But Jim Weddle refused to do the same and instead implemented a freeze on hiring and compensation. He also challenged employees to share ideas for reducing costs by 10 percent over a three-month period, which they did, enabling a cost reduction that exceeded Weddle's goal without having to end anybody's employment.[22] As many others in the financial services industry experienced, the casualties of the Great Recession were not just the ones who lost their employment. The former coworkers who were left behind to absorb their workloads suffered as well, a scenario that would have been contrary to Ted Jones' dream of building an investment firm that treats its advisors as partners in success, not just as vehicles for generating fees and growing assets.

With Edward Jones' success over the years came the natural desire for growth and expansion. The firm grew beyond its Missouri roots to over twelve thousand branches throughout the United States with plans to expand further and spread its advisor network more densely than its competitors. Most organizations run into growing pains as they try to scale operations but don't compensate with a larger staff to handle the increased business. They scale their ambitions without also scaling their capacity and resources. Jim Weddle set a goal to add new advisors to Edward Jones' ranks by 2020, bringing its associate headcount to over twenty thousand.[23] The one-advisor-per-branch business model will mean a market nearly saturated with Edward Jones offices giving associates at every location more bandwidth to handle their respective workloads and focus more on cultivating strong client relationships. The company has a saying about the culture of support its advisors can rely on when building their individual businesses: "You go into business for yourself, but not by yourself." It's the kind of reassurance that engages and inspires employees to do more because they have more in terms of help and resources.

LOOKING AHEAD

Throughout this chapter we discussed the negative effects an unreasonable workload and inadequate resources can have on employees and, in some instances, customers as well. Subscribers of the Stepford Employee Fallacy believe they can pile inordinate amounts of work on their staff without any impact on engagement or productivity. Even with a relatively manageable workload, employees who have not received the tools or training to perform their duties in a satisfactory manner will eventually check out or burn out. When employees reach that breaking point and decide to quit or, worse, stay and retaliate in some form or another, their employers will often be quick to allege disloyalty. But workers really can't be blamed for taking a stand when their employee experience just isn't up to snuff.

The following chapter will conclude Part II by covering the final belief in the Stepford Employee Fallacy: that employees will remain loyal no matter how they are treated or whether they are fulfilled by their jobs. What leaders must understand is that loyalty is not unconditional. It actually takes an effort on their part to earn their employees' loyalty and that includes treating them well, recognizing their efforts, and giving them opportunities to develop in their careers. Just as we learned in previous chapters, an organization cannot expect engagement from its employees without a compelling employee experience. The same goes for loyalty in that regard. A loyal employee is indeed a valuable partner in action. However, as you will see in the coming pages, there are actions an employer can take to foster that loyalty—and actions that will have the opposite result.

NOTES

1. Goodman, Christopher and Mance, Steven. *Bureau of Labor Statistics. Employment Loss and the 2007-09 Recession: An Overview.* April 2011. https://www.bls.gov/mlr/2011/04/art1full.pdf

2. Sullivan, Teresa. "Greedy Institutions, Overwork, and Work-Life Balance." *Sociological Inquiry.* Volume 84. Issue 1, 1-15. December 10, 2013. http://onlinelibrary.wiley.com/doi/10.1111/soin.12029/abstract

3. "83% of Americans Are Stressed out at Work." *Everest College - The Official Blog.* June 13, 2013. https://everestcollege.wordpress.com/2013/06/10/83-of-americans-are-stressed-out-at-work/

4. Salmela-Aro, Katariina, Upadyaya, Katja, and Vartiainen, Matti. "From Job Demands and Resources to Work Engagement, Burnout, Life Satisfaction, Depressive Symptoms, and Occupational Health." *Burnout Research.* Volume 3. Issue 4, 101-108. December 2016. https://www.sciencedirect.com/science/article/pii/S221305861630002X

5. Noguchi, Yuki. "Many Grouchy Error-Prone Workers Just Need More Sleep." *NPR.* April 26, 2016. https://www.npr.org/sections/health-shots/2016/04/26/475287202/many-grouchy-error-prone-workers-just-need-more-sleep

6. Kronos. *The Employee Burnout Crisis: Study Reveals Big Workplace Challenge in 2017.* January 2017. https://www.kronos.com/about-us/newsroom/employee-burnout-crisis-study-reveals-big-workplace-challenge-2017

7. McClellan, Steve. "Dentsu Employee's Suicide Linked to 'Overwork.'" *MediaPost.* October 10, 2016. https://www.mediapost.com/publications/article/286556/dentsu-employees-suicide-linked-to-overwork.html

8. McKee, Martin, Reeves, Aaron, and Stuckler, David. "Economic Suicides in the Great Recession in Europe and North America." *The British Journal of Psychiatry.* Volume 205. Issue 3, 246-247. September 2014. http://bjp.rcpsych.org/content/205/3/246

9. "France Telecom Suicides: Prosecutor Calls for Bullying Trial." *BBC News.* July 7, 2016. http://www.bbc.com/news/world-europe-36733572

10. Michel, Alexandria. "Burnout and the Brain." *Association for Psychological Science.* January 29, 2016. https://www.psychologicalscience.org/observer/burnout-and-the-brain

11. Centers for Disease Control and Prevention. "Heart Disease Facts." Retrieved January 9, 2018. https://www.cdc.gov/heartdisease/facts.htm

12. Oracle. *From Theory to Action: A Practical Look at What Really Drives Employee Engagement.* 2016. https://www.oracle.com/webfolder/s/delivery_production/docs/FY16h1/doc31/Oracle-HCMGlobalSurveyiPaperV12RG.pdf

13. Goldberg, Kevin. "The True Cost of Downtime." *AppDynamics.* June 27, 2016. https://blog.appdynamics.com/product/the-true-cost-of-downtime-infographic/

14. Lauby, Sharlyn. "Employee Turnover Caused by Bad Onboarding Programs." *HR Bartender.* (Blog). May 22, 2012. https://www.hrbartender.com/2012/recruiting/employee-turnover-caused-by-bad-onboarding-programs/

15. Udemy. *At the Breaking Point: The State of Corporate Training Programs in America.* 2015. https://info.udemy.com/rs/udemy/images/Udemy-State-of-Corporate-Training.pdf

16. Mulder, James. "Unreported Break-in, Untrained Staff, Missing Resident at James Square." *Syracuse.com.* June 29, 2017. http://www.syracuse.com/health/index.ssf/2017/06/drugged_intruder_barges_into_residents_rooms_at_james_square_nursing_home.html

17. Carleton, Heather, et al. "Burnout in the Nursing Home Health Care Aide: A Systematic Review." *Burnout Research.* Volume 3. Issue 3, 76-87. September 2016.

18. Stallard, Michael. "Why Edward Jones is Built to Last." *ExecuNet.* (Blog) March 31, 2016. https://www.execunet.com/edward-jones-built-last/

19. French, Kristen. "Due Diligence: Edward Jones Has an Edge at Training in an Industry That Stinks at It." *Wealth Management.* February 21, 2012. http://www.wealthmanagement.com/content/due-diligence-edward-jones-has-edge-training-industry-stinks-it

20. Leonhardt, Megan. "Drivers of Advisor Satisfaction: Technology and Efficiency." *Wealth Management.* December 1, 2014. http://www.wealthmanagement.com/2014-broker-report-card/drivers-advisor-satisfaction-technology-and-efficiency

21. "Edward Jones." *Great Place to Work.* July 31, 2017. http://reviews.greatplacetowork.com/

edward-jones?utm_source=fortune&utm_medium=referral&utm_
content=reviews-link&utm_campaign=2017-fortune100-list

22. Weddle, Jim. "Commentary: Jim Weddle on What Makes Edward Jones a Top Private Company." *St. Louis Business Journal.* May 11, 2017. https://www.bizjournals.com/stlouis/news/2017/05/11/commentary-jim-weddle-on-what-makes-edward-jones-a.html

23. Rusoff, Jane W. "Where Edward Jones is Tapping Talent." *Think Advisor.* May 27, 2014. http://www.thinkadvisor.com/2014/05/27/where-edward-jones-is-tapping-talent?page=2&slreturn=1515539281

CHAPTER 10

BELIEF # 7: ENGAGED EMPLOYEES WILL REMAIN LOYAL NO MATTER HOW THEY ARE TREATED OR WHETHER THEY ARE FULFILLED BY THEIR WORK

Employers spend a lot of money on labor costs. It's pretty much generally accepted that any organization's biggest expense is headcount. With most organizations today keeping a tight grip on expenditures, it makes sense that they would anticipate maximum return on the investments they *do* make. Each employee represents an investment. Cost-conscious business leaders also view employees as liabilities, because they could potentially do something disloyal that ends up hurting the company's bottom line. What happens if workers leave and join a competing firm? Don't they know it costs money to replace them? How much of a headache will they cause if they join together and try to negotiate higher wages or better working conditions? Shouldn't they just be grateful that they even have jobs? Engaged employees would never do anything as disloyal as quitting or demanding fair compensation, right? If only it were that simple.

As we've seen, engagement does not come without a phenomenal employee experience. When employees try to improve their work circumstances, either by negotiation or resignation, they aren't acting in conflict with the organization's interests nor are they being disloyal. The interests of workers and their employers don't have to be mutually exclusive. Yet, corporations today expect loyalty from employees even when they give little consideration to the needs and interests of those who make the business thrive. They unceremoniously terminate workers who gave decades of service and naively think the rest won't take notice. They mistreat, ignore, and fail to develop their talent and then become riled when employees assert their legal rights or quit. The point is, subscribers of the Stepford Employee

Fallacy believe their employees will display loyalty without any reason to do so. What's wrong with this belief is it ignores the most basic principle of loyalty in human relationships: if you show loyalty, you will get loyalty in return. Loyalty—true loyalty—cannot be bought or coerced, nor is it deserved if it is not also given.

One of the common frustrations that managers have today is employee attrition. Considering the high cost of turnover, it's easy to see why. There isn't much consensus about exactly how much of a cost (studies put the number anywhere between 20 percent and 213 percent of a departing employee's salary[1]), but lost productivity, advertising for a vacant position, and training a replacement can certainly get expensive. Millennial retention is a particularly difficult nut to crack. Of the many clichés about this generation's work behavior, job hopping seems to be one that causes the most consternation for business leaders because it is so costly.

Generation Y came into the workforce during very tumultuous economic times when they saw their Gen X and baby boomer colleagues being let go in droves. Shaken by the sense of uncertainty that they faced in the Recession and driven by both a need to gain financial independence as well as an affinity for meaningful work, millennials will leave an organization that does not offer the kind of employee experience that aligns with their work-life goals. Instead of complaining that younger workers don't stick around very long, leaders should look to this generation to define what it takes to earn employees' loyalty going forward. Over the next ten years, the talent market will become increasingly saturated with members of the millennial cohort. It would be wise for organizations to focus on developing strategies to gain their loyalty, because, if a millennial employee leaves—voluntarily or not—her replacement will very likely be someone from the same age group.

Some employers are quick to bid good riddance to employees they see as disloyal, but they never look in the mirror and ask what they could have done to engage them. Rather, they continue with the same business practices, ignorant of the fact that they are the very reason that their employees are leaving. A revolving door culture won't win the hearts and minds of talent nor will it inspire loyalty from the people you rely upon for your organization to succeed. To get loyalty, it must also be given. That truth is conspicuously disregarded in the unequal modern workplace where employers demand sworn allegiance without pledging any in kind.

THE LEGALITY OF DISLOYALTY

Before there were unions and labor laws to protect workers from employer mistreatment, companies could get away with paying poverty-level wages while requiring sixteen-hour workdays, employing young children, and forcing labor to work in unsafe conditions. The lure of economic prosperity supported by *laissez faire* capitalistic sentiment emboldened business owners with avaricious disregard for employee welfare, much less morale.

Even after the passing of historic workplace legislation like the National Labor Relations Act (NLRA) of 1935, employers and their unfair labor practices were still protected by the doctrine of *at-will employment* which states that either party in an employment relationship can terminate it for any reason, so long as that reason does not violate an existing statute. That left employers with fairly broad leeway to implement policies and behave in ways which were technically legal, albeit disadvantageous to workers. However, the NLRA does provide employees the right to engage in what is called "protected concerted activity" whether they are unionized or not. If two or more employees join efforts to address working conditions—like pay or hours—their activities are considered protected and free from retaliation by their employer.

As an example, in recent years, public social media postings between co-workers discussing work-related matters have raised the ire of employers who felt the potential damage to their brands represented a terminable offense and took action against those involved. The National Labor

Relations Board (NLRB), which administers the NLRA, intervened in cases in which employees were fired because the activity was protected under statute. The NLRB remains a thorn in the side of companies that wish to discipline employees for what they perceive to be disloyal behavior, only to have their dreams of a workforce comprised of Stepford Employees crushed when the Board steps in. Instead of designing a more attractive and engaging employee experience, organizations today spend time and money trying to skirt labor laws or fighting legal battles against the very people whose loyalty they should be striving to earn. It's counter-productive and does nothing to foster a sense of loyalty from employees who just want to be treated with fairness and dignity.

Six Jimmy John's franchise employees from Minneapolis were fired in 2011 for what the restaurant owner believed was disloyal conduct after they posted flyers on site and in their community criticizing an unfair sick leave policy.[2] The employees were attempting to win a union campaign through Jimmy John's Worker's Union and secure collective bargaining rights to negotiate sick leave benefits. They weren't asking for anything extraordinary. All they wanted was paid sick leave; a benefit most full-time employees take for granted these days. At a minimum wage of $7.25 per hour, Jimmy John's employees could not afford to lose any days of work if they fell ill. Worse, if they were absent for any reason, illness or otherwise, management would require them to find a replacement to cover their shifts or else they would face discipline up to and including being fired.

For workers at this particular franchise, getting sick meant losing money and potentially even losing their jobs. So they went to work even if they were suffering from a bout of influenza, putting customers at risk of contamination. The flyers distributed by union organizers showed pictures of two identical sandwiches with a caption asking customers whether they could tell which one was prepared by an employee sick with the flu. Additional verbiage informed customers of the labor dispute and encouraged them to contact the franchisee and let him know they would not eat tainted food. The owner, who had (allegedly) been engaging in union-busting activities at the time, like creating an anti-union Facebook page to disparage the organizers, retaliated by terminating six of them.[2] Those individuals filed charges with the NLRB. After review, the Board found that the terminations violated the National Labor Relations Act and subsequently ordered that their employment be reinstated and their lost wages repaid. The Eighth Circuit Court of Appeals overturned the NLRB's decision in 2017, reasoning that the flyers were so malicious and disloyal that they caused Jimmy John's reputational harm that could outlast the labor dispute and, therefore, the employees' activity was not protected under the NLRA.[3]

Another NLRB ruling on the subject of employee disloyalty involved the case of DirecTV contract workers protesting an unfair compensation policy whereby their pay was reduced if they failed to sell customers a service they did not want. DirecTV contracted service technicians through a company called MasTec and required them to pressure subscribers into connecting satellite TV service through their landlines. This would allow DirecTV to offer upgraded features and monitor customer viewing trends, but subscribers balked. DirecTV lowered payments to MasTec if its technicians did not connect at least half of all new customers via phone service.

MasTec balanced the lost revenues by implementing pay cuts for employees who didn't meet the goal. This, of course, did not sit well with the technicians after they saw their paychecks shrink, but their wholly justified protests fell on MasTec management's deaf ears. They contacted a local news station and gave an interview detailing the controversy which prompted DirecTV to tell MasTec that the employees who participated could no longer install their equipment. That led to the workers being terminated. When the NLRB heard the case, they determined that the employees' statements to news reporters were protected concerted activity related to working conditions and their firings were illegal. MasTec and DirecTV appealed, but the Court of Appeals for the District of Columbia Circuit affirmed the Board's decision.[4]

Although there were different outcomes for these two examples of disengaging employment practices, the argument of employee disloyalty given by both companies highlights a common business theme in the modern workplace. Employers demand unquestioning fidelity from their workers, but do nothing to earn it. Or, as was the case with Jimmy John's and DirecTV, they implement and enforce policies that harm employees and then wonder why loyalty is in such short supply. The old adage "Don't bite the hand that feeds you" probably rings true for most employers who cry foul when the people on their payroll betray them (i.e. stand up for themselves). However, I would complement that saying by giving them the following advice: don't kick the dog that protects you, lest you someday feel its bite. I'm not talking about (or condoning) theft, or espionage, or workplace violence. What I'm referring to is our natural desire to seek justice when we are wronged.

The workers at Jimmy John's and DirecTV approached their employers in vain attempts to resolve their respective grievances. When that didn't work, they engaged in protected concerted activity to collectively request assistance from the public in aiding their cause. They didn't attack the quality of their employers' products for sport or out of malicious spite. In fact, they did a public service in raising awareness of questionable business practices that were not in consumers' best interest. The NLRB found that these workers' activities arose from labor disputes and were not the kind of reckless or dishonest endeavors that would merit termination. Even though the Board's ruling did not stick for Jimmy John's, the company still had to cover their legal expenses as they pursued a favorable outcome. Had they only paid for this very basic employee benefit and made it safe for workers to be sick without jeopardizing their jobs, they could have avoided the exorbitant costs of ongoing litigation, lost business, and a demoralized, disengaged team.

Appealing to your employer's good nature has historically never worked in securing better labor conditions. Companies are motivated by money, not by magnanimity. That is why strikes are really the only persuasive tool a disenfranchised workforce has to effect change. So, as we've seen throughout this book, it makes better financial sense to create an engaging employee experience than it does to be cheap. Too many organizations ignore this lesson and instead place their bets on the system working in their favor. They take a chance that their employees will still somehow be loyal no matter how they are treated. It doesn't work that way. As long as human beings are employers' main source of labor, and as long as they have laws to protect them, their loyalty will be conditional.

YOU BETTER RECOGNIZE

As children, we sought the approval of our parents because it made us feel safe and loved. From the early days of mankind, social acceptance meant the difference between life and death. Our tribal ancestors relied on each other for food, shelter, and safety by maintaining strong social bonds. Rejection by other members of the tribe could have quite literally meant one's demise. Humans and other members of the animal kingdom have adapted to prefer social behavior because it ensures survival.

Our brains have been programmed by nature to recognize and seek out social acceptance. Again, the brain's engagement button—the ventral striatum—within its reward center is especially responsive to social interaction. A mother gives positive attention to her child, releasing the pleasure hormone dopamine in the child's brain. Thus, showing a child love and affection reinforces her need for that social recognition because we are all wired that way from birth.[5] In adulthood, the same desire for acceptance is seen with the employer/employee relationship. Feelings of security and stability come from a steady paycheck. When our boss gives us praise for doing well at work, it engages us as members of a tribe, so to speak. It activates the brain's reward center circuitry, makes us feel safe and loved, gives meaning to our efforts, and strengthens the bond between us and the leaders for whom we work.

Automation and globalization have injected widespread uncertainty into the modern workplace. Employees today feel more vulnerable and disengaged than in previous decades because the sense of connection to secure and fulfilling employment has all but disappeared. The business world is indeed changing at an ever-increasing speed, and leaders might not be able to restore the certainty of simpler industrial times; but they *can* build community and loyalty by satisfying employees' need for recognition.

Plenty of managers today do not believe it is their job to praise or recognize their employees and that a paycheck is sufficient reward for the work they accomplish. However, by adopting this sort of jaded leadership mindset, they are missing a precious opportunity to bridge the gap between employees seeing themselves as replaceable cogs in the corporate machine and as valued members of a team (i.e. safely integrated into a tribe).

Praise and recognition are powerful tools for driving engagement in the workplace. They just aren't utilized nearly enough. Regularly finding a way to convey a simple "great job" can engage employees and trigger their desire to continue doing their best. In my experience, not many management professionals do this. They ignore accomplishments, big or small, alienating their employees when they should be earning their loyalty.

In my early days working in IT, one of my colleagues received a very moving commendation from one of his business partners whom he helped with preparations for a critical customer demonstration. The test environment for our new e-commerce system was experiencing intermittent problems that jeopardized the presentation and could have negatively impacted roll out. He worked with our vendor well into the night in an attempt to resolve the issues, but to no avail. The day of the demo, he ended up recreating our business partner's work sample in a different test environment just in time for her to meet with the customer. That afternoon, she sent an e-mail to my colleague's supervisor and manager praising him for saving the day and for his tireless dedication. The message went totally unacknowledged by his superiors, even when he reminded them about it, leaving him to wonder if his work meant anything to them or whether he should take his talents elsewhere.

Unfortunately, in terms of praise and recognition, the most managers seem to do today is send infrequent, half-hearted e-mails saying, "Thanks for all you do! Keep up the good work..." It takes all the effort of typing a grocery list to send employees a mass e-mail as an expression of thanks. Engaging employees with meaningful recognition takes time, effort, and a personal touch. There is no such thing as being too busy to make time for thanking your team. If one of your employees couldn't complete a task because they didn't have enough time, would you simply let them off the hook? I highly doubt it. Nor should you shirk your leadership responsibilities by using the excuse that you don't have time to show thanks. The time element also involves frequency. How often you show genuine appreciation for your team is an indicator of their level of engagement and the quality of their employee experience. Putting a note in your employee's yearly performance appraisal thanking her for her contributions just doesn't cut it. Recognition should be frequent. Think of how often you catch employees doing something right versus something wrong. Focusing on the right builds them up. Focusing on the wrong breaks them down.

I worked with an executive who almost never recognized his employees' efforts and only focused on the work they *weren't* getting done. One of the managers from another department nominated a business analyst on the executive's staff for an IT vendor's excellence award without his knowledge. It was the first time any of his team members had received such recognition, a fact made even more embarrassing for the executive because he was not the one to make the nomination. When another manager praises your employees to keep them motivated because you don't do it nearly often enough, that should be an obvious sign that you, as their leader, have to step up your recognition game.

The more effort you put into saying thank you to your employees, the more it will pay dividends down the road in the form of higher engagement.

Moreover, it should make *you* feel good because it's the right thing to do! I'm not saying you need to throw a parade outside your office every Friday, but you have to put on your thinking cap and get creative. Effort does not necessarily mean grand, expensive gestures. As they say, it's the thought that counts. At one company where I worked, the supervisors would occasionally serve us full breakfast in the break room. It wasn't much, but the effort was certainly appreciated because they actually had to get up from their desks and stand in front of catering pans dishing out scrambled eggs, bacon, and pancakes to the entire office staff. That's just one idea if you have the budget. And it really wasn't even that costly. As a matter of fact, putting in an effort doesn't have to cost anything at all. Just getting up from your desk and walking over to an employee's cubicle to tell her "good job" is a small effort that won't go unnoticed.

A personal touch also can make a big difference as far as recognition goes. Don't send a mass e-mail to your employees with the same tired boilerplate "Thank you for your contributions" language. It's woefully impersonal. Unless you're a very senior executive working at an organization with hundreds of thousands of employees, you can't get away with this. That's not to say C-level executives should not still dedicate large chunks of their calendars to getting face time throughout all areas of the organization and take every opportunity to personally thank employees. Despite their hectic schedules, some CEOs will even personally write notes to employees thanking them for all they do. If you're not the CEO, then you most definitely need to personalize your gratitude. And I don't just mean hand writing a note. Find out your employees' individual engagement levers and pull them when you want to show appreciation. You'll send a message to your employees that you value them as people, not as numbers.

Discussion of employee appreciation always seems to pair rewards with recognition. I have purposely limited coverage of the former here because the latter is more conducive to long-term engagement. The promise of monetary rewards like bonuses, vacations, or other gifts might push employees to perform in the hope of receiving them, but that is not a sustainable engagement strategy for most organizations. For one thing, it's not cheap to be giving out extravagant rewards as often as is necessary for recognition to be effective. Also, monetary rewards and incentives don't really engage employees as much as they create competition among them. Organizations today are smartly dropping relative performance ranking systems that give performance-based rewards because they promote a dog-eat-dog atmosphere and discourage teamwork. I'm not suggesting that rewards are inherently bad for business. They do have a place within an effective employee engagement framework, but they should supplement, not replace, social recognition as a form of appreciation in the workplace.

Now, I need to provide a caveat about showing appreciation for employees' work. As we've discussed previously, unless the most basic elements of your organization's employee experience are in place—fair compensation, quality leadership, a safe work environment—any gesture of appreciation or recognition will be seen as tone-deaf and disingenuous. Think back on the more egregious examples of a terrible employee experience mentioned throughout this book and compare them to the positive examples from our case studies. The line workers at Tyson Foods would not feel any more engaged by thank-you notes from their supervisors when they can't even take bathroom breaks. But if the partners at Starbucks receive the same recognition, for them it would crystallize the organization's already strong commitment to a phenomenal employee experience. Do you see the difference? Remember the analogy between employee engagement and house construction from Chapter 4. Start with a foundation of quality leadership and move on to the fun and fancy stuff once the structure of a solid employee experience is built. That doesn't mean rewards and recognition are not important. In fact, they can make the difference between being an employer of choice and being just another company that takes great talent for granted.

YOU'LL GET PROMOTED . . . WHEN SOMEBODY RETIRES OR DIES

I mentioned Maslow's hierarchy of needs in Chapter 5 when talking about our basic fear of losing the security of a job. This fear is rooted in our primal need for the safety of employment and the basic needs it can fulfill in modern capitalistic society, like paying for food and shelter. These needs sit at the bottom of Maslow's Hierarchy and are prerequisite to those higher up, such as social acceptance—which is not to say that higher-level needs aren't important. On the contrary, when employees' needs at each level are met, they are all the more inclined toward engagement. The top two levels involve accomplishment and self-actualization, both being employee engagement levers that separate average organizations from ones that engage their talent with rewards, recognition, and promotion.

It is promotion that fulfills the need for self-actualization because we are achieving our potential as we make progress in our careers. When we advance to another role within an organization, we feel accomplished in our efforts and aligned with our sense of self as competent professionals. But if there is nowhere to advance, if we stay stagnant, then we start to disengage and seek another opportunity for growth.

Consider the immense popularity of massively multiplayer online role-playing games. Perhaps the most well-known is the game *World of Warcraft*. Games like *Warcraft* immerse their players in rich environments with limitless opportunities for players to level up, which allows them to gain new abilities and explore new areas. These types of video games are especially engaging for players because, if they are skilled and persistent enough, they can progress from level to level. Without this built-in functionality, players would become bored and stop playing. It's the challenge and subsequent reward that keeps them engaged. The same can be said for employees and career growth. Promotions that give employees new titles, greater responsibilities, more pay, and exposure to other parts of the business will fulfill their needs for achievement and actualization. When these needs aren't met, it is more likely that employees will seek fulfillment with a competitor than engage as partners in action with their current employer.

WorldatWork, a non-profit Human Resources association, published a report in 2016 based on a survey of over seven hundred organizations in the public and private sectors detailing job promotion trends.[6] Their findings showed a marginal increase in the average number of promotions across all industries compared to previous years—9.3 percent versus 9.0 in 2015—which is not terribly encouraging. Nearly a third of organizations have no formal guidelines pertaining to promotions, and 13 percent do have a policy but abstain from sharing it with employees. More than two-thirds of respondents said they do not advertise career development as a major aspect of their employee experience when recruiting new hires.

These statistics do not indicate a high degree of effort on the part of employers to make promoting their workers much of a priority. True, employees must be proactive in pursuing opportunities that are presented to them, and some are perfectly comfortable remaining in the same role for their whole careers. But when those who wish to ascend the corporate ladder have no way to do so with their current employers, they will leave. In fact, most employees tend to only see salary increases and upward job movement when they quit and go to work for another organization, which is a shame for two reasons. First, coworkers will notice their colleagues leaving for greener pastures and believe that the only way for them to succeed is to do the same. Second, departing employees carry a wealth of institutional knowledge that takes years to build and is invaluable to other companies just waiting to snatch up their competitors' malcontents. This accumulated knowledge of the organization and its history, processes, and inner workings cannot be easily replaced. Can you really blame employees for leaving, though? If they are not given clear expectations about when they will be promoted and do not have specific guidelines on how to get there, then they have no way of knowing if they will ever advance at their current employer.

It's not disloyalty when employees resign because they are not promoted; it is simple microeconomic strategy. Why should an employee remain blindly loyal to a company that does not reward or recognize her skills, contributions, and achievements when she could realize greater earnings and career growth with the next highest bidder? Adherents of the Stepford Employee Fallacy believe workers will show unwavering loyalty and active engagement when they are stuck in the same dead-end jobs for years with no hope of ever receiving a meaningful promotion.

Promotions are, indeed, critical to employee engagement, but I'm not suggesting that every employee can or should be promoted. On the contrary, I believe there are some who should not be promoted into certain roles, specifically management positions. Organizations typically justify promotions on the basis of either merit or tenure. However, neither necessarily guarantees that someone is capable of engaging leadership. A competent individual contributor might have the technical skills to be considered more than proficient in his role, but that does not mean he has the soft skills—like empathy, curiosity, and humility—to be the kind of leader who inspires true engagement. Be very careful about promoting people to management positions, and watch them like a hawk if you receive any complaints about them. If employees witness that type of person being rewarded with a fancy title and going on to treat his staff poorly, then they will think the promotion process at your organization is rigged against people who really deserve to make it.

When employees can see that their leaders worked hard to get to where they are and know that it is realistic for them to someday reach that same level of professional fulfillment, they will engage as partners in action and as agents of their own career development. In order for both to occur, leaders and HR need to create a comprehensive and employee-focused talent management strategy, one that promises bright and fulfilling careers as a sign of loyalty to their employees.

A few years ago, I was doing some work in a Boston high-rise cafe when I started eavesdropping on a conversation between a young employee and an older gentleman who appeared to be his supervisor. The employee was listening intently and jotting down notes while his supervisor dispensed some of the most tired and clichéd career advise I'd ever heard. It was clear that the employee had asked for this meeting to learn how he could get a promotion, and his supervisor's guidance over the course of their fifteen-minute conversation amounted to the following: "Keep your nose to the grindstone, come in early, stay late, and that's how you'll get ahead." At that, the supervisor glanced at his watch, stood up, and announced that he had to run to another meeting, leaving the bewildered young man adrift with no clear plan or timetable for getting promoted. My heart went out to him, because I had heard similar counsel given by managers in organizations where promotion was a mysterious and excruciatingly long process. At one company, we had a pretty dark joke that you would only be promoted if someone retired or died. Organizations that mismanage talent development are not just doing a disservice to employees; they are planting seeds of frustration that will eventually grow into disengagement.

CASE STUDY

ENTERPRISE RENT-A-CAR

These days it seems as though career advancement at the same company is out of reach for many aspiring professionals. The career ladder no longer exists in the majority of organizations, which frustrates employees who want to advance without having to deal with the hassle of interviewing somewhere else. When they do move on—if they manage to find an opportunity—they are seen as disloyal, but their employers have no career development strategy in place to retain them. It's a self-sustaining problem. For Enterprise Rent-A-Car, however, that is not the case. As the largest vehicle rental company in the United States, Enterprise has maintained a tight grip on top talent with a comprehensive, highly structured career development program that many competitors within and outside the industry cannot match.

Nearly every entry-level Enterprise recruit is hired into the company's management training program, which is an eight-to-twelve-month training experience that prepares new employees for long-term career progression with specific milestones and support along the way.[7] Each management trainee gains exposure to the myriad business facets of running an Enterprise branch, from marketing and fleet maintenance, to customer service and budget management. This practical learning strategy benefits the company with higher engagement and retention because employees are given a clear, predetermined path for career success as future leaders.

If management trainees meet their goals, they can expect a promotion to the next level of management assistant within a few months. They are then promoted to assistant manager and, with hard work and dedication, can come to manage their own branch not long after first being hired. From there, they are able to apply for leadership positions in sales, the Commercial Truck division, or continue on their rental path in area, group, and regional management roles. It is a representation of the company's firm commitment to a promote-from-within philosophy. In 2015, Enterprise promoted nearly fifteen thousand of its employees, roughly 16 percent of its workforce[8]—almost twice the average promotion rate in the United States. That is definite evidence of a company that values talent and is willing to help them grow in their careers.

There is probably no better person to epitomize a culture of internal promotion than a CEO who started with the company in an entry-level role and worked her way to the top. And that's just what happened with Enterprise's President and CEO Pamela Nicholson. She joined the company as a management trainee in 1981. Nine months after her hire, she was promoted to assistant manager of a branch in St. Louis. She then moved to California to help grow the company's business in Southern California.

Eventually, she was promoted to be the regional vice president, overseeing all SoCal. operations before returning to St. Louis as the corporate vice president at Enterprise global headquarters. After a two-year stint running operations in New York, Enterprise's second-largest market, Nicholson came back again to St. Louis and was named president and COO in 2008. In 2013, she became the CEO of Enterprise Holdings.

Nicholson credits the promote-from-within culture for not only her rise through the ranks, but many on her executive team as well.[9] It's not uncommon for senior management to have tenures spanning more than two decades with the organization. This kind of talent management practice sends an encouraging message to the entire workforce: Employees can be assured that their leaders went through the same management training program that they did, and someday they can look back with the same level of accomplishment.

Acting in your own interest might get you promoted at other organizations, but not at Enterprise Rent-A-Car. There, managers are promoted mainly on the basis of their proficiency at developing and training their own direct reports. It's not about how much money they saved with a new program they created or how well their branches did compared to others. Enterprise measures its leaders by how many more leaders they nurture and develop. Managers, especially those managing new employees, are expected to work very closely with their teams in teaching them the skills they need to be effective in their roles and progress to the next level. Their training methodology follows a proprietary system called SOS Training.[10] SOS stands for show, observe, and shape. First, the manager shows employees how to execute a certain task while also explaining the reason why Enterprise does it that way. Next, he or she observes the employees applying their knowledge and then offers immediate feedback on any areas that need improvement.

Promoting from within requires a qualified bench of available talent, which is why Enterprise targets candidates to fill spots in its management training program in order to prepare them for a future with the company. In terms of talent acquisition, Enterprise recruits heavily from colleges for entry-level management trainee positions. The company works with a variety of networks serving African Americans, Latinos/as, and former college athletes to attract young talent from diverse backgrounds. In 2014, the Talent Acquisition team sourced and hired about eighty-five hundred college graduates into management trainee roles.[11] That explains why those positions represent the majority of ERAC jobs posted on job boards like Monster and Indeed. You'll see few other types of jobs available, and that's because Enterprise fills higher-level positions internally. They really do walk the talk when it comes to their promote-from-within philosophy that started with the company's founding in 1957 and continues to this day.

LOOKING AHEAD

As we wrap up our examination of the beliefs that constitute the Stepford Employee Fallacy, it's fitting to end on the topic of loyalty. Without organic loyalty, there cannot be real engagement. All of the behaviors that define employee engagement stem from a sense of loyalty toward one's employer. Each belief in the Stepford Employee Fallacy represents a way in which employers drive their employees to disengage, whether that manifests via withholding discretionary effort, speaking negatively about the organization, or showing contempt for management. Loyalty is not fixed or durable. It is fragile, like glass. Once shattered, it becomes something sharp and jagged, cutting whoever foolishly and callously broke it. Engagement requires an employee experience that takes great care in shaping and preserving the loyalty of your workforce.

Part III begins with another myth about employee engagement: it is a two-way street. This premise turns engagement into a transaction, which only corrupts its true meaning. In Chapter 11, we will delve into the process of creating a phenomenal employee experience, which is far more effective than the commonly accepted *quid pro quo* engagement model. At the beginning of this chapter, we talked about the inherent reciprocity of loyalty. That's different from the transactional view of employee engagement for reasons we will see in the coming pages. How is loyalty earned from employees and how does that loyalty turn into engagement? The answer takes a bit of explanation, but it will give you a clear view of what true engagement looks like, as well as the knowledge to apply this new paradigm in your own organization. Engagement is possible anywhere. It just requires dedicated effort and openness to change. Having read this far, you can probably guess that I'm not referring to employees here. Leaders, this is where your real work begins.

NOTES

1. Boushey, Heather and Glynn, Sarah Jane. Center for American Progress. *There Are Significant Business Costs to Replacing Employees.* November 16, 2012. https://www.americanprogress.org/wp-content/uploads/2012/11/CostofTurnover.pdf

2. "Trial of Jimmy John's Bosses for Mass Firing of Whistleblower Workers Begins Today: Organizers Vow to Continue Fight for Change at Poverty-Wage Corporate Chains." *Industrial Workers of the World.* February 14, 2012. https://www.iww.org/cs/content/trial-jimmy-johns-bosses-mass-firing-whistleblower-workers-begins-today-organizers-vow-conti

3. MikLin Enterprises, Inc., d/b/a Jimmy John's v. National Labor Relations Board. 14-3211. United States Court of Appeals for the Eighth Circuit. 2016. *Labor Relations Today.* July 3, 2017. https://laborrelationstoday.lexblogplatformthree.com/wp-content/uploads/sites/312/2017/07/NLRB-Jimmy-Johns-Appeal-070317.pdf

4. DIRECTV, Inc. v. National Labor Relations Board. 11-1273. United States Court of Appeals, District of Columbia Circuit. 2016. *FindLaw.* Retrieved January 10, 2018. http://caselaw.findlaw.com/us-dc-circuit/1748332.html

5. Lieberman, Matthew. "Social: Why Our Brains Are Wired to Connect." New York: *Broadway Books.* 2014.

6. WorldatWork. Promotional Guidelines *Survey.* September 2016. https://www.worldatwork.org/adimLink?id=80657

7. Winter-Hercher, Amy. "Understanding Enterprise's Millennial Strategy." *Auto Rental News.* January 29, 2016. http://www.autorentalnews.com/channel/rental-operations/article/story/2016/01/understanding-enterprise-s-millennial-strategy.aspx

8. "Training Program Drives Promote-From-Within Philosophy at Car Rental Company." *HR Daily Advisor.* January 26, 2017. http://hrdailyadvisor.blr.com/2017/01/26/training-program-drives-promote-within-philosophy-car-rental-company/

9. Enterprise Rent-a-Car. "Moving up with Enterprise: Our Promote-from-Within Philosophy." Retrieved January 10, 2018. https://go.enterpriseholdings.com/moving-up-with-enterprise/

10. "World's Largest Car Rental Company Earns Accolades for Training and Development." *PR Newswire*. February 3, 2016. https://www.prnewswire.com/news-releases/worlds-largest-car-rental-company-earns-accolades-for-training-and-development-300214586.html

11. Suzono, Melissa. "How Enterprise Recruits and Develops Diverse New Grad Talent." *After College*. October 15, 2014. http://employer.aftercollege.com/enterprise-recruits-develops-diverse-new-grad-talent/

PART III

THE REALITY OF EMPLOYEE ENGAGEMENT

An ancient Hindu parable tells the story of three blind men who came across a strange animal none of them had ever encountered before: an elephant. Each touched a part of the elephant in an effort to describe the beast to his friends. The first man ran his hand along the elephant's trunk and declared that the mysterious animal must resemble a snake. The second took hold of the elephant's tail and said it was more like a rope. Finally, the third man touched the elephant's leg and told the other two he was certain this creature was shaped like a tree. Of course, the elephant looked like, well, an elephant. But, to the men in the story, it was something different based on their experience. Their interpretation of reality wasn't necessarily incorrect because reality, for them, was subjective.

Speaking of four-legged beasts, I happen to love dogs. Whenever I go to a social gathering at someone's house and they have a dog, I usually find myself spending at least as much time with the dog as I do with the other partygoers. But, for one of my friends, the experience is a little different. He's allergic to dogs, you see. If he spends too much time around them his eyes begin to itch terribly, and the party turns into an uncomfortable experience for him. It's not that he dislikes dogs. His experience with them is simply different from mine. Dog lovers could try to make an argument that their canine buddies are objectively fun to be around, but that isn't the case for everyone. For some, their reality diverges from the reality of others, and that is something that cannot be dismissed or ignored however convenient it might be to do so.

So, what do elephants and dogs have to do with employee engagement? When we talk about employee experience as either the stimulant or the inhibitor of employee engagement, we are referring to the subjective reality of working for a particular organization. This is where business leaders fail to see the impact that employee experience has on engagement levels. They are blind to the fact that employees could be experiencing reality quite differently than they are, even though they work within the same organization. And that subjective reality is what determines the intensity and sustainability of employee engagement there. In order to engage employees, leaders have to understand their reality and empathize with them. One of the most fundamental and unalterable aspects of human nature is our need to be understood in spite of our differences or the reality of our experience.

Part III centers on the importance of understanding employees and the realities they face under your leadership. In Chapter 11, we will study the flawed reciprocal model of employee engagement and discuss why it is not supported by the actual mechanics of how engagement really works. We will also look at the process of creating an engaging employee experience through feedback and why this model is so dissimilar to the way workplaces currently operate. Leaders today often have a distorted view of how their organizations operate for a number of reasons. First, they are focused on bigger picture concerns like market forces and shareholder satisfaction, and they are more attuned to these factors than to their employees' experiences. They are not involved in or exposed to the minutiae of doing business, so it is difficult for them to perceive reality at lower levels of the organization. The second reason leaders cannot see the reality of employee engagement is employees do not openly share feedback about their experience at work. Either they are punished for criticizing the company and its managers, or their concerns fall on deaf ears, so no change happens. Employees learn that there isn't any point in giving feedback, no matter what the reality of their experience happens to be, whether that is abusive management, ineffective tools, an unbearable workload, or substandard work conditions.

Listening to employees is an important step toward understanding them, but leaders need to actually care in order to meaningfully engage them. That is where the critical skill of empathy comes in. Chapter 12 covers empathy from both a natural and a business standpoint. It also explains why the modern workplace is seemingly devoid of empathy and offers suggestions for ways leaders can become more empathetic (and thus, more engaging). Finally, Chapter 13 presents true stories from the modern workplace to underscore a point that has been made throughout this book: employees are real people, not just human capital, and certainly not robots. These stories will hopefully give you an appreciation for what employees face today, and how their engagement indeed reflects their reality.

We humans tend to think of reality as fixed and immutable. An elephant is an elephant and a job is a job. We cannot change an elephant into something it isn't, no matter how strongly we believe our own reality. Similarly, our feelings about work do not change the fact that there is a job to be done. However, our perceptions and experiences mean reality is different for each of us. What if one of the blind men from the Hindu parable were nearly crushed by the elephant after he pulled on its tail? The elephant would have become a source of pain and fear for him, shaping the reality of his experience with it. Now think back over the employee experiences detailed throughout this book: the employees who were punished for having miscarriages or cancer or life-threatening injuries, who had to choose between caring for loved ones and keeping their jobs, who had to soil themselves because they weren't allowed bathroom breaks, who were sexually harassed and then bullied for speaking out, and whose unbearable workloads drove them to suicide.

Although one cannot expect to significantly change the behavior of an angry twelve-thousand-pound pachyderm, leaders do have control over the employee experience they create or allow within their organizations. That is the reality of employee engagement. It requires intervention from leaders to transform the reality of what it is like to work in their organizations.

In reality, a pile of wood is just that. It does not become a brilliant fire until someone kindles it. Leaders have the same power over employee engagement. They can leave it alone and expect employees to engage themselves. Or they can ignite it. Once it's lit, they can either stoke it or smother it. Decisions you make as a leader determine the reality of your team's employee experience and, as a result, whether or not they are engaged.

CHAPTER 11

EMPLOYEE ENGAGEMENT IS NOT A TWO-WAY STREET

A relationship is often described as a two-way street. Both parties engage in a fair and equal exchange in order to sustain the relationship while drawing mutual benefit from it. Business leaders tend to think of employment relationships in this conditional sense. An employer pays its employees wages in return for their labor. It's a simple economic exchange that reflects a transactional view of relationships as two-way streets, each side giving and taking. The *quid pro quo* model holds up until the concept of employee engagement is introduced into the mix.

Leaders who hope to capture the holy grail of employee engagement, discretionary effort, but still view the relationship as a two-way street will find it nearly impossible to engage their employees. That's because employee engagement requires employees to feel *inspired* rather than obligated. Engagement happens when an employer creates a work experience that's inspirational for employees. If leaders were to apply the conditional relationship approach to their employee engagement strategy, they would gain no traction at all. Here's how it would look in practice:

> We'll pay you a fair wage, but only if you work extra hard to earn it.
>
> We'll promote work-life balance, but only if your life is balanced in favor of the organization.
>
> We'll inspire you with a clear vision for our company's success, but only if you agree to never question us or tell us what we need to change.
>
> We'll treat you like a competent and trustworthy adult, but only if you conform to our ideal of how employees should think and work.

We'll give you the tools you need to do your job, but only if you generate a substantial return on our investment.

We'll support your career and personal development, but only if you give us your unqualified loyalty.

We'll recognize and reward your efforts, but only if you consistently exceed our unrealistic expectations for performance.

There's nothing inspirational about working for an employer who turns the most basic elements of a positive employee experience into a series of transactions. Employees won't want to go above and beyond for leaders who will only treat them well if the company's needs are met first. If you wait for your employees to engage themselves and you refuse to take any further steps toward bettering their employee experience until they do, then you're going to be wasting a lot of time just trying to make a point. Again, these are the elementary building blocks of employee experience we're talking about here, not the coolest and fanciest perks that are normally associated with engagement. They are nonnegotiable and should be unconditional.

Now look back over those seven statements again. What if each condition after the stated action were replaced with something else that conveyed a spirit of altruism and camaraderie? For example, consider if a leader were to say "We'll recognize and reward your efforts because we want you to feel inspired and proud working here. We want you to help us make this an amazing place to work, and to let us know how we can get even better." You see, employee engagement isn't transactional. It's inspirational. It's a virtuous circle that begins and ends with leadership.

THE VIRTUOUS CIRCLE OF EMPLOYEE ENGAGEMENT

Leaders set the tone and strategy for their organization, hire the best people for the right roles, treat them well, give them the tools and support to develop and become leaders in their own right, and the cycle continues. Employees feel inspired to go above and beyond for an organization that cares about them, and they provide honest feedback along the way for areas needing improvement. Leaders then implement changes to create a more engaging employee experience. Therein lies the unique nature of engaging employment relationships. Leaders need employees to be committed to the organization, but they must continually earn and build that commitment with a great work experience. The quality of that experience is predicated on leaders' openness to improve it based on feedback from employees. This is where many people get confused with the employee engagement concept. They insist that employees are responsible for engaging themselves, or, at the very least, that is a matter of give and take. If there is anything I have proven in the preceding chapters, it's that this couldn't be further from the truth.

Leaders are the ones who have the power and wherewithal to shape the employee experience in their organizations. They control money for training, staffing, compensation, technology, leadership development, and other areas that directly affect what it's like for employees to work for them. They establish the cultural tone within their organizations either through their direct actions or their tacit approval of others' actions. Leaders have control over every step within the Virtuous Circle of Employee Engagement and are therefore responsible for not breaking it. A breakdown at any point in the circle can negatively impact employee experience and provoke disengagement.

Engaging Purpose

The first step in the Virtuous Circle is formulating the organization's Engaging Purpose. Simon Sinek's popular TEDTalk, *How Great Leaders Inspire Action*, challenged leaders to look at their organization's mission not through the lens of what they do but why they do it.[1] Disney doesn't just make movies and sell theme park tickets. Its employees create magical moments because Walt Disney believed in the power of imagination, and his company continues to capture imaginations around the world with that guiding principle. Starbucks doesn't just sell coffee. It believes in making a positive difference for the customers and communities it serves through a love of coffee. This extends far beyond a mission statement that is painted on the wall of a company's main office. It is the very essence of a company's existence, its purpose.

Recall our discussion of meaning in the workplace and its impact on engagement. Meaningful work starts with an understanding of why an organization does what it does and how employees' efforts connect with that reason for doing business. It is the vision for what the organization is, where it is going, and why. With the Engaging Purpose clearly visualized, ask employees if they understand what it means, if they understand how their work is in alignment with it, and if it even makes sense based on what they know to be true about their area of the organization. Think back to our prior discussions of meaning and brand ambassadorship as they relate to employee engagement. Employees who find meaning in your organization's Engaging Purpose will speak positively about their work experience, which can help you attract the best talent and continue to refine *what* you do because *why* you do it is so engaging.

Engaging Talent Management

Next is talent management. Once you've established your Engaging Purpose, you need to staff your organization with people who have a passion for what you do. I've said all along that employees don't engage themselves, and that is still true. Having a passion for one's vocation is not the same as engagement. It does, however, make engagement easier to sustain. That's why the hiring process is so critical. When you bring people on board and they have little to no interest in the work they will be doing, it becomes almost impossible to fully engage them.

Hiring in your organization should be a thoughtful, streamlined activity based upon generally accepted standards for determining a candidate's fit for a particular role and for the organization itself. This is where leaders will need the input and expertise of their partners in Human Resources who can advise on best practices and market trends. For years,

HR has been warning that the hiring process in the modern workplace is broken, that it takes far too long and they do not have the capacity to effectively assess applicants. Companies have installed barriers to Engaging Talent Management in the form of archaic applicant tracking systems and endless bureaucratic red tape. They relegate the recruiting function to a necessary headache along the way toward getting warm bodies in chairs. This creates a painfully drawn-out candidate experience that deters passionate talent and results in far too many bad hires. Notice I said "bad hire" and not "bad employee" there. Yes, I put the blame for an employee failing in his or her role on the organization and its leaders because, somewhere along the line, there was a breakdown in the talent management process.

Recruiting, interviewing, and onboarding should give prospective employees a feel for what it would be like to work at your organization, and it should treat them like they are valued every step of the way. A great candidate experience is the preview to a phenomenal employee experience. Ask candidates, employees, and HR staff for their thoughts on the hiring process and where more attention or resources are needed. The better your hiring and onboarding processes are, the more likely you are to recruit top talent who will become partners in action. This is where you perfect your employee value proposition for new and existing talent.

Engaging Employee Experience

The third step on the Virtuous Circle represents the bulk of work leaders must do to engage employees: the employee experience. We've previously discussed what employee experience is and what elements of the organization's existence encompass it. As I stated earlier in this chapter, every piece of a company's employee experience is under the control of its leaders, from the technology workers use to the kind of supervisors they have. This step is where leaders can choose to drop every belief from the Stepford Employee Fallacy and co-create an exceptionally Engaging Employee Experience with their talent. I want to carefully explain the concept of co-creation here because it can be confusing for those unfamiliar with it and because it is misused by others who subscribe to the Stepford Employee Fallacy. Co-creating an employee experience does not mean employees simply decide to make the best of whatever their circumstances at work happen to be. It also does not mean allowing a free-for-all work environment without rules, expectations, goals, or standards. It specifically entails the feedback mechanism, which is present in the other two steps of the Virtuous Circle, but is most vital with employee experience.

Market-leading companies develop products and services with customers' input, so it is the same with employees. Consumer feedback is invaluable to these organizations in their efforts to shape a winning customer experience. Employers of choice take a similar approach to ensuring the experience of working for them is inspirational and engaging. Don't worry if you only have a modest budget to improve areas of your employee experience, because there is one particular area that has the greatest impact on engagement and it costs nothing to enhance: leadership.

Indeed, leadership is the force that keeps the Virtuous Circle of Employee Engagement in motion. It enables and empowers, rouses and compels. We've covered in great detail the influence Engaging Leadership has on the quality of employees' work experience, and this piece of the Virtuous Circle serves as the culmination of those points. Further, organizations with an Engaging Employee Experience will nurture and support employees toward becoming leaders, themselves. The next generation of engaged leaders proceed to hone and carry on with the organization's purpose, thus completing the Circle and starting the cycle anew.

Figure 11.1: The Virtuous Circle of Employee Engagement

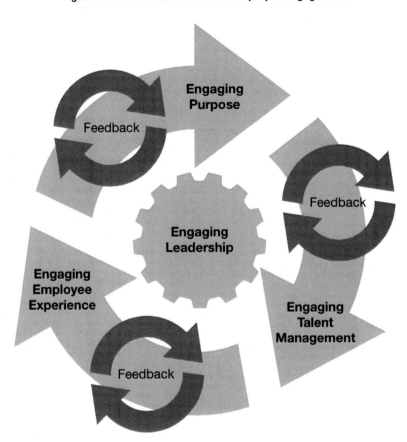

FEEDBACK IS A GIFT

I specifically chose to describe employee engagement using this model because of the nature of virtuous circles. They are concentric, continuous feedback loops that reinforce positive outcomes. Here, the outcome is employee engagement. At each step along the Virtuous Circle of Employee Engagement, leaders seek feedback from employees about their experience working in the organization or their recommendations for what the company can do better, and then they act on it. Most organizations today go through the exercise of administering annual satisfaction surveys to give the impression that they value their employees' thoughts. This is not an effective method for eliciting feedback and it does not fit into the kind of meaningful engagement strategy we are talking about here. Why? Because employees have no faith in it and managers do not act on it.

Nearly half of employees believe annual surveys have little to no value. About 80 percent of employees believe their managers will not act on the survey results. Neither of these statistics should seem very surprising given that over 50 percent of managers report that they review survey results, but take no action. Worse, more than a quarter of managers never even look at the results.[2] Also consider that employees in toxic, fear-driven work environments are hesitant to provide honest answers, which corrupts survey data with biased responses and a lower response rate. A tool as useless and infrequent as a yearly employee survey is a poor substitute for the robust culture of genuine, welcome feedback needed to stoke engagement within an organization.

Feedback is how we learn and grow when we might be blind to aspects of ourselves that are preventing us from being the best professionals we can be. It's like a magnifying mirror to give us a closer, often uncomfortable, but definitely necessary view of our imperfections. Managers and HR professionals gladly hold a feedback mirror up to their employees' faces, but when employees turn the mirror around, things can get ugly. Unfortunately, the modern workplace is not one where workers can safely share candid feedback or constructive criticism about their employee experience or the organization itself. I personally learned this lesson the hard way.

About a year into my first full-time job out of college, I decided to go back to school and get my master's degree. The curriculum dovetailed perfectly with my passion for employee engagement, and I couldn't wait to apply everything I learned about engaging employees through great leadership. The final course in the program was an action research project. Students had to work with their employers to identify a problem or need within the organization, research it, and develop viable solutions. I chose a topic I was pretty familiar with: engaging millennials. Specifically, I wanted to determine why employees from this age group were leaving the company and driving turnover costs. I reached out to my HR business partner to tell him and his manager about the project, how I planned to research the problem, and asked for their guidance. I told them that I planned to survey and interview current employees, then use my findings to lay out what was causing millennial attrition. They seemed enthusiastic about helping me . . . until they read my report that showed the company had some aspects of its employee experience in need of improvement.

Even though I was completely forthcoming with HR, they decided I hadn't painted a flattering enough picture of the organization. So they called me into a meeting while I was on vacation putting the finishing touches on the project. I should have known how the meeting was going to go when the HR manager grabbed a box of tissues before inviting me into her office. In short, they blackmailed me into abandoning the project altogether by threatening termination and a subsequent lawsuit unless I gave in to their demands. I'll never forget the phony look of pity on the HR manager's face when I angrily asked what exactly I was supposed to do after they initially gave me their blessing and I had all but finished the thesis. "That's on you," she flatly replied. It was a Sophie's choice: lose my job and possibly be sued, or fail the final course in a master's program that I had worked my ass off to complete.

But they didn't stop there. HR contacted my school to tell them what happened and to ensure I wouldn't just turn in the project anyway. Fortunately, the administration and faculty were on my side and couldn't have been more supportive. The dean told me she was shocked by the company's actions and my professor was none-too-thrilled by what they did to me, either. They allowed me to choose another research topic and offered to give me an extension for completing the course. Still, it meant throwing out all of the work I had done on the original project and starting over from scratch. Facing a much more powerful adversary, I acquiesced. I then had two weeks to finish a completely different project. Except, you can't finish a master's thesis in two weeks. Through sheer determination and willpower I managed to do just that with the help of family and friends who served as research participants. I even turned in the paper on time and received an A- in the course. A few weeks later, I graduated with honors. I left that company the following year and went on to work for a competitor.

When employees work in an environment that discourages the sharing of bottom-up feedback, they usually suffer in silence, slowly becoming disengaged from the organization's goals and objectives. Or they eventually throw caution to the wind and let their superiors know exactly what they think. That's what one retiring Pennsylvania Turnpike Commission employee did when he sent his exit interview responses to literally everyone in the organization.[3] In a nutshell, this employee completed his exit interview in the form of a survey and had some pretty blunt feedback on the state of the PTC. Rather than send his responses to Human Resources, he e-mailed them to everyone who worked at the Turnpike Commission, including the chairman. Not long after the newly retired worker clicked the Send button, the chairman replied with an e-mail of his own (also sent to every Turnpike employee) which read in part: "I don't believe we ever met, and after reading your Exit Questionnaire, I am grateful that we didn't . . . Best of luck in your retirement." The chairman followed up on his response with comments to the media, refuting the points raised in the exit survey.

Let's first address the commissioner's immediate e-mail response. It was a dismissive, impulsive mistake of a message wrapped in fake well wishes. The commissioner labeled the employee's exit interview as "disingenuous," but there are few things *less* genuine than wishing someone well after telling him you're glad the two of you never met. He was upset with the retiring worker's feedback, and his decision to 'Reply All' with this response just made him look arrogant and defensive in front of the remaining two thousand employees. Clearly the commissioner took issue with the fact that this employee felt it was necessary to e-mail his exit survey to every employee in the Turnpike Commission. He claimed there would have been a better way to deliver this feedback than sending a mass e-mail laying out the organization's deficiencies. Here's the thing: employees who take this kind of action are fed up and know full-well that quietly delivering constructive feedback to management would, at best, be an effort in futility. This employee worked at the Turnpike Commission for thirty-five years, so he was aware of the political land mines he might detonate simply by telling the truth. The commissioner's stonewalling to the media clearly indicates what he would have done with this worker's feedback if it were given in a different forum: nothing.

The commissioner also tried to shoot down the employee's claims that senior leadership was "out of touch" while at the same time patting himself on the back for having such hands-on, communicative managers. Now, of course we don't know the details of how the Pennsylvania Turnpike Commission is run. But if it's like any other large organization, the upper echelon probably makes all kinds of decisions that negatively affect their workers because they are too far-removed from the work that's being done. They surely don't want to admit they're wrong, so any dissent is likely to be squashed right quick. Based on the many examples of disengaging leadership cited throughout this book, it's safe to assume that the reason this employee sent his negative feedback to everybody working at the Turnpike Commission was because he knew it would have been ignored or even punished if given any other way. The commissioner and his leadership team seemingly brought this on themselves, just as leaders in plenty of other organizations foster a culture where employees are afraid to speak truthfully about how they feel until the moment they're walking out the door.

When faced with such a jarring feedback dump from an obviously disengaged employee, leaders have a choice: they can either grow defensive and learn nothing from the experience, or they can consider it a wake up-call that gives them the chance to improve the way honest communication takes place within their organizations. If something like this happens in your organization, it is a sign that the feedback mechanism in your Virtuous Circle of Employee Engagement is broken. You cannot expect your employees to be engaged when you won't listen to them. The Pennsylvania Turnpike commissioner should have sent an e-mail to every employee explaining that he is going to ensure the culture at PTC allows for open and honest communication throughout all layers of the organization. He should have conveyed the expectation that all managers will encourage employees to give feedback on how they can be better leaders, what in the organization isn't working, or how their work experience could be improved. Finally, it should have been explicitly stated that any manager who retaliates against an employee for telling the truth will face discipline up to and including termination. That's how serious you need to be about creating a culture where employees feel safe enough to give feedback and feel confident that their leaders will hear what they have to say.

If you give your employees a reason to think that their feedback doesn't matter, then you won't just have a morale problem on your hands. One need only look at what happened with the Columbia space shuttle disaster back in 2003, a well-known and tragically grim example of what happens when employee feedback is rejected. A NASA engineer tried to alert his superiors to safety issues with the shuttle, and their refusal to heed his warnings resulted in the deaths of all astronauts aboard the Columbia when it disintegrated upon reentry.[4] This is an extreme scenario, but it illustrates that there can be serious consequences for disregarding employee feedback.

How do leaders foster a culture of feedback in their organizations? You'll recall our discussion of curiosity and humility from Chapter 7. These leadership attitudes should be instilled and required at all levels of management. Curious and humble leaders are receptive to feedback from their employees. But employees need to be comfortable and willing to share feedback in the first place. This is where the power of trust comes into play. As social creatures, human beings will feel a sense of trust and community among those with whom they have built positive, mutually respectful relationships. Trust plays a critical role in social interaction between parties who exchange information that could be perceived as sensitive or relevant to one or both of them. Feedback would definitely fall under this description.

Employees don't trust leaders unless they have proven themselves to be trustworthy. Yet, throughout this book, we've seen example after example of leadership behaviors, decisions, and interactions that undermined employee trust and broke the Virtuous Circle. From Wells Fargo throwing employees under the bus, to Walmart punishing employees for getting sick, to Volkswagen ignoring engineers' warnings, to Tyson Foods not letting employees take bathroom breaks, these organizations (allegedly) made terrible mistakes that created distrust and disengagement among their workers. There's one final piece to the trust equation, and it is absolutely the most important: empathy. I have saved the topic of empathy for its own chapter because it is hugely crucial, so we will learn about the relationship between engagement and empathy in Chapter 12. But as far as trust goes, relating to employees as human beings and putting yourself in their shoes can lay the groundwork for a relationship that encourages the sharing of candid feedback.

You're probably familiar with the practice of having an open door policy when it comes to fostering relationships with employees. The idea is to make yourself available for employees to approach you with feedback or concerns about matters related to their work experience. While this has become a fairly typical management trope, it does not guarantee that any conversations will yield effectual or even positive outcomes. At best, the feedback is ignored. At worst, the messenger gets shot, as we've seen in our earlier examples. This ends up discouraging employees from bothering to share their two cents going forward, leaving the organization shortchanged and leaders unaware of key information.

Some practitioners recommend that not all employee feedback should be given the same weight, that leaders should only listen to a select few who they deem to be engaged, accountable high performers at certain levels of the organization. During a chat with a colleague about an upcoming client engagement with a small community bank, I mentioned my intent to conduct focus groups at each branch office so I could get a pulse on the level of engagement from those working closest with customers. My colleague, an HR executive, told me I shouldn't really waste too much time talking with the bank tellers because they are low-level employees who usually have no prior work experience, the implication being that their feedback carried no worth. I was stunned by his suggestion. Shutting down the dialogue—or even the opportunity for dialogue—with employees is highly detrimental to engagement. It doesn't force employees to sit back and wonder whether their feedback is worth sharing, nor does it make the feedback from the sycophants and superstars any more valuable. All it does is disengage real people in your organization from becoming your partners in action. Positive relationships with employees require leaders to have more than open doors; they must have open *minds*.

LOOKING AHEAD

Imagine going out to dinner for your birthday with your spouse. At the end of the meal, he or she hands you a small wrapped box that you open to discover a very expensive watch. You're delighted, but before you can say anything, your spouse says, "I bought you this watch, so I expect you to buy me a new car for my birthday, or else I'm divorcing you." Such an astonishing statement would probably cheapen the gift's significance and make you question whether you wanted to stay married to someone who treats your relationship like a series of transactions.

Although employment relationships are very different from those of the romantic variety—they more closely mirror the relationship between a company and its customers—the basic premise of reciprocity relies on genuine feelings of inspiration and admiration, not obligation. Employee engagement is not a two-way street in the same way that a marriage is not a cold, transactional arrangement. As with a successful marriage, employee engagement takes care and communication, but the difference lies in the onus for engagement being almost entirely on leaders. In the case of engagement, leaders open the lines of communication through continuous feedback about the organization, its employee value proposition, and its employee experience.

Care is not a word one thinks of when talking about business, but it means something specific in this context: empathy. There is a dearth of empathy in the modern workplace, and I believe that is the primary cause of any organization's employee engagement struggles. In Chapter 12, we will examine what it really means to be empathetic in an organizational setting, that it isn't a touchy-feely *kumbaya* notion, and that it is in fact the most important business skill leaders need to master in order to engage their employees. No matter what form a relationship takes, empathy is the force that connects both parties and inspires them to care for one another. The best employers understand this axiom of human behavior and use it to formulate a winning engagement strategy.

NOTES

1. Sinek, Simon. "How Great Leaders Inspire Action" (Lecture) TEDxPugetSount. September 2009. https://www.ted.com/talks/ simon_sinek_how_great_leaders_inspire_action

2. Fermin, Jeff. "12 Mind-Blowing Employee Survey Statistics." (Blog). *Office Vibe*. September 9, 2014. https://www.officevibe.com/blog/ employee-surveys-infographic

3. Murphy, Jan. "Turnpike Chairman Put off by Retiring Employee's Widely-Shared Exit Questionnaire." *Penn Live*. December 5, 2016. http://www. pennlive.com/politics/index.ssf/2016/12/turnpike_chairman_put_off_by_r.html

4. *Beaumont, Peter. "NASA Chiefs 'Repeatedly Ignored' Safety Warnings." The Guardian. February 2, 2003. https://www.theguardian.com/science/2003/feb/02/ spaceexploration.usnews3*

CHAPTER 12

AN ENGAGEMENT DRIVER ALL GREAT WORKPLACES HAVE IN COMMON

People often confuse the terms sympathy and empathy. That's understandable given that both involve emotions, and, for many, emotion is an uncomfortable topic, particularly in the workplace. Sympathy refers to one's ability to feel sorrow for another's misfortune, whereas empathy is the act of imagining one's self in another's emotional, psychological, or somatic condition in order to understand what they are feeling. For some highly sensitive people, empathy means literally feeling the emotions or sensations of others. Still, it's difficult for many people to fully grasp the experience of being in another's position and tend to dismiss—or at least not fully appreciate—the other person's reality.

Take, for example, childbirth. For centuries, women have endured the painful miracle that is bringing life into the world while their mates stood by only partially understanding the pangs of birth as sympathetic observers. A recent social media trend helped to close the childbirth empathy gap when couples partook in the Childbirth Simulator Challenge on YouTube. Essentially, a woman would attach electrodes to her partner's abdominal muscles and switch on a device that used electrical currents to simulate the frequency and intensity of labor contractions. The men's reactions were, of course, hilarious, and they gained a clearer appreciation for what mothers go through.

Empathy is incredibly powerful because it forges a connection between parties who otherwise might not see eye to eye but rely on each other to accomplish a common objective. If that objective were, say, ensuring continued success and innovation for their organization, then that company's leaders would have to somehow inspire their employees to reach that goal. That's where the concept of employee engagement comes in. If leaders do not empathize with their employees and use that empathy to build an engaging culture, then they will have a workforce that merely goes through the motions instead of engaging as partners in action.

There has always been an understood tension between leaders and their employees, generally accepted as the essence of the employment relationship: labor versus management, worker bees versus those at the top, us versus them. It doesn't have to be that way, though. Effective leaders know how difficult it is to execute organizational goals if there is a constant feeling of distrust between managers and workers. The most forward-thinking leaders know that engagement is the key to fostering trust and inspiring their employees to perform. Unfortunately, the traditional "us versus them" work dichotomy, by its nature, is not conducive to an engaging culture in which employees would *want* to bring their A game on a consistent basis. But the power of empathy—putting yourself in your employees' shoes and then flexing your leadership interactions, behaviors, and decisions—is its ability to bridge the gap between leaders and their employees. Empathy builds a teamwork mindset among colleagues who mutually respect and trust one another, and work together toward achieving goals. This mindset is what enables and promotes engagement. It is something all the best organizations have in common.

DO YOU FEEL WHAT I FEEL? THE SCIENCE OF EMPATHY

As I've said many times in the preceding pages, employees are human beings. In order to understand and elicit engagement, leaders must first come to accept that fact and work within the parameters of the human condition, specifically the way people relate to one another. Humans are emotional creatures who determine how much of an investment they want to make in a particular aspect of their lives based on how it makes them feel. If they feel that they are treated well, then they will go above and beyond for their employer and its customers. That is the only way to secure true, sustainable engagement and, more importantly, how to prevent disengagement.

Empathizing with employees doesn't mean forgetting that you have a business to run. It means treating the people who run your business with the dignity, respect, compassion, and consideration that you would expect if you were in their exact same position. The problem is most leaders have lost touch with what it's like to *be* in that position, so their empathic facility is diminished. That's not to say people in management roles are incapable of empathy. They are also humans, after all. And all humans have a built-in mechanism for relating to each other. You can probably guess what that might be. Yes, again, we will look to that wonderful and complex bundle of neurons and gray matter in our heads: the brain.

In the 1990s, doctors from the University of Parma were studying the neurological activity of primates. They noticed the same neurons firing in the brains of macaque monkeys if they grabbed an object and saw another monkey perform the same action.[1] Each neuron was linked to a specific action. If a monkey ate a peanut, then the same neuron was triggered when the subject witnessed another monkey eat a peanut. The researchers coined the term "mirror neurons" to describe what they observed. Years later, using neuroimaging, the same researchers identified similar brain activity in humans. In one study, participants breathed in fetid odors and were then shown video of a person looking disgusted. In both scenarios olfactory neurons in the participants' brains fired. This was a breakthrough in terms of understanding why people seem to experience the feelings of others, at least to a certain degree. We are hard-wired with the neurological circuitry to be empathetic. It is interesting that the same brain activity occurs in our closest biological relatives, pointing to an evolutionary reason for this gift.

Our tribal ancestors relied on each other for survival in a dangerous and unpredictable world. They evolved with a sense of empathy to form connections and insure succession of the tribe. One could draw a parallel to organizations relying on their employees' engagement to ensure continued innovation and success in the business world. This research would suggest that leaders have the innate capability to empathize with employees, but, as we've seen, they are failing to do so. Further research offers a clue as to why this might be happening.

A 2013 study in the *Journal of Neuroscience* involved participants attempting to accurately gauge each other's feelings in a series of experiments.[2] Each subject was instructed to look at a screen with two images: one assigned to them and the second they were told was assigned to another participant. The images depicted either pleasant or unpleasant situations or things. In some scenarios, both images matched, while in others the images were discordant. Regardless of the scenario, participants were also instructed to put their hands into a box and touch something that corresponded to their assigned image: faux fur to go with an image of a bunny or rubber worms to mimic the feel of maggots.

After touching the object that represented their image, a participant was then asked to rate their level of comfort or discomfort on a ten-point scale, as well as estimate what the other participant felt vis-à-vis the second image on their screen. For example, a subject looking at images of a swan and a raw liver while touching a feather (to imitate the feel of a swan) would rate the level of discomfort he thought the subject touching toy slime (representing the liver) felt. Likewise, a subject looking at images of two swans would rate the level of comfort felt by the other participant who was also touching a feather. In the experiments with matching images, participants more accurately rated the feelings that their counterparts reported in their own scenarios. However, when the images were mismatched, subjects underrated their fellow participants' feelings.

To understand what was happening neurologically during these experiments, researchers scanned participants' brains using functional magnetic resonance imaging. In scenarios with mismatched images, the scans showed increased activity in an area of the brain called the right supra marginal gyrus (rSMG), which resides in what is called the mirror neuron system. Unsure as to exactly what neurological role this region played in the participants' ability to empathize with one another, researchers tried disrupting the rSMG using magnetic stimulation and then re-ran the experiments to see if the subjects were better or worse at empathizing. The results showed much poorer performance in each test scenario, proving that the rSMG serves as an empathy actuator in the human brain. Researchers learned another interesting property of this empathic function when they reduced the amount of time given for participants to assess each other's emotions. When rushed through the experiments, subjects performed just as poorly as they had with magnetic disruption of the rSMG. In other words, the less time they had to consider the feelings of their fellow participants, the less empathetic they were.

So, what do these findings tell us? What do they mean? The purpose of the study was to comprehend what is called egocentricity bias in the emotional domain. That's just a fancy way of saying the researchers wanted to understand the way we are selfish about our own emotions and mostly ignorant or uncaring about the feelings of others. When we are in a pleasant situation, it's difficult for us to fully grasp how someone in a not-so-enjoyable position might feel and, therefore, tend to trivialize whatever negative emotions that person is experiencing.

In a business context, this is seen with executives and managers who are so disconnected from the experience of being an employee that they cannot comprehend the plight of a disengaged workforce. From their positions of power and prosperity, leaders are, on the whole, numb to the damaging effects their decisions and behaviors have on the people who work for them. Compounding this desensitized leadership condition is the mercurial, hurried nature of the modern workplace. No one really has the time to stop and think about the needs or experiences of anyone but themselves, hindering their capacity for empathy. Nowadays, it's every man/woman for himself/herself. The rise of the gig economy is undoubtedly a direct response to the state of today's workplace wherein employees are treated like human capital instead of human beings. Given the levels of corporate apathy, exploitation, and relentless greed showcased throughout this book, it's no wonder workers have stepped away from long-term commitment and engagement to their employers and sought out opportunities for freelancing or consulting. This is bad news for organizations that rely on an engaged workforce to compete in their respective markets. Luckily, there is a business case to be made for raising the level of empathy in your talent strategy. Believe it or not, it actually pays to be more empathetic toward employees.

THE BUSINESS CASE FOR EMPATHY

When I first started my consulting business, I had a mentoring session with a senior HR executive to discuss my message and how I would differentiate myself from other practitioners. I talked about my passion for empathy and how I believe empathetic leadership is the key to employee engagement. My mentor expressed concern that business leaders would be turned off by an abstract, visceral concept like empathy. Her concerns were not unfounded. Empathy is not a topic that's given much consideration in the modern workplace or within the realm of business affairs. You certainly would not find reference to empathy anywhere in an MBA curriculum. Is there even a way to quantify the impact empathy can have on business results? It turns out that there is.

Since 2014, British-based think tank, The Empathy Business, has been studying businesses that epitomize true empathy in their dealings with employees and customers. The Empathy Business analyzed the CEO performance, cultural climate, ethical integrity, and brand perception of one hundred seventy global companies to compile their *Ethical Index* report.[3] Companies like LinkedIn, SAP, Southwest Airlines, Starbucks, and Whole Foods earned some of the highest empathy scores, with Facebook taking the top spot. The research methodology used to assess each company's empathy score measured financial performance and the number of ethical breaches (like fraud) as well as qualitative data in the form of social media commentary, Glassdoor reviews, and customer feedback. The findings make a compelling case for being more empathetic. The top ten companies with the highest empathy scores were 50 percent more profitable than those at the bottom of the list. Moreover, there was a strong correlation (80 percent) between high-performing employees and more empathetic work environments.

A survey by employee benefits technology firm Businessolver showed that there is a disconnect between leaders' assumptions about empathy in the workplace and employees' perceptions. Two-thirds of CEOs believe their organizations to be empathetic, whereas less than a quarter of their employees agree. Over 30 percent of employees think their managers value profits over people.[4] These are some pretty sobering statistics, especially after looking at how much better empathetic organizations perform in comparison to their cold, uncaring peers.

With everything we have covered about the nature of employee engagement in previous chapters, there is a strong argument to be made for a correlation between empathy and engagement. We can also safely conclude that a lack of empathy corresponds with higher levels of disengagement.

At the other end of the empathy spectrum lies the darker side of the human psyche, one characterized by egocentricity, selfishness, manipulative tendencies, grandiosity, and the need for control. Narcissists—true narcissists who exhibit the aforementioned personality traits and can be classified using the *Diagnostic and Statistical Manual of Mental Disorders*—all have a common psychopathic modus operandi in their dealings with other people: no empathy. It's frightening enough to know that there are psychopaths walking among us. Studies suggest 1 percent of the general population fit the DSM criteria for psychopathy. However, research points to a more disturbing statistic about the number of psychopaths in the upper strata of corporate hierarchy. Approximately one in five executives displays narcissistic and even psychopathic behaviors. That number is more in line with the percentage of psychopaths in the prison system.[5] The same callous disregard for humanity that causes violent criminal activity is what seems to be rewarded in the modern workplace. Cutthroat business tactics and a single-minded focus on the bottom line form the leadership creed of many top executives who believe employees are disposable pawns, and they, the exalted kings.

The competitive nature of business invites manipulation, coercion, self-centeredness, and cruelty from narcissistic managers whose ambitions for success and glory do produce notable financial results. Thus, their conduct is rewarded and reinforced, even though they are also the cause of disengagement in the workforce. Researchers from Florida State University studied the effects of narcissistic leadership on the work experiences of twelve hundred employees, and the results confirm a direct link between narcissism among leaders and disengagement among employees. Respondents in the study who worked for narcissistic bosses reported feeling more stress and frustration, lower discretionary effort, increased frustration, and less pride in their employer, and noted that they found their work lacked meaning.[6]

There are very real consequences for allowing narcissists to thrive and progress within organizations, even if those effects aren't immediately visible on a balance sheet or within the annual report. When Al Dunlap was brought in to salvage Sunbeam Corporation from collapse in 1996, he was already established as a corporate turnaround genius who had an impressive track record of rescuing struggling organizations and transforming them into streamlined, highly profitable enterprises. Prior to accepting the position of CEO at the home appliance manufacturer Sunbeam, Dunlap orchestrated a turnabout for Scott Paper, growing the company's value to $9 billion—an increase of $6.5 billion—during his two-year tenure as the chief executive, a job that netted him $100 million in total compensation.[7] His approach was to dramatically cut costs and restructure organizations over the course of a few years, restoring shareholder confidence and reaping substantial stock payouts before moving on to the next company.

Dunlap allegedly took pleasure in laying off workers as part of his rescue plan for each company, earning him the nickname "Chainsaw Al." He was described as cruel, aggressive, money-hungry, unable to handle criticism, and totally insensitive to the suffering of employees whose jobs he axed. In his first year at Sunbeam, he laid off six thousand workers (half of the company's workforce) and shuttered thirty warehouses and production facilities. While at Scott Paper, he terminated 35 percent of the organization's employees, rescinded Scott's charitable giving pledges, and eliminated the corporate morale officer's role of promoting employee engagement. He possessed a management style that left employees with no uncertainty as to where they stood in terms of importance. Shareholders, he proudly declared, were his only constituents. Growing shareholder returns along with his own personal wealth were all that mattered to him. If that sounds familiar, it's because this is just one of many other stories of corporate greed involving allegations of fraud or corruption. Mr. Dunlap was fired in 1998 amid charges from the Securities and Exchange Commission that Sunbeam had misrepresented profits and undervalued its inventory to artificially boost stock prices. Sunbeam subsequently filed for bankruptcy and the SEC barred Al Dunlap from ever again serving in an officer or director capacity in a publicly traded company.[8]

IT'S NOT ROCKET SCIENCE

One of the most common questions I'm asked when I preach the value of empathetic leadership is whether empathy can be taught. It's a legitimate challenge to what most business-minded adults consider impractical, hokey mush. But empathy is not anathema to business; it is integral to business. Specifically, it is the catalyst for employee engagement and the inoculant against disengagement. That is why I firmly believe empathy not only can be taught, but *should* be taught. Empathy should be a must-have requirement for all new hires, especially any and every person who will be working in a management capacity. It should be expected that managers have a clear and intimate appreciation for what their employees experience working at their organization day in and day out.

A chief complaint among workers in any industry is that their leaders are out of touch, that the lofty perspective from their ivory towers blinds them to the challenges and realities of working at the ground level. This is the first way leaders can learn to be more empathetic: Experiential Empathy. You might ask, "Are you suggesting that I, a senior executive/director/manager, go spend my very limited time toiling in a lowly plebeian job after I have worked years to reach this respected position?" Why, yes. That is exactly what I'm saying. Immerse yourself in your organization's employee experience. If you are head of sales, spend a month at a sales desk making cold calls, struggling to reach the ambitious quotas that you insisted could be reached. If you are head of operations for a large hotel chain, spend a few weeks housekeeping guests' rooms or preparing meals or doing janitorial tasks. The point is this: As a manager, you cannot expect your employees to be engaged until you sit at their desks, stand at their stations, walk in their shoes, and then ask yourself whether those same circumstances would engage you or disengage you.

Bryon Stephens, president and COO of Marco's Pizza, spent time working in one of his pizzerias for an episode of *Undercover Boss*. The experience opened his eyes to the value of empathizing with front-line workers. He implemented a policy that every Marco's executive must spend at least one day per year working at one of their stores to learn exactly what it is like being an employee and to gain insights directly from the people serving their customers.[9] Empathy by experience is a powerful mechanism to connect with employees and see beyond the blind spots that prevent you from perceiving what your workforce struggles with every day.

The second way leaders can learn to be more empathetic is by practicing what I call Situational Empathy. Whereas Experiential Empathy is literally occupying the same space as one of your employees to experience exactly what she does, Situational Empathy is more cerebral. It involves taking a particular situation that an employee (or employees) is facing and mentally processing how you would feel if you were in their place. Say, for instance, you have an employee with an apparent performance problem. She's been late for work, missing deadlines, short-tempered with colleagues, and making mistakes. The typical managerial response would be to bring these issues to the employee's attention, clearly intimate that her performance is unacceptable, implement a performance improvement plan to show her that her job is in jeopardy, and begin the termination process if she does not satisfactorily improve. To most, that would seem pretty fair and reasonable: standard procedure for performance management. Except there is something missing in this process. Empathetic leaders choose to look beyond the business need for high-functioning human capital and seek to fulfill the human need for empathy present in each of their employees.

Instead of following the cold, bureaucratic path that most organizations have laid out for dealing with an underperforming employee, an empathetic leader would first ask if there is anything going on with her that could be causing the decline in her work. He would *ask*, not accuse. In this example, before even thinking the words "performance management," the manager opens the lines of communication to inquire about how the employee is doing and then just listens. He learns that the employee's wife had an affair, is divorcing her to marry her best friend, and is leaving the country while the employee must support their two small children. Now imagine if you had found yourself in that same situation. Your spouse cheated on you with your closest friend. You now must go through the agony and cost of divorce while trying to care for your young children on your own. What would that feel like? How would that affect your ability to do your job? How would you want your boss to treat you during this painful period? Would you expect a little decency and consideration? How would you react to the callous indifference of an employer that cares more about your productivity than your adversity? Viewing an employee's situation through an empathetic lens gives one the clarity necessary for understanding how to engage that employee and avoid disengaging her.

When I worked in the technology space training employees on how to use new e-commerce systems, I had a certain mindset about the whole process that seemed to help with user adoption and satisfaction. My approach was simple, really. I trained people the way I would expect to be trained if I were learning something new. Personally, I take a little longer than most to learn a new skill, so I can relate to the difficulty some feel when they don't immediately grasp something being taught to them. I spent as much time as was needed, explained concepts and functions as many times as it took for employees to feel confident, and remained patient when they became frustrated or confused. The end goal was for them to learn. In order for that to happen, they had to *want* to learn. I had to create an encouraging, supportive learning experience that made it safe for them to absorb information at their own pace and gave them ample time to bridge any knowledge gaps. In other words, I needed to engage them and take care not to disengage them.

I recall being trained for a new role years ago. My co-worker, who was a senior member of the team, had become agitated with my failure to acclimate as quickly as someone who had been doing the job for ten years, as well as my tendency to ask questions about tasks she had already demonstrated. "It's not rocket science!" she flippantly told me. Unsurprisingly, her attitude wasn't helpful and made it much more difficult for me to be effective at the start of that job.

As a leader, when you empathize instead of criticize, you acknowledge the other person's situation or reality, whether they are faltering because of a personal hardship or stumbling as they try to learn the ropes of a new job. However, this can be exceptionally challenging for people in leadership positions because of the effect power has on their brains. Researchers at the University of California discovered that position power causes the same disruption in the frontal lobes of the human brain as a traumatic head injury.[10] The mirror neurons responsible for feelings of empathy we discussed earlier in the chapter happen to be located in the frontal lobes. Individuals with damage to their frontal lobe regions are more aggressive and care less about the thoughts or feelings of others. Unlike irreparable brain damage, however, power does not permanently handicap one's ability to empathize. Even if someone is not readily inclined toward empathy, that doesn't mean he or she cannot take steps to become more empathetic. Yes, empathy may seem like an abstruse concept for the powerful, but it is not impossible to learn. All it takes is a willingness to change your perspective.

LOOKING AHEAD

As we conclude our discussion on the very important and timely subject of empathy, I want to reiterate a point I have raised over and over within these pages. In fact, I would say that it is the central theme of my overall message: employees are human beings. If you empathize with them, you can engage them. The vast majority of employees want to do a good job. But they have their limitations. They have their bad days, their foibles, their privations and tragedies, their needs, their fears, and their motivations. Leaders who agree with the Stepford Employee Fallacy are willfully ignorant of their employees' very human nature, much to the detriment of engagement within their organizations. We are not machines. We do not engage and go above and beyond in the workplace but for leaders who embrace our humanity and make decisions that elevate the quality of our employee experience.

Fittingly, the final chapter of this book is a compilation of stories from real people whose work experiences reflect the true state of the modern workplace: the good, the bad, and the ugly. These stories are intended as a rebuttal to the Stepford Employee Fallacy; as evidence that employees are indeed so much more than the compliant automatons that their managers hope they would be. The following pages give a voice to those who felt like they had none after working in a disengaging environment for far too long. They also include stories from workers who were lucky to have found the opposite: an employer that owns responsibility for employee engagement and treats talent like the valued partners in action they are capable of being if they are so inspired. Tahir Shah once wrote that "stories are the communal currency of humanity." From these stories, I hope you, as a leader, can glean value in the knowledge that we are all human. Because what makes us human is the same thing that either begets or deters our engagement in all areas of life, including work.

NOTES

1. Winerman, Lea. "The Mind's Mirror." *American Psychological Association.* Volume 36, Number 9. Page 48. October 2005. http://www.apa.org/monitor/oct05/mirror.aspx

2. Lamm, Claus, Ruff, Christian, Silani, Giorgia, and Singer, Tania. "Right Supramarginal Gyrus Is Crucial to Overcome Emotional Egocentricity Bias in Social Judgements." *Journal of Neuroscience.* September 25, 2013. Volume 33. Issue 39, 15,466-15,476. http://www.jneurosci.org/content/33/39/15466

3. Parmar, Belinda. "The Most Empathetic Companies 2016." *Harvard Business Review.* December 1, 2016. https://hbr.org/2016/12/the-most-and-least-empathetic-companies-2016

4. BusinessSolver. *2017 Empathy Monitor.* 2017. https://www.businessolver.com/2017-empathy-monitor-executive-summary?hsCtaTracking=9e006e63-8034-41e9-ac00-19227993b694%7Cd49f67a6-5d50-4439-9241-5ec2bb24321f#

5. "Corporate Psychopaths Common and Can Wreak Havok in Businesses, Researcher Says." *Australian Psychological Society.* September 13, 2016.

6. Hochwarter, Wayne. "Researcher: Narcissistic Bosses Destroy Morale, Drive Down Bottom Line." *Florida State University.* August 7, 2009. https://www.fsu.edu/news/2009/08/07/narcissistic.bosses/

7. Sider, Don. "The Terminator." *People.* November 26, 1996. http://people.com/archive/the-terminator-vol-46-no-22/

8. Norris, Floyd. "S.E.C. Accuses Former Sunbeam Official of Fraud." The New York Times. May 16, 2001. http://www.nytimes.com/2001/05/16/business/sec-accuses-former-sunbeam-official-of-fraud.html

9. Stephens, Bryon. "Going 'Undercover' Changed How I Run My Business." *Business News Daily.* August 24, 2016. https://www.businessnewsdaily.com/9355-undercover-boss-marcos-pizza.html

10. University of California. "How Power Makes People Selfish." (YouTube Video). January 13, 2015. https://m.youtube.com/watch?v=0vvl46PmCfE

CHAPTER 13

THE TRUTH, AS TOLD BY EMPLOYEES

"We do not err because truth is difficult to see.
It is visible at a glance. We err because this is more comfortable."

Alexander Solzhenitsyn

REBA'S STORY

Reba worked in the IT department for a property management company that was struggling to attract and retain talent. The organization was set to undergo a cultural makeover, shifting toward a more positive work environment, and Reba was part of the team tasked with making that happen. To kick off the transformation, each department head would be presenting the company's new cultural values at a town hall meeting attended by every employee. Reba and her team were to prep the CIO for his part in the presentation by researching talking points and writing his speech. Unfortunately, the CIO was not receptive to the idea of creating a better employee experience. When Reba explained to him that engaged employees lead to better business results, his response was succinct, albeit less-than-encouraging: "Bullshit." He had an old-school leadership mentality that wasn't exactly conducive to the engaging culture that the company was trying to foster. He would tell his employees they were lucky just to have a job and gave little thought to quaint frivolities like work-life balance. The toxic environment he had created caused significant turnover and hiring problems. Exit interviews consistently named the CIO as the reason for departure, and the company had a difficult time replacing employees who quit, yet he was still somehow able to keep his job.

Reba eventually ended up leaving and took a 20 percent pay cut to join another firm mainly because its culture was so markedly different from that of the property management company. One day, while working at her new job, she received an e-mail from a coworker whose guitar had gone missing. He wanted to give his brain a rest and play some music but couldn't find his instrument. So he sent an e-mail to the entire company asking for help. This struck Reba, because her old company was not the kind of place where an employee could send a company-wide e-mail saying he wanted to take a break from his work so he could play the guitar. It also was not the kind of place where many employees wanted to continue their careers or share their talents. The CIO had simply pushed them to the point where they walked out the door and never looked back.

TYLER'S STORY

Automotive sales can be a tough gig for even the most seasoned professionals. High-volume, high-pressure dealerships are enough to really test a salesperson's mettle. Add the stress that terrible leadership can cause and a grueling job becomes downright miserable. Tyler loved working in car sales. He had been doing business development at the same dealership for about five years and sold more than a few cars and trucks in his time there. However, neither his nor his coworkers' accomplishments seemed to be enough for the general sales manager who ran the dealership like a monarchy and believed respect was his birthright. During their weekly sales meetings, the sales manager would pontificate and denigrate, reprimanding employees like children for even the smallest mistakes.

A few years into Tyler's tenure, a new employee joined his team and their friendship developed into something more. Office romances were not unheard of at the dealership; another couple had been dating for a while before Tyler and his boyfriend started their relationship. The employee handbook did not stipulate that any kind of fraternization was against the rules, but Tyler still decided to do the right thing and be forthcoming with management anyway. Much to his surprise, the dealership's owner launched an aggressive investigation and brought in an attorney to interview Tyler and his boyfriend. The owner advised him that a new company policy prohibited dating a coworker. He told Tyler that he had a choice: fire his boyfriend or they would both be unemployed. So, with no other option, Tyler went home and had to be the one to tell his own partner that he no longer had a job. When his boyfriend started suffering from seizures caused by the stressful situation, Tyler knew it was time to give his notice. Interestingly, the other office couple—a heterosexual pair—were never bothered by management, kept their jobs, and continued their romance.

Not one to let a negative work experience at this dealership ruin his love for cars, Tyler interviewed with a smaller, family-owned dealer and secured a role managing their Internet sales. He knew very quickly that he had found an employer that truly cares for its employees as individuals. A month after he was hired, the dealership's owner came into his office just to talk. She asked about Tyler's life outside of work, showed a genuine interest in learning about him as a person, and encouraged him to share ideas about how to make their Internet sales department more successful. He felt (and still feels) accepted and that he could be totally authentic at work as an out gay man. One of his initiatives became the dealership's primary marketing campaign for LGBT clientele and substantially increased overall sales, garnering Tyler much praise and support from management. The cultural difference between this dealership and his last employer is amazing. The weekly sales meetings are upbeat and solution-oriented, in contrast to the other dealership's climate of immediacy and fear where employees were constantly wondering, "Now what did I do wrong?" At the new dealership, the owner's one mandate for all employees is that they can't be mean to each other. Everyone is treated with the same respect that you would give a family member or friend. Even in a sales environment, it seems there's a place for engaging, empathetic leadership.

KIMBERLY'S STORY

Kimberly Jones was an IT business analyst working for a large consumer products manufacturer. She and her project manager, Mariya, were frequently at odds over differences of opinion on how certain tasks should be accomplished, making for a strained working relationship. Mariya, being an overbearing and relentlessly exhausting manager, was largely to blame for the situation. She would stomp over to Kimberly's desk and loudly criticize her work and her ideas in front of other employees. Instead of calmly brainstorming a better approach, Mariya would stand over Kimberly's desk berating her: "Kimmy! No! Kimmy! No!" During team meetings, Mariya would share her dissatisfaction with some of the team's failure to follow set procedures and humiliate Kimberly by using her as an example. "We're getting better at documenting progress on deliverables, but a few people still aren't doing what's required . . . ahem . . . Mrs. Jones."

Finally, at a customer presentation, Mariya grew frustrated with Kimberly's approach and belittled her while their business partners sat as uncomfortable witnesses to a grown woman being treated like a child by her boss. After the meeting, Mariya asked Kimberly to remain in the conference room so she could carry on nagging her, and she finally snapped. "You're always badgering me!" she exclaimed in anger. Taken aback, Mariya promptly left and told the department executive what happened. The executive, who did not tolerate "insubordination" of any kind, immediately phoned office services and told them to deactivate Kimberly's employee badge while she was out to lunch. She found out that she had been fired when she returned to the building and realized she no longer had access to the elevator banks: one final indignity to reassure her that she had indeed been working with a company and management team that neither respected nor engaged her.

ALICE'S STORY

A company that genuinely values its employees is a rarity in today's business world, but that's just what Alice found with her employer. The company not only treats its employees like human beings, but it considers them to be valuable business partners whose feedback and expertise are frequently solicited and acted upon. The biotech firm aims to be seen as a great employer, so employee survey results are taken very seriously.

Executives attend "speak up sessions" after the survey period has ended to hear directly from staff what their concerns and recommendations for improvement are. In fact, upward feedback is a common theme within the organization. Managers at all levels attend "leader chats" that are low-structure, informal social gatherings with employees to build rapport and camaraderie. They even dress in costumes when these events fall on Halloween. Supervisors and managers also hold individual check-in meetings and skip-level chats to solicit process improvement ideas from each employee. Indeed, leaders there—including C-level executives—insist on pushing decision-making to the lowest possible level.

Alice's manager allows her the autonomy to create training and development initiatives for their department and supports her in these efforts, reinforcing the company's values statement: "Everybody deserves a great manager." Even without feedback from employees, the company is constantly looking for ways to enhance its employee experience. A market review of pay revealed that employees were in need of salary increases, so everyone, including Alice, received a raise. Every aspect of the organization's employee experience—from its generous paid leave programs, to its free shuttle transportation for all employees, to its rule that no one sends e-mails between 6:00 p.m. Friday and 6:00 a.m. Monday—is purposefully implemented in alignment with senior leadership's goal to be one of the best places to work. With a very low turnover rate and hundreds of job applications for each open position, it's clear that the company has achieved its objective of being an employer of choice.

ERYN'S STORY

Imagine growing up feeling as though you don't belong in your own body; how confusing, frightening, frustrating, and depressing that must be. Think of what it must be like to live your life as someone you know, deep down, you are not. For almost her entire life, Eryn felt this way. She was born a boy, but felt and presented like a girl up until she reached the age of ten. From then on, she repressed her truth and conformed to her outward male appearance. She graduated college and entered the work-force still wearing the guise of a body that wasn't hers. She dressed like a man, looked like a man, and, for a period of her life, thought she was a man simply because of the gender she was assigned at birth. Then some-thing changed. She reflected on whether she was truly living an authentic life and finally came to terms with something she had known from a very young age but had never fully acknowledged until that point: Eryn was transgender.

After finally taking the life-changing first step of accepting who she is—who she truly is—Eryn faced the daunting task of telling the rest of the world. Coming out as transgender to one's inner circle has its own set of challenges, but making such a personal and sensitive announcement in the workplace can be especially tough. How would her coworkers and superiors react? Would she be ostracized and made to feel like she no lon-ger belonged in a job she loved? There was only one way to find out. One Friday, she met with her team and told them that she wanted to be her self at work—her real self. Everyone was refreshingly supportive. One of the directors even became emotional, tearfully telling Eryn that she was so happy for her. Eryn's chief of staff was initially shocked when she came out to him, but joined the rest of her colleagues in their acceptance.

Eryn then met with the CEO to tell her story and nervously explained how she had felt like a girl ever since she could remember. She indicated that she wanted to start the process of transitioning so the way she looked on the outside would match how she felt on the inside. His initial reaction was one of concern. He asked her how she was feeling about her decision to come out and how people in the office were treating her. The CEO was just as caring toward Eryn as everybody else had been. His only request in regards to her transition was that she would refrain from wearing Christian Louboutin designer shoes to the office, lest his girlfriend ask for her own pair. It was just the kind of levity a newly out transgender woman needed from her boss in this situation.

The CEO looked at Eryn's transition as a positive development for their small company. "You will be teaching our organization a lot, and that is a good thing," he told her. He asked Eryn if she felt comfortable announcing this to the entire company at their next all-staff meeting, which she did. Following the meeting, Eryn overheard one employee from another department remark, "Wow, what a cool day!" She received an outpouring of support from across the organization, including letters and e-mails telling her how she had touched other employees with her courage. People started using inclusive language in the office, such as adding their preferred gender pronouns to their e-mail signatures in a show of solidarity. HR invited Eryn to lead a working group on crafting more inclusive personnel policies. The CEO even raised the transgender flag outside the company headquarters. Management gave Eryn the work flexibility she needed during her transition journey, which made the process far less difficult than many transgender people experience with their employers. The amount of support and empathy Eryn received from all levels at her organization strengthened her sense of engagement there. Today, her coworkers cannot even remember when she presented as a male. To them, she is, and has always been, Eryn.

ANN'S STORY

Ann had always admired the vice president of her department. She thought she was an extremely intelligent woman and believed that they had a positive relationship, that is until Ann and her colleagues missed an error that cost their employer $50,000. The mistake was no small matter, for sure. But instead of trying to understand how it happened and coaching the team to learn from it, Ann's boss launched into a fifteen-minute vitriolic tirade excoriating them for their "fucking irresponsible incompetence." The VP was a very well-respected member of management who had the CEO's ear, and Ann feared retaliation if she were to report the incident. She had heard about the VP quashing another employee's career prospects for daring to cross her, so it seemed that Ann's only option was to look for another job.

Reflecting on her experience, Ann remembered how a previous employer had been much more sensitive to the fact that employees are human beings. While at this company, Ann's mother had been battling lung cancer. Everyone there—from the VP down to her manager—made it very clear that she should spend whatever time she needed to with her family. Nobody questioned her and every one of her colleagues offered to cover for her. It can be pretty reassuring (and certainly engaging) when employees receive support if they hit a low point, whether that's a major failure or a personal hardship. Unfortunately, not all leaders are so accepting of an imperfect workforce.

WILLIAM'S STORY

It's ironic that, often times, those who work in the human services field are the ones treated most inhumanely. The ones who give so much of themselves often get taken by those in a place of power. It was one such situation that, for William, really spoke to just how low someone will go to knock another individual one rung down the ladder, professional or otherwise.

William worked as a behavioral therapist in San Diego, providing direct home-based therapy services to children and young adults with an autism spectrum disorder (ASD). He really had a knack for the job. He loved the clients he worked with and they, in return, loved him for being a pillar of support. William was incredibly proud of his work and thought his supervisors would be as well. They were . . . mostly. The company's clinical director, Kennedy, was not his biggest fan. "To this day, I'll never know quite what I did to make me such a permanent fixture on her shit list." Regardless, there he was, firmly in her crosshairs, and she wasn't shy about making it known through her words and actions.

It was December, and the company was holding its annual holiday boat cruise on the beautiful Mission Bay in San Diego. The night consisted of dancing, singing, laughing, eating, and plenty of drinking. Kennedy was a good three to four drinks ahead of the rest of the team, and she decided to once again make William the target of her spiteful invective. As William made his way to the dance floor, he noticed an area of the floor being avoided by all. Turning to a friend, he asked, "What's going on?" Apparently, somebody had spilled wine on the floor and everyone was scared it might be blood. William marched boldly to the center of the dance floor, bent down, touched his finger to the offending spill, gave it a sniff, and informed the room of his findings: Clearly it was red wine. Kennedy, in her opportunistic cruelty, took this moment to shout to the rafters: "William has HIV! William just got HIV for the company! HIV! HIV!"

William walked off the dance floor and to the top of the boat to calm himself and get some much-needed fresh air. *Take the high road, William,* he thought to himself. *Take the high road. She's trying to get a rise out of you. She's drunk and wants you to make a scene. Don't take the bait.* He didn't take the bait, and the moment passed. When he resigned six months after the incident, he used his exit interview to express how incredibly offended he was by Kennedy's HIV comments and that he hoped no other employees need suffer her wrath after his departure. Eight months later, he received word that Kennedy left the company in disgrace and had become a full-time marriage counselor. William took the high road and karma, as it tends to do, took care of the rest.

BARBARA'S STORY

When Barbara started her career in insurance as a claims adjuster, she had supportive managers who recognized her as a hard worker and fast learner. She excelled at her work, and they promoted her very quickly. Then a regime change brought in new leadership for the claims department as well as new management in Barbara's office. The changes were accompanied by a shift away from recognizing employees' efforts toward closely tracking metrics and wringing maximum productivity from staff. Barbara continued to give the same effort she always had, even going out of her way to help struggling colleagues who were overwhelmed with impossible workloads. She brought work home with her to barely keep up with management's impractical demands, but that was still not good enough. She was shocked by her performance review that stated she underperformed in her role and that she was not a "team player" because she was vocal about concerns over poor management decisions, such as forcing adjusters to use their personal phones for company business.

Being crushed under the relentless weight of her work and told that she had a "bad attitude" about it made Barbara feel as though she were set up to fail, a sentiment many of her coworkers shared. It wasn't until after she lost her job that she learned the company was making its way through a black list of long-term employees in the top quartile of their salary ranges, methodically finding ways to fire them or constructively discharge them. Years of service and excellence meant nothing to the company. Senior management preferred to have low-cost, low-maintenance Stepford Employees who could hit their numbers with no questions asked.

After a frustratingly difficult job search, Barbara finally secured a claims role with another insurance carrier. She brought with her the same tenacity and work ethic that she displayed in her previous position, hoping her new bosses would be satisfied enough to keep her on board. In the self-assessment portion of her first annual performance review, she rated herself as merely average because she had grown so accustomed to feeling as though her work did not exceed expectations. To her surprise, Barbara's supervisor disagreed, telling her that she deserved a much better rating and rewarded her with the highest possible raise for that year. The differences between her old and new employers are like night and day. Rather than focusing on the negative, the company actually looks for ways to acknowledge the things employees do well. Her supervisor sends e-mails to the department manager bringing Barbara's accomplishments to her attention. And unlike management at the old company, Barbara's supervisor monitors and adjusts her case load to ensure she is not overworked. The amount of care, support, and recognition Barbara now feels translate to a much more engaging work experience. "I know I'm doing a good job because they tell me so."

CONCLUSION:

COMMITTING TO CHANGE THE MODERN WORKPLACE

So where do we go from here? We have taken a journey that started with surveying the desolate employee engagement landscape of the modern workplace, and then quashed myths that are responsible for causing this undesirable state. We came to a better understanding of how engagement really works and heard stories from actual employees illustrating these points. Each chapter contained lessons that, taken together, present a nigh-impossibly tall order for leaders who are anxious to emend the state of engagement within their organizations. These lessons might also be frustratingly obvious for managers who really do get it when it comes to employee engagement, but they face opposition or indifference from senior leaders.

Now that we have the answers about employee engagement, what, if anything, can be done with them to effect change in the modern workplace when the problem of disengagement only seems to be getting worse? I would like to propose three radical changes that I believe will have a transformative impact on the concept of employment as we know it, as well as the quality of employee experience on a large scale.

These changes will require a commitment from business leaders to implement them, and how they are implemented is a matter of social and economic debate. Should regulations be put in place for widespread workplace reform? Or should businesses be left to manage the changes on their own, relying on market forces to dictate the extent and longevity of modification? Does it necessarily have to be an either/or proposition? It's certainly an interesting conversation, and arguments could be made for a particular approach. Regardless of *how* these changes are put in place, I am positive that they will lead to higher engagement, better business outcomes, and overall happier employees. In other words, I believe changing the modern workplace is the only way to bring about true employee engagement.

CONTROL EXECUTIVE COMPENSATION

The first change is arguably the easiest to measure but probably the most controversial to discuss. We briefly covered the topic of executive pay in Chapter 5 where it was noted that CEOs today earn, on average, $274 for every dollar in the typical employee's paycheck. One could make the argument that senior leaders are paid so handsomely for a reason: they are rewarded for their ability to effectively marshal a complex organization's limited resources toward achieving optimal performance, thus increasing profitability and shareholder value. That's no small task, and those who succeed at it deserve to be compensated accordingly. Except this leaves broad latitude for C-level executives to execute their responsibilities in particularly disengaging (and sometimes unethical) ways.

Wells Fargo's former CEO, John Stumpf, impressed shareholders and Wall Street analysts alike as the bank raked in record profits under his command. And his compensation package reflected the value his constituents placed on his continued delivery of stellar financial results. As the CEO, he received hundreds of millions of dollars in salary, bonuses, and stock awards, along with an additional multi-million-dollar severance payment after the fraudulent account scandal cost him his job. The thousands of Wells Fargo employees who were caught up in the mess didn't get the same treatment when *they* were fired. Recall "Chainsaw" Al Dunlap and the Sunbeam Corporation debacle wherein his brutal cost-cutting strategy yielded impressive short-term gains for the company and put $70 million in his pocket. He commanded a prodigious stipend for his work turning around ailing companies, but the controversy surrounding Sunbeam's downfall also shone light on the darker side of executive job performance.

As is the case with most executive compensation packages, Stumpf's and Dunlap's pay was tied to the bottom-line growth of their respective companies, regardless of their means for making it happen. Had their pay been modified by the quality of their organizations' employee experience, their bank account balances would now have fewer commas. That is the change I am suggesting. Tie executive compensation to employee experience so they have a tangible incentive to engage their workforce (and avoid disengaging them). We have established that employee engagement drives measurable organizational results and that high engagement is the outcome of a phenomenal employee experience. So, it makes sense that an organization's senior leaders should only realize such sizable financial rewards if they achieve outstanding results by engaging their employees.

For example, if a CEO's contract stipulated a $1 million salary with a $6 million long-term-incentive bonus based on year-over-year growth in profitability, the entire compensation package would be subject to a sliding scale modifier depending on the overall employee experience. The worse the employee experience, the more the compensation is reduced. If the employee experience translated to a two on a ten-point scale (i.e a relatively poor employee experience score), then the CEO would forfeit the bonus and only receive 10 percent of his projected pay, or $100,000. If the employee experience score were one, then he would only receive 1 percent and should probably start looking for a new job. The funds that would have otherwise been paid to the CEO are then put toward ameliorating the areas of employee experience most in need of improvement, like staffing levels, wages, technology, or leadership training. It's a simplistic model, but it shows a clear consequence for the CEO allowing or potentially creating a lousy employee experience. This acts as a check and balance against the tendency for leaders to utilize disengaging business strategies in the myopic pursuit of big revenues and low costs. Linking executive compensation to employee experience can have a substantial impact on engagement in the modern workplace by putting an actual dollar value on the leadership decisions that benefit the whole workforce, not just those at the top.

HOLD MANAGERS TO A HIGHER STANDARD

A Michigan Cracker Barrel retail manager was fired in 2010 over her use of racially inflammatory language during arguments with her African American employees while at work. She had expressed her disdain for employees accepting public assistance—specifically the Michigan Bridge Card, which she referred to as the "ghetto card"—and refused to dispense paychecks to workers who participated in the program. An assistant manager witnessed these exchanges and reported the manager to his superiors. Although both the manager and her staff had violated the company's non-discrimination policy by uttering racially offensive terms like "ghetto card" in their altercations, she was terminated for her misconduct while the employees were merely reprimanded. She sued Cracker Barrel for reverse discrimination but lost her case in summary judgment. The court ruled that Cracker Barrel was reasonable in holding a member of management to a higher standard of conduct than non-management employees and that it did not commit any discriminatory action by firing the manager. Michigan's Sixth Circuit Appellate Court affirmed the lower court's judgment.

Everybody, at some point in their careers, has worked for bosses who made them question how these managers could possibly continue to keep their jobs or why they were even promoted in the first place. Some people simply should not be in management positions, regardless of their abilities or the results they produce. As we discussed in Chapter 7, managers have an influential and quite powerful effect on their employees' engagement, and that should be the litmus test for their efficacy. Just as a CEO should be accountable for the overall employee experience of her organization, managers at all levels must be held to a higher standard for engaging their employees. Specifically, the decisions, behaviors, and interactions of every manager should happen with the employee experience in mind—from the manner in which they give team members feedback to the amount of praise and recognition they bestow. The Cracker Barrel manager might not have been the only one to use distasteful language in her interactions with employees, but she should have known better.

When one has the privilege and responsibility of working in a management position, it comes with the expectation that he or she will behave as a true leader should. Indeed, engaging leadership is the standard to which all managers must be held. And organizations should act quickly to remove any managers who conduct themselves in ways that are demoralizing, abusive, or disengaging. The modern workplace gives managers far too much leeway in their treatment of workers and they are nearly always assumed to be in the right anytime there is an employee relations issue. Their titles confer immunity from criticism or retribution, emboldening them to perpetuate the traditional autocratic management mindset that is mainly responsible for so much disengagement in organizations today. It is time to stop protecting bad managers and hold them accountable for the negative employee experiences they create. This is the second change we must make to foster a more engaging workplace.

How does an organization go about implementing higher standards for its managers' conduct? First, it should communicate the expectation that all members of management—front-line supervisors all the way up to senior executives—are to exemplify the qualities of engaging leadership, that they should lead with empathy, curiosity, and humility at all times. The times of managers acting as overseers and enforcers are over. If an organization hopes to achieve its goals with a workforce of engaged employees, then it needs to staff its management ranks with engaging *leaders*. That means first administering a robust leadership development program and requiring all managers to complete continuing leadership education that is geared toward maintaining a great employee experience. Second, it means identifying managers who fall short and either moving them into non-management roles or ending their employment with the company altogether. Organizations can glean information about their managers' performance from frequent employee feedback, but the key is to act on it. This is not about turning the leadership function into a popularity contest wherein the most lenient and complacent managers succeed. Leaders should still be responsible for ensuring work is carried out, that employees receive the constructive feedback they need, and that sound processes are followed. I'm not suggesting that managers are no longer needed. But we do need to hold them to a higher standard for the *way* they manage if there is to be a change in the state of employee engagement.

REWRITE THE SOCIAL CONTRACT

In medieval times, wealthy European nobles permitted the peasantry to live on land that they controlled in exchange for labor. The peasants, known as serfs, entered into a social contract of sorts with the lords: serfs and their families lived on a plot of land and were allowed to farm a portion of it, promising service and fealty to the feudal lord in return. This system of feudalism could be considered an early form of pre-industrial employment. Fast-forward a few hundred years to the Industrial Revolution in which factory owners paid laborers paltry wages as they were forced to work in hazardous conditions for long hours with no breaks. This social contract showed a clear imbalance of power between the employer and the employed, one that shifted in the twentieth century with the rise of unions and the enactment of labor laws. Union sway in the working world was relatively short-lived, however, as the nature of the employment relationship began to regress backwards. The 1980s represented a sharp turning point marked by deregulation and hypercapitalism. By the 2000s, layoffs, the decline of unions, economic turmoil, wage stagnation, and the political influence of corporations brought the social contract even closer to its feudalistic origins. Workers had little say in the quality of their employee experience because they had few alternatives to earn a living outside of powerful employers that dictated the terms of employment.

It seems that the employment relationship has come full circle to arrive at what scholars have dubbed neo-feudalism. Large companies not only own the capital and means of production to keep fair, robust competition at bay, but they also expect to own the people who work for them (their *human capital*). Employees must be fully engaged and committed to their organization no matter how they are treated if they hope to keep their jobs. Sure, they can quit and try to find work elsewhere. But the system is fixed so that there's no guarantee another employer will be any better. Still, that doesn't mean employees will stop being human or accept unfair work circumstances. Neo-feudalism simply ignores this in favor of a more convenient narrative. Employers continue to believe employee engagement means unquestioning devotion, discretionary effort, and tireless performance in exchange for a middling paycheck. The Stepford Employee Fallacy has become the new social contract in the modern workplace, and it is unsustainable. The contract, once again, needs to change.

If organizations continue to use the Stepford Employee Fallacy as the basis for their social contract with the workforce, then the system will eventually collapse under the weight of its own inequity. With the balance of power so grossly stacked in favor of employers and the income gap widening over time, society's middle class—universally acknowledged as the backbone of a healthy economy—will slowly disappear. What will remain is a social hierarchy similar to sixteenth century France: an isolated, affluent minority controlling the bulk of wealth and the serfs below them. You might recall from your high-school history class what happened in France when the poor had nothing left to eat while the rich feasted in comfort. The French Revolution restored equity to a country that had a broken social contract. One of the Revolution's most dramatic and fundamental changes to French society was the abolition of feudalism.

Following a shift away from feudalistic societal structure, the subsequent industrialization of Europe and western nations changed the way economies function by giving essentially anyone the opportunity to make a living and own property. This opportunity became what is now known as the American Dream in the United States. There was a time, not long ago, when Americans could count on lifetime employment with a company, earning a livable wage that was enough to purchase a home, grow a family, and save for a comfortable retirement. Now the American Dream is more of a pipe dream for most, particularly those just starting their careers. And yet, employers have their own dreams of perfectly engaged employees driving them toward success without realizing (or perhaps not caring) that their new social contract is, in fact, corrosive to engagement.

The point of this history lesson is we, as a society, need to move away from the unsustainable social contract of the modern workplace. Employees aren't happy. They're not engaged. A disturbing percentage of them hate their jobs for a variety of reasons we've covered over the course of this book. The current social contract is broken and many of today's business leaders are either too greedy or too unconcerned to fix it. But, as the French landlords learned a few hundred years ago, a society cannot properly function as an oligarchy. Are we already walking down that dark path? Perhaps not. But we are certainly facing that direction. I call upon leaders everywhere to have courage, stand alongside their employees and say that we deserve better. Our families, friends, neighbors, and colleagues deserve a better working world than what callous, corporate hegemony has created for us: a massive-scale, unending rat race. We scratch and scramble for crumbs of cheese and are told we should be grateful for the opportunity to compete. Eventually the game will grow tiresome for the hordes of disengaged employees craving more from life than to serve exigent, gluttonous employers who desperately cleave to their ideas of what employment is supposed to look like.

It's time to ditch the Stepford Employee Fallacy in favor of something better; something that will save the modern workplace from the malaise of disengagement and benefit society as a whole. That should be the true purpose of a social contract. Instead of higher profit being an organization's sole and primary objective, it should strive to always do good in the world, especially for its employees. Google had the right idea with their original corporate motto, "Don't be evil." We must replace the current social contract with one that weighs every organization's activities against a simple test: how does the action benefit employees, customers, the community, and society at large? If any of these stakeholders are harmed by a decision or an action, then the organization has failed in its duties under the new social contract. The idea that an organization has no responsibility to society and the people within it is the biggest fallacy of all. The disengaging leadership behaviors, decisions, and interactions occurring in the modern workplace have an aggregate impact on our society. In order for society to endure and thrive in a complex global economy, we must commit to making work fairer for workers and stop expecting them to be Stepford Employees.

LET'S GET TO WORK

I came up with the concept for *The Stepford Employee Fallacy* quite some time ago. Over the years, I have heard and read about employee engagement from management consultants, HR practitioners, and other organizational development thought leaders who professed to have the definitive answers on this topic. Something about what they were all saying just didn't sit right with me, though. These were people who hadn't been employees for many years, yet they claimed to know better than employees how engagement works. Thinking back over my career, I reflected on all of the mistreatment I had witnessed and experienced in the workplace. And yet, all of the employee engagement experts were saying that workers are responsible for choosing their own level of engagement in spite of the quality of their employee experience. I knew that it did not work that way. I knew employees want to raise their voices and tell leaders exactly what they think of this whole employee engagement thing. But they can't. Not now, anyway. Now they must be happy, smiling, committed, dutiful Stepford Employees. Within these pages, I decided to say what they cannot: the truth.

This book is a much-needed dose of truth about what's really going on in the modern workplace. It is a reality check to let organizations and their management teams know if they truly want to have engaged employees, they need to start treating them with empathy. No more punishing employees for being human. No more holding them to impossible standards. No more insisting that they act like perfect, servile robots. We need to transform work from an ugly, depressing four-letter word into something meaningful, positive, and, dare I say, engaging. At the very least, we should change the way companies relate to their employees so work is no longer *dis*engaging. It can be done. Every organization in every industry can bring about this change through the determined, courageous actions of those with the power to make it a reality. Employee engagement—true employee engagement—begins and ends with exceptional and empathetic leadership. So let's get to work, leaders.

NOTES

1. Martinez, Mary v. Cracker Barrel Old Country Store, Inc. 11-2189. United States Court of Appeals for the Sixth Circuit. 2013. *Government Publishing Office*. January 10, 2013. https://www.gpo.gov/fdsys/pkg/ USCOURTS-ca6-11-02189/pdf/USCOURTS-ca6-11-02189-0.pdf

Index

D

E

unpaid overtime. *See* wage theft

unrealistic goals 47

V

values 98, 102, 162, 228

ventral striatum 90, 121, 142, 178

victim-blaming 101

Virtuous Circle of Employee Engagement 198

Volkswagen 41, 209

W

wage theft 141

walking meetings 139

Wall Street 8

Walmart 82, 209

Walt Disney Company 61, 199

Walton family 83

Warren, Elizabeth 46, 48

Washington 46

Weddle, Jim 165

Weinstein, Harvey 117

Wells Fargo 46, 209, 240

whistleblowers 41

Whole Foods 218

Wilson, Woodrow 125

Winterkorn, Martin 41

work

  defined 57

  pointless busywork 67

work-life balance 84, 197

work-life integration 71

work martyrdom 131, 144

work output 143

workplace democratization 113

workplace prisoners 20

workplace violence 177

WorldatWork 184

World Economic Forum 13

World of Warcraft 183

World War I 143

World War II 151

Y

Yahoo 143

Yellen, Janet 24

Yelp 11, 91

yoga 152

YouTube 213

YUM! Brands 128

Z

Ziglar, Zig 89

ABOUT COGNIZE CONSULTING

The word *cognize* means to perceive or understand. That's what leaders need to do in order to achieve organizational goals through the power of an engaged workforce. Cognize Consulting helps leaders craft an attractive employee experience by giving them guidance to see, understand, and engage the people who drive their organization's success. We teach leaders how to effectively engage their employees and, more importantly, how to stop disengaging them. A paycheck alone is no longer sufficient to inspire today's talent. Employee experience is the currency of the modern workplace. We specialize in diagnosing employee experience shortfalls and creating interventions to facilitate real, sustainable engagement. For more information about our products and services, including our Engaging Leader Toolkit™ with resources to help you become a more engaging, empathetic leader, visit our website: www.cognizeconsulting.com.